Frommer's®

Boston
day BY day
3rd Edition

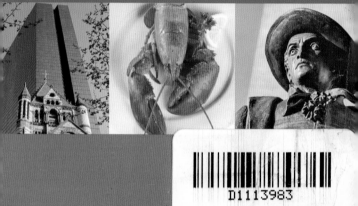

D1113983

by Marie Morris

FrommerMedia LLC

Contents

Published by:

FrommerMedia LLC

Copyright © 2014 Frommer Media LLC, New York, NY. All rights reserved. No part of this publication may be reproduced, stored in a retrieval system or transmitted in any form or by any means, electronic, mechanical, photocopying, recording, scanning or otherwise, except as permitted under Sections 107 or 108 of the 1976 United States Copyright Act, without the prior written permission of the Publisher. Requests to the Publisher for permission should be addressed to http://www. support@frommermedia.com.

Frommer's is a trademark or registered trademark of Arthur Frommer.

ISBN: 978-1-62887-020-6 (print); 978-1-62887-050-3 (ebk)

Editorial Director: Pauline Frommer
Editor: Alexis Lipsitz Flippin
Production Editor: Lindsay Conner
Photo Editor: Seth Olenick
Cartographer: Roberta Stockwell
Page Compositor: Julie Trippetti
Indexer: Cheryl Lenser
Front cover photos, left to right: Hancock Tower © Alfgar; Lobster © Marco Mayer; Bunker Hill Memorial © Jorge Salcedo.
Back cover photo: Leonard P. Zakim–Bunker Hill Memorial Bridge © Robbie Shade.

For information on our other products and services, please go to Frommers.com/contactus.

Frommer's also publishes its books in a variety of electronic formats. Some content that appears in print may not be available in electronic formats.

Manufactured in China

5 4 3 2 1

About this Guide

Organizing your time. That's what this guide is all about.

Other guides give you long lists of things to see and do and then expect you to fit the pieces together. The Day by Day guides are different. These guides tell you the best of everything, and then they show you how to see it in the smartest, most time-efficient way. Our authors have designed detailed itineraries organized by time, neighborhood, or special interest. And each tour comes with a bulleted map that takes you from stop to stop.

Hoping to walk in the steps of the Founding Fathers? Or watch a baseball sail over the Green Monster? Or even walk into a bar where everybody knows your name? Whatever your interest or schedule, the Day by Days give you the smartest routes to follow. Not only do we take you to the top attractions, hotels, and restaurants, but we also help you access those special moments that locals get to experience—those "finds" that turn tourists into travelers.

The Day by Days are also your top choice if you're looking for one complete guide for all your travel needs. The best hotels and restaurants for every budget, the greatest shopping values, the wildest nightlife—it's all here.

Why should you trust our judgment? Because our authors personally visit each place they write about. They're an independent lot who say what they think and would never include places they wouldn't recommend to their best friends. They're also open to suggestions from readers. If you'd like to contact them, please send your comments our way at support@frommermedia.com, and we'll pass them on.

Enjoy your Day by Day guide—the most helpful travel companion you can buy. And have the trip of a lifetime.

About the Author

Marie Morris is a freelance writer and editor based in the North End of Boston, where she has lived long enough to pass for a native but long enough not to acquire a Boston accent. She grew up in New York and graduated from Harvard, where she studied history. Marie has worked for Newser.com, *02138* magazine, the *Boston Herald, Boston* magazine, and the *New York Times*. She's the author of numerous Frommer's guides to Boston and a co-author of *Frommer's New England Day by Day*.

An Additional Note

Please be advised that travel information is subject to change at any time—and this is especially true of prices. We therefore suggest that you write or call ahead for confirmation when making your travel plans. The authors, editors, and publisher cannot be held responsible for the experiences of readers while traveling. Your safety is important to us, however, so we encourage you to stay alert and be aware of your surroundings.

Star Ratings, Icons & Abbreviations

Every hotel, restaurant, and attraction listing in this guide has been ranked for quality, value, service, amenities, and special features using a star-rating system. Hotels, restaurants, attractions, shopping, and nightlife are rated on a scale of zero stars (recommended) to three stars (exceptional). In addition to the star-rating system, we also use a **kids** icon to point out the best bets for families. Within each tour, we recommend cafes, bars, or restaurants where you can take a break. Each of these stops appears in a shaded box marked with a coffee-cup-shaped bullet ☕.

The following abbreviations are used for credit cards:

AE	American Express	DISC	Discover	V	Visa
DC	Diners Club	MC	MasterCard		

Frommers.com

Frommer's travel resources don't end with this guide. Frommer's website, www.frommers.com, has travel information on more than 4,000 destinations. We update features regularly, giving you access to the most current trip-planning information and the best airfare, lodging, and car-rental bargains. You can also listen to podcasts, connect with other Frommers.com members through our active-reader forums, share your travel photos, read blogs from guidebook editors and fellow travelers, and much more.

A Note on Prices

In the "Take a Break" and "Best Bets" sections of this book, we have used a system of dollar signs to show a range of costs for 1 night in a hotel (the price of a double-occupancy room) or the cost of an entree at a restaurant. Use the following table to decipher the dollar signs:

Cost	Hotels	Restaurants
$	under $130	under $15
$$	$130–$200	$15–$30
$$$	$200–$300	$30–$40
$$$$	$300–$395	$40–$50
$$$$$	over $395	over $50

How to Contact Us

In researching this book, we discovered many wonderful places—hotels, restaurants, shops, and more. We're sure you'll find others. Please tell us about them, so we can share the information with your fellow travelers in upcoming editions. If you were disappointed with a recommendation, we'd love to know that, too. Please write to: Support@FrommerMedia.com

14 Favorite
Moments

14 Favorite **Moments**

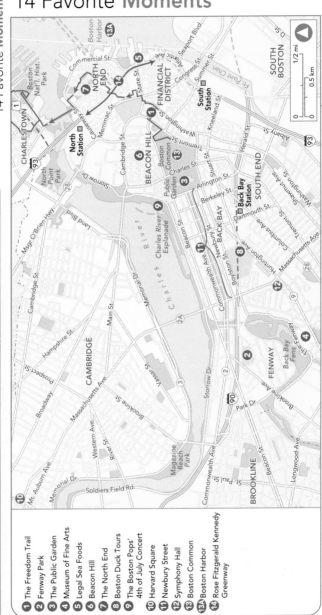

Previous page: Washington statue.

Once in a while, just for a moment, I get a new perspective on my adopted hometown. The sun emerges from behind a cloud and makes the harbor seem to glow. I can't take my eyes off the lush green of the Fenway Park outfield or the sapphire blue of the Charles River. In the Public Garden, a delighted child's laughter rings out. The familiar feels new, and I realize yet again what an endlessly fascinating city Boston is. I'd love to help you find some serendipitous moments of your own. Let's look around.

1 Treading in the footsteps of the Founding Fathers. Only a handful of American cities have histories as rich and varied as Boston's. A walk along the Freedom Trail covers the highlights. See p 42.

2 Feeling like a kid again at Fenway Park. Whether you're a lifelong baseball fan or you've never been to a game, the oldest park in the major leagues (it opened in 1912) will capture your heart and stay in your memory. Take in a game, or save some time and money and take a tour. See p 133.

3 Savoring spring in the Public Garden. Boston's loveliest park is gorgeous year-round, but there's something special about the atmosphere when the bitter New England winter finally recedes. Maybe it's the sheer beauty of the beds of tulips. Or maybe it's just that the pasty-white Bostonians all seem so excited about the change of seasons. See p 91.

4 Seeing old friends at the Museum of Fine Arts. Strolling through the MFA, you may find greetings forming on your lips. Hello, Degas dancer. How's everything, Vincent van Gogh? Are your teeth bothering you, President Washington? They may not be the most valuable or significant of the museum's holdings, but the most familiar ones feel like home. See p 13.

Two fans at Fenway Park.

5 Devouring a lobster. It doesn't matter how much I rave about a stylish bistro or unfamiliar ethnic cuisine—my out-of-town visitors want seafood, preferably of the bright-red variety, and I can't complain. Legal Sea Foods, here we come. *See p 109.*

6 Imagining yourself as an American aristocrat. Picturesque Beacon Hill has been a blueblood bastion for almost 400 years. Visitors stroll the cobblestone streets and marvel: "This is exactly what I thought Boston would look like." *See p 46.*

7 Savoring a taste of Italy. Rush, rush, rush. Sightsee, photograph. Wait—what's this? A cafe that serves perfect espresso? Is this the North End we've been hearing so much about? Why, yes, we really could use a break. A cappuccino would be lovely, thanks. *See p 50.*

8 Riding on a Duck (Tour). My favorite tour is amphibious and unforgettable: It trundles around the city streets before slipping into the placid waters of the Charles River basin. *See p 14.*

The deep, sheltered harbor helped Colonial Boston rise to prominence.

9 Wishing the United States a happy birthday. You may think your town makes a big deal about the Fourth of July. Bostonians celebrate for a week. Boston Harborfest is a citywide event that culminates in a free outdoor concert by the Boston Pops. Hundreds of thousands of revelers attend. *See p 129.*

10 Channeling a college student. Skip the body art and ill-fitting pants and head to Harvard Square, the heart of a city that's also an age-old, cutting-edge college town. Beyond the brick walls and wrought-iron gates of Harvard Yard is a festival of trendy shopping, gourmet ice cream (maybe *that* explains the baggy pants) and alfresco music. *See p 18.*

11 Wearing the numbers right off your credit cards. Boston offers unique merchandise of all descriptions at all price points. Begin with an inspirational stroll along Newbury Street. *See p 32.*

12 Tapping your foot in time to the music. From the world-famous Boston Symphony Orchestra to the noisiest street buskers, Boston's live-music scene creates a unique soundtrack. We must be spoiled, because we take it for granted. *See p 128.*

13 Oohing and ahhing over fireworks. The best night of the year for pyro (technic) maniacs is New Year's Eve, when fireworks explode over Boston Common at 7pm and over Boston Harbor at the stroke of midnight. *See p 164.*

14 Taking a walk on a mile-long park. The Rose Kennedy Greenway is a mile long and only about a block wide, but it's packed with flowers, fountains, food vendors, sculpture, and even a carousel. *See p 23.* ●

1 The Best **Full-Day Tours**

The Best in One Day

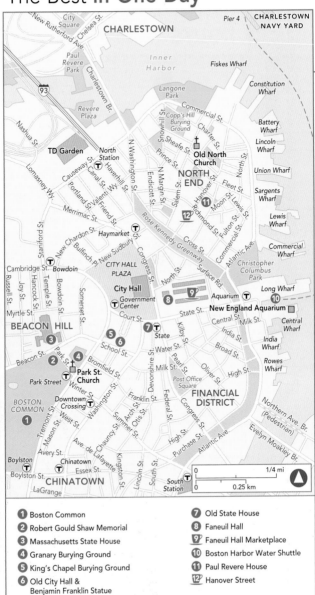

1. Boston Common
2. Robert Gould Shaw Memorial
3. Massachusetts State House
4. Granary Burying Ground
5. King's Chapel Burying Ground
6. Old City Hall & Benjamin Franklin Statue
7. Old State House
8. Faneuil Hall
9. Faneuil Hall Marketplace
10. Boston Harbor Water Shuttle
11. Paul Revere House
12. Hanover Street

Previous page: St. Luke Drawing the Virgin.

With just 1 day to spend in Boston, focus on the compact downtown area. You'll follow part of the Freedom Trail, which presents an opportunity to explore three-plus centuries of history. My best advice is twofold. Don't concentrate so hard on the trail that you forget to look around. And wear comfortable shoes. START: **Red or Green Line T to Park Street**

❶ ★ Boston Common. The oldest public park in the country (bought in 1634, set aside in 1640) is a welcome splash of green in red-brick Boston. As a boy, philosopher Ralph Waldo Emerson herded his mother's cows here on the way to school. ○ *5 min. Bordered by Beacon, Park, Tremont, Boylston, and Charles sts. Free admission. Daily 24 hr. T: Red or Green Line to Park Street.*

❷ ★★★ Robert Gould Shaw Memorial. The literal and figurative high point of the Common is this magnificent bronze sculpture by Augustus Saint-Gaudens. It honors the first American army unit made up of free black soldiers, the Union Army's 54th Massachusetts Colored Regiment, which fought in the Civil War under the command of Col. Robert Gould Shaw (1837–1863). Read the plaque on the back before or after taking in the incredible artistry of the front, a relief that took 14 years to design and execute. Unveiled in 1897, the sculpture is one of the finest public memorials in the country. ○ *10 min. Beacon St. at Park St. Free admission. Daily 24 hr. T: Red or Green Line to Park Street.*

❸ ★ Massachusetts State House. The state capitol is one of the signature works of the great Federal-era architect Charles Bulfinch. Note the symmetry, a hallmark of Federal style, in details as large as doors and as small as moldings. Tours (self-guided and, by prior arrangement, guided)

explore the building. Allow time to investigate the statues and monuments that dot the grounds; my favorite is President Kennedy captured in midstride. ○ *10 min. to explore outside; 40–45 min. with tour. Beacon St. at Park St.* ☎ *617/727-3676. www.sec.state.ma.us/trs/trsgen/genidx.htm or www.malegislature.gov/engage/statehousetours. Free admission and tours. Mon–Fri 9am–5pm (tours 10am–3:30pm). T: Red or Green Line to Park Street.*

❹ ★★ Granary Burying Ground. Established in 1660, yet not even close to being the oldest in Boston, this cemetery is my favorite for its variety of designs and high-profile occupants. Consult the map near the entrance for help in locating the graves of, among

Robert Gould Shaw, who was white, led the 54th Massachusetts Colored Regiment in the Civil War.

A simple tombstone at the Granary Burying Ground.

others, Paul Revere, Samuel Adams, and John Hancock, whose monument is almost as ostentatious as his signature. For more information, see the "Boston's Colonial Cemeteries" tour on p 96. ⏱ *15 min. Try to visit in the morning, before tour groups clog the walkways. Tremont St. at Bromfield St. Free admission. Daily 9am–5pm (until 3pm in winter). T: Red or Green Line to Park St.*

⑤ ★ King's Chapel Burying Ground. The oldest graveyard in the city dates to 1630, the same year Europeans settled the peninsula. The chapel was completed in 1754. For more information, see the "Boston's Colonial Cemeteries" tour on p 96. *Tremont St. at School St. Daily 8am–5:30pm (until 3pm in winter). T: Green or Blue Line to Government Center.*

⑥ Old City Hall & Benjamin Franklin Statue. The seat of local government from 1865 to 1969, this ornate French Second Empire building now holds offices and a steakhouse. In front is the city's first portrait statue, a likeness of Benjamin Franklin, who was born a block

away. *School St. at City Hall Ave. (end of Province St.). T: Blue or Orange Line to State.*

⑦ ★ kids Old State House. Like a flower in a forest of skyscrapers, this fancy little brick building sits amid towering neighbors. The Old State House opened in 1713, when Massachusetts was a British colony and State Street was named King Street. (In the 1630s, when the Puritan settlement was in its infancy, the whipping post and stocks awaited sinners on this site.) During a visit to Boston in 1789, George Washington watched a parade from the balcony. The building served as the state capitol from Revolutionary times until the present State House opened in 1798. Today it houses the city's history museum, a fascinating amalgamation of permanent and temporary displays. The engaging photographs in the permanent collection, which figure in many rotating exhibits, are worth the price of

The Declaration of Independence was read from the Old State House balcony in 1776.

admission. On the exterior are vestigial traces of British rule—a lion and a unicorn, both royal symbols that predate the Revolution. ⏱ *40 min. 206 Washington St., at State and Court sts.* ☎ *617/720-1713, ext. 21. www.revolutionaryboston.org. Admission $8.50 adults, $7.50 seniors and students, free for kids 18 and under. Freedom Trail Ticket (with Old South Meeting House and Paul Revere House) $13 adults, $2 kids 6–18. Daily 9am–5pm (until 6pm May–Sept). T: Blue or Orange Line to State.*

8 ★ kids **Faneuil Hall.** Many of the great orators of the past 2-plus centuries inspired audiences to rebellion, reform, and protest here, earning the building the nickname "the cradle of liberty." One of the best-known speakers was the revolutionary firebrand Samuel Adams (yes, like the beer), whose statue stands outside the Congress Street side of the building. Originally erected in 1742, Faneuil Hall was a gift from prominent merchant Peter Faneuil. Charles Bulfinch designed the 1805 expansion. National Park Service rangers staff the first-floor visitor center and give brief, interesting talks in the second-floor auditorium that tell the story. Note the address—Dock Square—and the fact that there isn't a dock, or indeed any water, nearby. The seemingly random shapes and patterns etched into the stone at the foot of the Samuel Adams statue show the shoreline at various points in the past 3-plus centuries, illustrating how landfill has transformed the city. ⏱ *10 min.; 30 min. for tour. Dock Square (Congress and North sts.).* ☎ *617/242-5642. www.nps. gov/bost. Free admission. Daily 9am–5pm (visitor center until 6pm); talks every 30 min. until 4:30pm. Ground-floor shops close later. T: Green or Blue Line to Government Center, or Orange Line to Haymarket.*

Samuel Adams spoke frequently at Faneuil Hall.

9 ★★ kids **Faneuil Hall Marketplace.** The five-building complex incorporates shopping, dining, drinking, live entertainment (think juggling), and people-watching. The Quincy Market building holds a huge food court. At lunch, follow the office workers—lines form at places that earn repeat business. ⏱ *30–60 min. Morning is least busy, but afternoons are most entertaining, especially in warm weather. Bordered by State, Congress, and North sts. and Atlantic Ave.* ☎ *617/523-1300. www.faneuilhallmarketplace.com. Mon–Sat 10am–9pm, Sun 11am–6pm; many restaurants open earlier and close later. T: Green Line to Government Center, Orange Line to Haymarket or State, or Blue Line to Aquarium or State.*

10 ★★★ kids **Boston Harbor Water Shuttle.** A classic open secret. The $6 round-trip adult fare for the commuter ferry that connects downtown Boston and the Charlestown Navy Yard might be the best money you spend during your visit. If time is short, consider riding across the Inner Harbor, turning around, and coming right back. There's plenty to look at on either end: Long Wharf adjoins the New England Aquarium, and the Charlestown pier is a 5-minute walk from USS *Constitution* ("Old Ironsides") and its museum. But the point is the journey, not the destination—find a place on the deck in good weather, and enjoy feeling the wind in your face as you dream of running away to sea. In inclement weather, this is still a fun excursion, with excellent views from the enclosed cabin in all but the worst conditions, but do bundle up.

🕐 *10 min. each way; allow 1 hr. total to include wait time and a bit of exploring at either end; steer clear during the morning and evening rush hours, when regular commuters are all business. Long Wharf, 1 block from State St. and Atlantic Ave.* ☎ *617/222-4321. www.mbta.com. One-way fare $3 adults, free for kids under 12 with a paying adult. Mon–Fri 6:30am–8pm, Sat–Sun 10am–6pm. T: Blue Line to Aquarium.*

⓫ ★★★ **kids** **Paul Revere House.** The more I learn about "midnight rider" Paul Revere, the better I understand that he was a regular guy. On a visit to his North End home, you get a sense of what daily life was like for a successful colonial craftsman. Outfitted with 17th- and 18th-century furniture and fascinating artifacts (including silver pieces created by Revere), the little wood structure is open for self-guided tours, a visitor-friendly format that allows you to set your own pace. A talented silversmith who supported a large family—he had eight children with each of his two wives—Revere played an important role in the fight for independence. As tensions between British troops and colonists escalated in the last years of colonial rule, he monitored the royal soldiers' activities and helped to keep the Americans apprised of the progress of the rebellion. He left this cozy house over and over again, working to bring about what would end up being the American Revolution—and risking his neck

The architectural style of the Paul Revere House is usually described as Tudor or folk Gothic.

Top Attractions: Practical Matters

A CityPass (☎ 888/330-5008; www.citypass.com/boston) is a booklet of tickets—so you can go straight to the entrance—providing admission to the Museum of Fine Arts, Museum of Science, New England Aquarium, Skywalk Observatory at the Prudential Center, and either the Harvard Museum of Natural History or the Old State House. If you visit all five, the price ($51 for adults, $36 for youths 3–11) gives adults a nearly 48% discount on buying tickets individually. An even better savings can be in time when lines at the attractions are long—especially if you have your heart set on visiting the aquarium. The passes, good for 9 consecutive days from the date of purchase, are on sale at participating attractions, through the website, and from some hotel concierge desks and travel agents.

every single time. Could I be that brave? Could you? ⏱ **40 min.** *Crowds fluctuate, but weekend afternoons are busiest. 19 North Sq., between Richmond and Prince sts.* ☎ *617/523-2338. www.paulrevere house.org. $3.50 adults, $3 seniors and students, $1 kids 5–17, free for kids 4 and under. Apr–Dec daily 9:30am–5:15pm (until 4:15pm Apr 1–15 & Nov–Dec); Jan–Mar Tues–Sun 9:30am–4:15pm. T: Green or Orange Line to Haymarket.*

12 ★★ kids Hanover Street.
This crowded street at the heart of the North End, Boston's best-known Italian-American neighborhood, overflows with restaurants, cafes, and out-of-towners. The increasingly sophisticated retail options include quirky boutiques on Salem and Hanover streets and some of the side streets that connect them. Explore a bit before settling down with a cappuccino, a cannoli, and an appetite for people-watching. My favorite destinations are Mike's Pastry (300 Hanover St., ☎ 617/742-3050, www.mikes pastry.com; $) and Caffè Vittoria

(290–296 Hanover St., ☎ 617/227-7606, www.vittoriacaffe.com; $). A tip: Don't call the North End "Little Italy," unless you want everyone to know you're a tourist.

Take a break at a North End cafe to enjoy some cannoli and a cappuccino.

The Best in **Two Days**

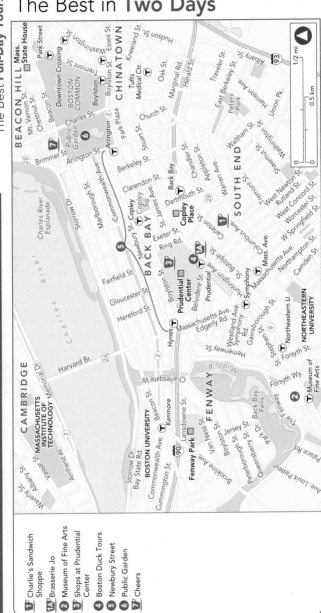

1 Charlie's Sandwich Shoppe

W Brasserie Jo

2 Museum of Fine Arts

3 Shops at Prudential Center

4 Boston Duck Tours

5 Newbury Street

6 Public Garden

7 Cheers

If you followed the 1-day tour, you have a feel for downtown Boston and its colonial legacy. In the 19th century, the city grew westward, building up the neighborhood now known as the Back Bay and spreading into the Fenway. Today you'll see a little of everything. Again, comfortable shoes are key. START: **Orange Line T to Back Bay or Green Line T to Copley**

1 ★ kids **Charlie's Sandwich Shoppe.** The Museum of Fine Arts doesn't open until 10am. Fuel up first at this long-time South End favorite, where specialties include blueberry pancakes and turkey hash. If it's Sunday, when Charlie's is closed, head to Brasserie Jo (see p 105). *429 Columbus Ave. (between Holyoke St. and Braddock Park).* ☎ *617/536-7669. $–$$. No credit cards.*

2 ★★★ kids **Museum of Fine Arts.** The familiar and the undiscovered meet here, creating an irresistible atmosphere that makes the MFA one of the best art museums in the world. Plan your visit beforehand—you might take a tour, concentrate on a particular period, or head straight to one specific piece. For me, that would probably be a Monet painting (the museum owns dozens), but I reserve the right to substitute a sculpture, a photograph, a mural, a vase, or even a piece of furniture. It's all here; use your time wisely. *See also the mini-tour of the MFA on p 27.* ⓘ *at least 3 hr. Arrive when the doors open, visit on a weekday if possible, and if you're traveling without kids, try to avoid school vacation weeks. 465 Huntington Ave. (between Museum Rd. and Forsyth Way).* ☎ *617/267-9300. www.mfa. org. Admission (good for 2 visits within 10 days) $25 adults, $23 seniors and students, $10 kids 7–17 on school days before 3pm, otherwise free. Free for kids 6 and under.*

Mary Cassatt's In the Loge.

Voluntary contribution Wed 4–9:45pm. Sat–Tues 10am–4:45pm, Wed–Fri 10am–9:45pm. Tours daily except Mon holidays 10:30am–3pm, Wed 6:15pm. T: Green Line E to Museum of Fine Arts or Orange Line to Ruggles.

3 kids **Shops at Prudential Center.** The Pru has a good, if generic, food court and several sit-down restaurants (including a branch of Legal Sea Foods; see p 109) that don't require reservations. If the weather's good, picnic in the courtyard. Depending on when your Duck Tour begins (see the next stop), you may want to grab a bite afterward instead. *800 Boylston St.; enter from Huntington Ave. near Belvidere St. or from Boylston St. between Fairfield and Gloucester sts.* ☎ *800/SHOP-PRU. www.prudential center.com. $–$$.*

The Public Garden, the first botanical garden in the country, is lovely year-round.

④ ★★★ kids Boston Duck Tours. The best motorized tour of Boston gives travelers a vantage point high above the street in a reconditioned World War II amphibious vehicle. The con-ducktors (ouch) are exceptionally well trained—they need licenses to operate the mammoth "Ducks" on both land and water, after which memorizing some historical highlights must feel like child's play. After a relatively brief but thorough tour on land, the vehicle rolls down a ramp and cruises around the Charles River basin for about 20 minutes. Whee! A captivating combination of unusual perspectives, cooling breezes, and fascinating narration. ⏱ *80 min. for tour. Timed tickets go on sale 30 days ahead online, 5 days ahead in person, and at 8:30 or 9am day of tour; aim for the afternoon, when the action on the river is liveliest, but don't pass up a morning tour if that's the only option. Boarding behind the Prudential Center at 53 Huntington Ave. between Ring Rd. and Exeter St., or at the Museum of Science, Science Park, off McGrath–O'Brien Highway (Route 28). Discounted (by $2–$3)* 65-minute tours leave from New England Aquarium; check ahead for schedule. ☎ 800/226-7442 or ☎ 617/267-DUCK. www.boston-ducktours.com. Tickets $34 adults, $28 seniors and students, $23 kids 3–11, $11 kids 2 and under. Mid-Mar to late Nov daily 9am to 1 hr. before sunset. No tours Dec to mid-Mar. T: Green Line E to Prudential or any car to Copley for Prudential Center; Green Line to Science Park for Museum of Science; Blue Line to Aquarium for New England Aquarium.*

⑤ ★★★ Newbury Street. The best-known retail destination in New England has something for everyone. Newbury Street is famous for art galleries and designer boutiques, and it's increasingly known for generic national chains. As a rule, the closer to the Public Garden, the nicer the neighborhood and the higher the price tags. Generally less expensive and more fun are the stores at higher-numbered addresses. Note that the cross streets go in alphabetical order. *Arlington St. to Massachusetts Ave.* ☎ *617/267-2224. www.newburystreetleague.org. T:*

This flag marks the location of America's most famous bar.

Green Line to Arlington, Green Line to Copley, or Green Line B, C, or D to Hynes/ICA.

6 ★★★ kids **Public Garden.** Boston's most beloved park is a perfect place to unwind. The Public Garden overflows with seasonal blooms and permanent plantings (the roses, which peak in June, are particularly lovely). No matter how crowded it gets, it feels serene. Stroll the perimeter, studying the delightfully miscellaneous collection of monuments and statues. Watch the ducks, the swans, and the iconic Swan Boats. Relax. For more information, see the tour of the Public Garden starting on p 90. *Bordered by Arlington, Boylston, Charles, and Beacon sts. www.friendsofthepublicgarden.org. Free admission. Daily dawn–dusk. T: Green Line to Arlington.*

7 kids **Cheers.** This is it, in all its touristy glory. I wouldn't even mention this bar, restaurant, and souvenir outlet, but it's across the street from the Public Garden, and hardly a week goes by without an out-of-towner asking me for directions. *84 Beacon St. (at Brimmer St.).* ☎ *617/227-9605. www.cheersboston.com. $–$$.*

Boston Duck Tour vehicles travel on both land and water.

The Best **in Three Days**

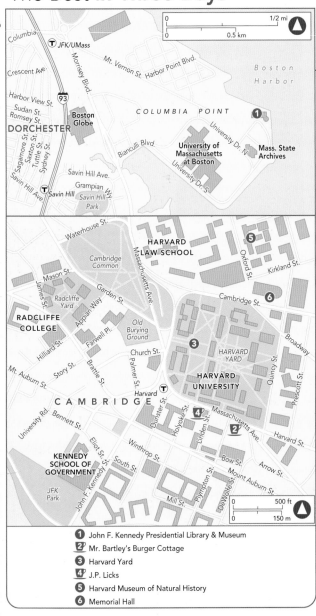

1 John F. Kennedy Presidential Library & Museum
2 Mr. Bartley's Burger Cottage
3 Harvard Yard
4 J.P. Licks
5 Harvard Museum of Natural History
6 Memorial Hall

After 2 days concentrating on central Boston, this is your chance to spread out a little. The city's Dorchester neighborhood is accessible on the Red Line and home to a unique attraction, Massachusetts native John F. Kennedy's presidential library. Harvard, his alma mater, is just a subway ride away, at the heart of an intriguing city that thrives in Boston's shadow. START: **Red Line to JFK/UMass**

I. M. Pei designed the Kennedy library to suit its location on Dorchester Bay.

① ★★★ kids **John F. Kennedy Presidential Library and Museum.** Whether or not they remember the Kennedy era, history buffs enjoy this wonderful museum. Copious collections of memorabilia, photos, and audio and video recordings illustrate the exhibits, which capture the 35th president in vibrant style. A 17-minute film about his early life narrated by Kennedy himself, using cleverly edited audio clips, kicks off your visit. The displays begin with the 1960 presidential campaign and proceed chronologically; by the time you reach the dim room where news reports of the assassination play, you'll want to shed a tear along with Walter Cronkite. ⏱ *2 hr. Arrive when the doors open and you may have the place to yourself; prepare for gridlock on summer weekend afternoons. Columbia Point, off University Dr. N. near UMass Boston.*

☎ *866/JFK-1960 or* ☎ *617/514-1600. www.jfklibrary.org. Admission $12 adults; $10 seniors and students with ID; $9 youths 13–17; free for kids 12 and under. Surcharges may apply for special exhibitions. Daily 9am–5pm (last film at 3:55pm). T: Red Line to JFK/UMass, then take free shuttle bus. Check website for driving directions.*

② ★★★ kids **Mr. Bartley's Burger Cottage.** Fantastic burgers are the thing here, but I've also had excellent veggie burgers, hummus, and cheese steaks. Make sure you try the unbelievable onion rings. On Sunday, when Bartley's is closed, grab lunch at the Border Café (see p 105). *1246 Massachusetts Ave. (at Plympton St.), Cambridge.* ☎ *617/354-6559. $–$$.*

❸ ★ **Harvard Yard.** Harvard, the oldest college in the country (founded in 1636), welcomes visitors and offers free guided tours when school is in session. Even without a guide, the stately main campus (two adjoining quads known as Harvard Yard) is worth a look. The most popular stop is the John Harvard statue in front of University Hall. The most popular stop should (according to me) be Sever Hall, where the rounded archway around the front door forms a "whispering gallery." Stand on one side and speak softly into the molding; someone standing next to you won't be able to hear, but a listener at the other end of the archway will. Across the way is majestic Widener Library; climb the steps for a sensational view. To begin exploring, visit the website or stop in at the Events & Information Center to take a free guided (1 hr.) or self-guided tour or to pick up a map. ⏱ *30 min.; longer if you take a tour. Events & Information Center, 1350 Massachusetts Ave. (between Dunster and Holyoke sts.)* ☎ *617/495-1573. www. harvard.edu/visitors. Tours Mon–Sat; check website for schedule. T: Red Line to Harvard.*

❹ ★★★ kids **JP Licks.** A break already? Hey, college is hard! You need gourmet ice cream, in flavors both plain and fancy. *1312 Massachusetts Ave. (between Holyoke and Linden sts.).* ☎ *617/492-1001. $.*

❺ ★★ kids **Harvard Museum of Natural History.** One of the university's most popular attractions, the museum is an intriguing destination that's just the right size for families with curious children. From dinosaurs to insects, the exhibits are both fascinating and educational. Also here are the world-famous Glass Flowers, 3,000 models of hundreds of plant species that might

just fool you. It's true—they look real. **Note:** If art is more your speed and you're visiting after mid–2014, check for information about the three Harvard Art Museums (www.harvardartmuseums.org). At press time, they're closed for renovations and scheduled to reopen in fall 2014. ⏱ *2 hr. Seldom truly mobbed, unless you run into a large school or camp group (which can be fun). 26 Oxford St. (near Kirkland St.).* ☎ *617/495-3045. www.hmnh. harvard.edu. Admission (includes Peabody Museum of Archaeology & Ethnology) $12 adults, $10 seniors and students, $8 kids 3–18, free for kids 2 and under; free for Massachusetts residents before noon Sun and after 3pm Wed. Daily 9am–5pm. T: Red Line to Harvard.*

❻ ★ **Memorial Hall.** Anything but a stereotypical red-brick Harvard building, "Mem Hall" is a Victorian-era (1874) structure in an unusual style known as Ruskin Gothic. Polychrome (multicolored) brickwork sets off quirky archways, and the floor plan mimics a Gothic cathedral. The nave is a dining hall, and the apse is Sanders Theatre, a lecture and concert hall. The walls of the transept hold memorials to the Harvard men who perished in the Civil War—but only if they fought for the Union. ⏱ *10 min. Stay away during mealtimes to avoid being trampled by hungry students. 45 Quincy St. (at Cambridge St.).* ●

Harvard's Widener Library.

The Best Special-Interest Tours

Boston with Kids

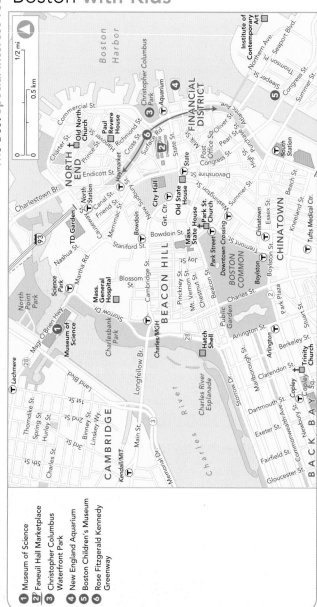

1 Museum of Science
2 Faneuil Hall Marketplace
3 Christopher Columbus Waterfront Park
4 New England Aquarium
5 Boston Children's Museum
6 Rose Fitzgerald Kennedy Greenway

Previous page: Leonard P. Zakim-Bunker Hill Memorial Bridge.

Every day in the summer, children shuffle along the Freedom Trail like prisoners on a chain gang, looking hot, tired, and seriously bored. Unless your kids are old enough to express an interest, spare them the history lesson. Boston offers so much else to see and do that you'll never miss the Freedom Trail. Before you plunge in, note that I suggest you visit either stop 4 or stop 5 (not both) depending on how old your kids are. START: **Green Line T to Science Park**

❶ ★★★ Museum of Science. This is the best indoor family destination in the Boston area. It can be a bit overwhelming, with some 500 exhibits—engaging hands-on activities and experiments, interactive displays, and fascinating demonstrations—but it's both educational and entertaining. I suggest that you pick a few subjects you find interesting and build your visit around them. For example, I especially like the sections that focus on the human body, dinosaurs, maps, and nanotechnology. Use the website before you leave home to rough out a route through the enormous museum, leaving room for inspiration to strike; the temporary exhibits are always worth a look. Also check the schedules for the on-premises butterfly garden,

A Tyrannosaur at the Museum of Science.

Omni theater, and planetarium, which can help you decide whether to budget the time and money for a longer stay—or a return visit.
🕑 3 hr. Buy tickets online in advance and arrive at 9am sharp to avoid the largest crowds. Science Park, off O'Brien Hwy. (Rte. 28). ☎ 617/723-2500. www.mos.org. Museum admission $23 adults, $21 seniors, $20 kids 3–11, free for kids 2 and under. Butterfly garden (with museum admission only) $5 adults, $4.50 seniors, $4 kids. Omni theater or planetarium $10 adults, $9 seniors, $8 kid. Discounted combination tickets available. Sat–Thurs 9am–5pm (until 7pm July 5 to Labor Day), Fri 9am–9pm;

Learn about electricity at a dramatic demonstration of the Van de Graaf generator at the Museum of Science.

theater and planetarium close later. T: Green Line to Science Park.

2 ★★ Faneuil Hall Marketplace. The counters that line both sides of Quincy Market are a smorgasbord with something for everyone, from hungry omnivores to picky vegetarians. Get your food to go, because you'll be picnicking across the street, away from the marketplace crowds. See p 9, bullet 9.

3 ★★ Christopher Columbus Waterfront Park. Across the Rose Kennedy Greenway from Faneuil Hall Marketplace is this lovely little park overlooking a marina. It has a small playground (to your left as you face the water), plenty of lawns and shady trees, a rose garden, benches beneath a graceful trellis, and an excellent fountain. The fountain doesn't run all the time; press one of the four buttons arranged around the edge to start the timed spray. ⏱ *45 min. Atlantic Ave. (State and Richmond sts.).* ☎ *617/635-4505. www.cityofboston.gov/parks. T: Blue Line to Aquarium.*

4 ★ New England Aquarium. Consider skipping this stop or the next one, depending on how old your kids are and whether marine life interests them. For preteens and teens that like aquariums, the thousands of fish and aquatic mammals here make this place a big hit. The centerpiece is the Giant Ocean Tank, which contains the sharks (and 200,000 gallons of water). The surrounding displays and hands-on exhibits are home to a vast variety of sea creatures. My favorites are the open-air marine mammal center, where seals and sea lions frolic, and the shark and ray touch tank, which lets visitors get up close and personal with the exhibit's leathery-skinned inhabitants. Other exhibits focus on penguins, the Amazon rainforest, the Gulf of Maine, and other seagoing creatures and habitats. Allow an extra hour if you plan to take in a 3D film in the adjacent theater. ⏱ *2 hr. Buy timed tickets online in advance or invest in a Boston CityPass (see p 11) to avoid the lines at the entrance. Central Wharf (½ block from State St. and Atlantic Ave.).* ☎ *617/973-5200. www.neaq. org. Admission $23 adults, $21 seniors, $16 kids 3–11, free for kids under 3. IMAX theater tickets $10 adults, $8 seniors and kids. Discounted combination tickets available. Aquarium July to Labor Day Sun–Thurs 9am–6pm, Fri–Sat & holidays 9am–7pm; day after Labor Day to June Mon–Fri 9am–5pm, Sat–Sun 9am–6pm. IMAX theater daily*

View seals, penguins, sharks, crabs, and fish galore at the New England Aquarium.

Kids will bubble over with excitement at the Boston Children's Museum.

starting at 9:30am. T: Blue Line to Aquarium.

❺ ★★ Boston Children's Museum.
If your kids are under 11 or so, or don't care for fish and their friends, skip the aquarium and head here. This is hands-on heaven: Visitors get physical on an illuminated dance floor, work construction, visit Japan, learn about Boston's African-American community, make giant soap bubbles, experiment with thinking like a scientist, and climb around in a gigantic three-story maze. And that's just scratching the surface. ⏱ *2 hr. Crowds are especially large on rainy summer weekdays. 300 Congress St. (Sleeper St., overlooking Fort Point Channel).* ☎ *617/426-6500. www. bostonchildrensmuseum.org. Admission $14, free for kids under 1; $1 for everyone Fri after 5pm. Sat–Thurs 10am–5pm, Fri 10am–9pm. T: Red Line to South Station, 10-min. walk.*

❻ ★★ Rose Kennedy Greenway.
A block wide and a mile long, the Greenway offers numerous options for family fun. Be as active or passive as you like: splash in a fountain, ride the custom-built

carousel, explore the labyrinth (in the Armenian Heritage Park at Commercial St.), or just relax on a lush lawn. Walking the whole Greenway without stopping takes about half an hour, but allow time for exploring and resting as you unwind from your busy day. If you want a snack, you have numerous options, including mobile food vendors (most plentiful at lunchtime, but some hang around until early evening). Check the website beforehand to see whether your visit coincides with a concert, market, movie, or other activity—the Greenway has evolved constantly since it was dedicated in 2004, and you never know what you might see. ⏱ *30 min., or as long as it takes you to wind down. The Greenway runs roughly parallel to the waterfront from North Station (Causeway St.) to Chinatown (Kneeland St.).* ☎ *617/292-0020. www. rosekennedygreenway.org. Carousel tickets (May–Oct) $3. Daily 7am– 11pm; 24-hour pedestrian access. T: Green or Orange Line to North Station or Haymarket, Blue Line or Inner harbor ferry to Aquarium, or Red Line to South Station.*

The Fenway

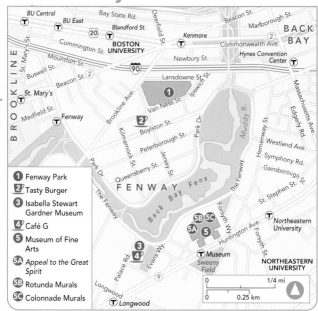

1 Fenway Park
2 Tasty Burger
3 Isabella Stewart Gardner Museum
4 Café G
5 Museum of Fine Arts
5A Appeal to the Great Spirit
5B Rotunda Murals
5C Colonnade Murals

The Fenway neighborhood offers a unique opportunity to visit two institutions that are virtual temples in their fields: Fenway Park and the Museum of Fine Arts. Weird combination? Maybe a little. But consider this: Both places celebrate the efforts of people who do what they do better than just about anyone else. START: Green Line T (B, C, or D train) to Kenmore

---

1 ★★★ kids Fenway Park.

The oldest and arguably most beloved venue in the major leagues is Fenway, which John Updike famously described as a "lyric little bandbox of a ball park." Cubs fans are likeliest to argue, but even they can't deny the appeal of this baseball icon, which opened in 1912. The magic isn't in the players or the unforgettable green of the field or even the story of the supposed "curse" that prevailed in the 86 years between World Series titles (1918–2004). It's in the whole experience, and you can't truly understand what the fuss is about until you see for yourself. You don't have to score expensive tickets to do so, either—tours run year-round. Tour specifics may vary, especially in the off-season, when construction is often going on. Visitors usually get to explore the stands and visit the press box and luxury seats, and they sometimes walk on the warning track and touch the left-field wall, nicknamed the "Green Monster." ⏱ 1½ hr. 4 Yawkey Way (Brookline Ave.); buy tour tickets at

Fenway's "Green Monster."

Gate D, Yawkey Way and Van Ness St. ☎ *617/226-6666 for tour info;* ☎ *877/733-7699 for game tickets. www.redsox.com. Tours $16 adults, $14 seniors, $12 kids 3–15, free for kids under 3. Daily 9am–5pm or until 3 hr. before game time. T: Green Line B, C, or D to Kenmore or D to Fenway.*

2 **kids** **Tasty Burger** This accurately named little place—in a renovated service station—also serves hot dogs, chicken sandwiches, salads, and a huge selection of drinks (alcoholic and non). *1301 Boylston St. (Yawkey Way).* ☎ *617/425-4444. www.tastyburger.com. $–$$.*

3 ★★ **Isabella Stewart Gardner Museum.** This engaging museum makes a perfect stop between Fenway Park and the Museum of Fine Arts; its namesake was a devoted Red Sox fan. An heiress and socialite, "Mrs. Jack" Gardner (1840–1924) was also an avid traveler and patron of the arts. The core of the museum is her private collection of paintings, sculpture, furniture, tapestries, and decorative objects. It includes works by Titian, Botticelli, Raphael, Rembrandt, Matisse, and Sargent. My favorite gallery is the Dutch Room, where the displays include a 17th-century silver sculpture of an ostrich and an actual ostrich egg. The largest artifact is the building itself, completed in 1901 and designed to resemble a 15th-century Venetian palace. Three floors of galleries surround the plant- and flower-filled courtyard. The terms of Gardner's will forbid changing the permanent exhibitions, so when the museum expanded in 2012, it did

The Gardner Museum courtyard.

John Singer Sargent's famous portrait of Isabella Stewart Gardner.

so by commissioning a whole new wing. The Renzo Piano design is a treasure in its own right. ⏱ *2 hr. 280*

The Fenway (Museum Rd.). ☎ *617/ 566-1401. www.gardnermuseum.org. Admission $15 adults, $12 seniors, $5 college students with ID, free for kids 17 and under, military and families, and adults named Isabella with ID. Wed–Mon 11am–5pm (until 9pm Thurs). T: Green Line E to Museum of Fine Arts.*

④ ★★ **Café G.** The Gardner Museum has an appropriately classy cafe that's a perfect place to indulge in some sweets and a cup of tea or a glass of wine. You can dine at the cafe without paying museum admission. *280 The Fenway (Museum Rd.).* ☎ *617/566-1088. $–$$.*

⑤ ★★★ **kids Museum of Fine Arts.** In addition to being one of the world's great museums, the MFA is an architectural landmark. The Art of the Americas wing (2010) is the work of Sir Norman Foster and his firm, Foster + Partners. I. M. Pei designed the Linde Family Wing for Contemporary Art (1981). And at the heart of the original building at this location (1909) is the rotunda. Let's take a closer look. See p 13, bullet ②.

Cyrus Dallin's **Appeal to the Great Spirit,** *outside the Museum of Fine Arts.*

Museum of Fine Arts

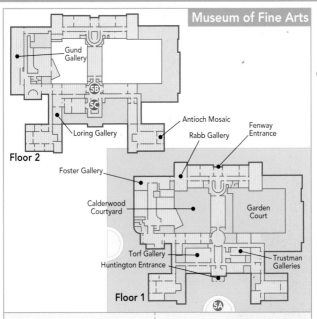

Floor 2

- Gund Gallery
- Loring Gallery
- Antioch Mosaic
- Rabb Gallery
- Fenway Entrance
- **5B**
- **5C**

Floor 1

- Foster Gallery
- Calderwood Courtyard
- Garden Court
- Torf Gallery
- Huntington Entrance
- Trustman Galleries
- **5A**

Most visitors enter the Museum of Fine Arts (1909) from Huntington Avenue or the Fenway. The Huntington Avenue entrance overlooks a lawn where you'll find **5A** *Appeal to the Great Spirit,* a bronze statue of an Indian on horseback. Cast in Paris in 1909, it's one of the finest works by American sculptor Cyrus Dallin.

Inside, a sweeping staircase leads to the rotunda, which holds one of the museum's signature elements: **5B** John Singer Sargent's Rotunda Murals. Sargent incorporated sculpture and architectural features with paintings to create the elaborate space; colorful murals depict mythological figures such as Apollo, Athena, the Muses, and Prometheus. The rotunda, which opened to the public in 1921, proved so popular that the museum wanted more. Return to the staircase, scoot out of the flow of traffic, and look up and around to take in Sargent's **5C** Colonnade Murals. Creating this space required substantial structural work; for example, the columns that allow light to pour in

Detail of Renoir's Dance at Bougival.

replaced solid walls. Apollo is here, too, as is a delightfully grisly representation of Perseus holding Medusa's severed head. This project was Sargent's final work: In 1925, the night before he was to sail from London to Boston to supervise installation of the last section, he died in his sleep.

Copley Square Architecture

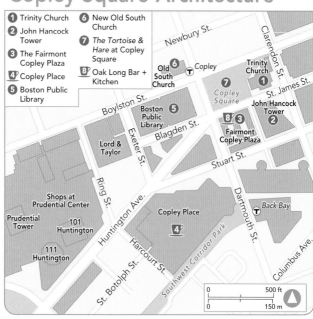

1. Trinity Church
2. John Hancock Tower
3. The Fairmont Copley Plaza
4. Copley Place
5. Boston Public Library
6. New Old South Church
7. *The Tortoise & Hare* at Copley Square
8. Oak Long Bar + Kitchen

opley Square is, in many ways, the heart of Boston. Landmark buildings occupy three sides of the lovely plaza, notable structures peek in from two corners, and a constant flow of pedestrians enlivens the area. A block from the 2013 Boston Marathon bombings, the square—named for the celebrated artist John Singleton Copley (1738–1815)—has since become a focal point for the attitude known as "Boston Strong." Copley Square is most enjoyable on Tuesday and Friday afternoons July to November, when a farmers' market anchors one side, but it's a visual treat year-round. START: **Green Line T to Copley**

---

1 ★★★ Trinity Church. One of the best-known church buildings in the country, Trinity Church is architect H. H. Richardson's masterwork. A native of New Orleans and a Harvard graduate, Richardson was a larger-than-life figure whose style was so distinctive that it now bears his name: Richardsonian Romanesque. Think of the prototypical New England church—white with a towering steeple, right? Trinity is anything but. Before you enter, stand back and take a moment to enjoy the busy yet harmonious design of the polychrome (multicolored) exterior. Consecrated in 1877, the building is granite, trimmed with red sandstone, with a roof of red tiles on the 221-foot (67m)

Trinity Church.

off-season hours. *T: Green Line to Copley.*

② ★★ John Hancock Tower.

This reflecting-glass behemoth is remarkable for what it isn't—obtrusive, distracting, or incongruous. It complements rather than competes with its neighbors, and it's so beautiful that I can almost forgive the wind-tunnel effect it creates for several blocks in all directions. While still under construction, the Hancock Tower gained worldwide notoriety for some unfortunate incidents in which huge panes of glass plummeted onto the sidewalk hundreds of feet below. (Yes, it was 4 decade ago, and the problem was corrected quickly, but it's still a great story.) The top-floor observation deck, for many years one of the most popular attractions in Boston, closed in 2001. *200 Clarendon St. (St. James Ave.)*

③ ★ The Fairmont Copley Plaza.

The relatively austere facade of the 1912 hotel conceals a riotously ornate interior that's well

The 60-story Hancock Tower is the tallest building in New England.

tower. The tower alone weighs 90 million pounds (41 million kg). Inside, barrel vaults draw the eye up to the 63-foot (19m) ceilings, and John La Farge's murals and decorative painting make imaginative use of colored plaster that complements the hues in the renowned stained-glass windows. Be sure to spend some time contemplating La Farge's window *Christ in Majesty,* in the west gallery. And take a tour, which will surely touch on the building's remarkable construction—the structure rests on 4,502 pilings driven into the mud that was once the Back Bay; the pilings must be kept wet so they don't rot. ① *1 hr. 206 Clarendon St. (Boylston St.).* ☎ *617/536-0944. www.trinitychurch boston.org. Free admission and free tours after Sunday service. Guided or self-guided tour $7 adults, $5 seniors and students, free for children 15 and under with an adult. Summer Mon–Sat 9am–5pm (until 6pm Tue–Thu), Sun 7am–7pm; check ahead for*

worth a look—be sure to check out the lobby ceiling. (**Bonus:** A black Labrador named Catie Copley hangs around in the lobby, and you can probably pet her if she's there.) Architect Henry Janeway Hardenbergh, who had help on this project from local architect Clarence Blackall, also designed New York's Plaza Hotel and Dakota apartment building. *138 St. James Ave.*

4 **Copley Place.** Boston's fanciest shopping center has a limited selection of places to grab a quick bite, but it's a good climate-controlled option for resting and refueling. *100 Huntington Ave.* ☎ *617/236-5800. $.*

5 ★★ **Boston Public Library.** Architect Charles Follen McKim of the legendary New York firm of McKim, Mead & White gets the credit for designing the main branch of the city's library system, but he was really the captain of an artistic all-star team. Take a tour if it fits into your schedule, or explore on your own. Pause outside to admire the way the arches across the granite facade of the Renaissance Revival building echo the design of Trinity Church, on the other side of the square.

The library's bronze doors are the work of sculptor Daniel Chester French (better known for the seated Abraham Lincoln at the presidential memorial in Washington, D.C., and the John Harvard statue in Cambridge), and Augustus Saint-Gaudens created the decorative seals above each of the three entrance arches. Inside, sculpture, painting, and elaborate architectural details abound. The walls of the entrance hall are rare yellow Siena marble, and the murals on the staircase and in the second-floor corridor, which represent the wisdom and knowledge collected in the building, are by Pierre Puvis de Chavannes. On the third floor is the Sargent

The Boston Public Library opened in 1895.

IN HONOR
OF THE
MASSACHUSETTS VOLUNTEER INFANTRY
AND IN REMEMBRANCE OF THE
OFFICERS AND MEN WHO FELL IN ITS RANKS
THIS MONUMENT HAS BEEN GIVEN TO THE CITY OF BOSTON

Gallery, which houses John Singer Sargent's murals illustrating religious themes. The celebrated portraitist worked on the murals from 1895 through 1916, and no matter how many times you view them, you'll always notice something new. Many consider this gallery their favorite part of the library; I love the interior courtyard, with its Roman arcade and eternally peaceful atmosphere. ⏱ *1 hr. 700 Boylston St. (Dartmouth St.).* ☎ *617/536-5400. www.bpl.org. Mon–Thurs 9am–9pm, Fri–Sat 9am–5pm, Sun (Oct–May only) 1–5pm. Guided Art & Architecture Tours free. Tours Mon 2:30pm; Tues & Thurs 6pm; Wed, Fri–Sat 11am; Sun (Oct–May only) 2pm. T: Green Line to Copley.*

⑥ ★ New Old South Church.

The Northern Italian Gothic church anchors its corner of Copley Square with authority. The multicolored facade (the technical term for the design on the entrance arches is zebra-striped) encloses a similarly vivid sanctuary, illuminated with stained glass throughout. Be sure to visit the chapel, to the left as you enter, where the Gothic influence is particularly evident in the design of the windows. Wondering about the name? The congregation of this church, constructed from 1872 through 1875, originated downtown in the building now known as the Old South Meeting House. *645 Boylston St.* ☎ *617/536-1970. www.oldsouth.org. Mon–Fri 8am–7pm, Sat 10am–4pm, Sun 8:30am–4pm. T: Green Line to Copley.*

⑦ ★ 𝗸𝗶𝗱𝘀 The Tortoise & Hare at Copley Square.

Trinity Church and the library are Copley Square's best-known features, but the neighborhood is even more famous for

New Old South Church.

being the destination of the Boston Marathon. The finish line, painted on the street outside the Boylston Street entrance to the library, stays in place year-round. In Copley Square proper is a whimsical reminder of the race, a three-dimensional illustration of the tortoise and hare fable created by Nancy Schön (also the sculptor of *Make Way for Ducklings,* in the Public Garden). *Off Boylston St. between Clarendon and Dartmouth sts.*

⑧ ★ Oak Long Bar + Kitchen.

This elegant establishment serves food and drink from early morning to late evening. In good weather, there's outdoor seating. *In the Fairmont Copley Plaza Hotel, 138 St. James Ave. (Dartmouth St.).* ☎ *617/585-7222. $$$–$$$$.*

The Best Special-Interest Tours

Newbury Street

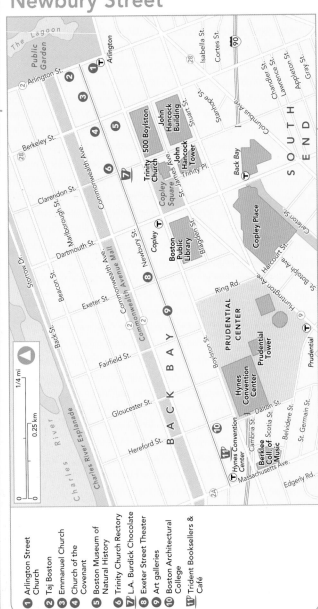

1 Arlington Street Church
2 Taj Boston
3 Emmanuel Church
4 Church of the Covenant
5 Boston Museum of Natural History
6 Trinity Church Rectory
7 L.A. Burdick Chocolate
8 Exeter Street Theater
9 Art galleries
10 Boston Architectural College
11 Trident Booksellers & Café

Newbury Street, Boston's foremost retail destination, is also an architectural treat. It originates at the Public Garden, where the real estate and merchandise are elegant and pricey, and extends past Massachusetts Avenue, growing less expensive (though hardly cheap) and more unusual with each passing block. This is one of the main streets of the Back Bay. Originally a marshy body of water, the neighborhood materialized when 19th-century landfill projects replaced the "bay" with dry land. For modern-day visitors, the result is a harmonious blend of sightseeing and shopping. START: **Green Line T to Arlington**

Louis Comfort Tiffany stained-glass window at Arlington Street Church.

1 ★ Arlington Street Church. Constructed from 1859 to 1861, this was the first building completed in the Back Bay (the congregation dates to 1729). Architect Arthur Gilman designed the exterior to resemble the Church of St. Martin-in-the-Fields in London's Trafalgar Square. The Italianate interior is famous for the stained-glass windows designed by Louis Comfort Tiffany between 1899 and 1929; they're considered some of the celebrated artist's finest work. Like Trinity Church in Copley Square, this building rests on wooden pilings. ⏱ *30 min. 351 Boylston St. (Arlington St.) ☎ 617/536-7050. www.ascboston.org. Visit office to be admitted to sanctuary. Mon–Fri 9am–5pm (closed Fri in summer), Sat–Sun 1–5pm. T: Green Line to Arlington.*

2 ★ Taj Boston. Constructed in 1927 as the Ritz-Carlton, this was the original hotel in the chain. It was once so exclusive that management evaluated prospective guests based on whether their names appeared in the Social Register or Who's Who. The architecture blends Regency and Art Deco details. The hotel is now part of the Mumbai-based luxury chain. *15 Arlington St. (Newbury St.).*

3 Emmanuel Church. The main part of this church was the first building completed on Newbury Street, in 1862. The Gothic Revival exterior unites three separate spaces; the loveliest is the Leslie Lindsey Memorial Chapel, which was consecrated in 1924. It bears the name of a Bostonian who died on her honeymoon in 1915 when a German U-boat torpedoed the

The Taj Boston offers champagne brunches with amazing views of the city.

Lusitania. Look closely at the stained-glass window representing St. Cecilia, who was modeled on the young bride. She died wearing the diamonds and rubies her father had given her as a wedding gift, and her parents sold the jewels to finance the construction of the chapel. Try to attend the Sunday service at 10am; from September through May, the liturgy includes Bach cantatas performed live by the orchestra and chorus of Emmanuel Music (www.emmanuel music.org). ○ *10 min. 15 Newbury St. (Arlington St.).* ☎ *617/536-3355. www.emmanuel-boston.org. T: Green Line to Arlington.*

❹ ★ Church of the Covenant.

Church of the Covenant is an interesting complement to its neighbor Emmanuel Church; another Gothic Revival edifice. Erected from 1865 to 1867, the church has an

Church of the Covenant's steeple.

elaborately decorated 240-foot (73m) steeple, which Oliver Wendell Holmes described as "absolutely perfect." (Emmanuel doesn't have a steeple.) Louis Comfort Tiffany and John La Farge designed the stained-glass windows, which were created by three of Tiffany's most esteemed artists. The best known is the Sparrow Window, which depicts Jesus at work, but I prefer St. Augustine, who sits beneath a passage of his own writing incorporated into the design (like graffiti!). The parish house holds **Gallery NAGA** (p 79), which specializes in contemporary art. ○ *30 min. 67 Newbury St. (Berkeley St.).* ☎ *617/266-7480. www.churchofthecovenant. org. Mon–Sat 11am–3pm. T: Green Line to Arlington.*

❺ Boston Museum of Natural History.

The 1864 building, a graceful French Academic design by William Preston, now houses a Restoration Hardware store. The museum—a forerunner of the Museum of Science—is long gone; originally a two-story structure, it retained its original roof when the building gained a third floor. *234 Berkeley St. (Newbury and Boylston sts.).*

❻ Trinity Church Rectory.

H. H. Richardson designed the rectory, which was completed in 1879, 2 years after the church (p 28, bullet ❶). The style is considered Richardsonian Romanesque, but this building is considerably less elaborate than the landmark house of worship. *233 Clarendon St. (Newbury St.)*

❼ ★★ L. A. Burdick Chocolate Shop.

This little cafe serves a wide variety of drinks—coffee and tea as well as hot and iced chocolate—and luscious pastries. This is also a retail location for the New Hampshire–based luxury chocolatier's

Tired of gallery-hopping? Take a load off at one of Newbury Street's many outdoor cafes.

dreamy confections. *220 Clarendon St. (between Boylston and Newbury sts.).* ☎ *617/303-0113. www. burdickchocolate.com. $.*

8 Exeter Street Theater. The 1884 Romanesque Revival building (get a load of the top-floor ornamentation on both the Exeter St. and Newbury St. sides) originally housed the First Spiritualist Temple. It was later a movie theater and now holds office space. *26 Exeter St. (Newbury St. and Commonwealth Ave.)*

9 ★★ Art galleries. Not all of the art on Newbury Street is bricks and mortar (or granite or puddingstone or other building materials). This tony thoroughfare is far better known for its huge concentration of art galleries. Take time now to check out some painting, sculpture, photography, or other work. Turn to the "Art" section of chapter 4 for specific suggestions. A good strategy if you don't have a particular destination in mind is to check the

website of the Newbury Street League (www.newburystreetleague. org) and pick out a couple of appealing merchants. Alternatively, as you walk along, pick out places to which you'd like to return. Be sure to keep an eye out for galleries below and above street level.

10 ★ Boston Architectural College. The main building of the BAC is an example of Brutalist architecture, with large glass windows on the Hereford Street side that make it far more appealing than another notable local Brutalist building, the inexcusable Boston City Hall. Take a couple of minutes to walk around to Boylston Street and see the west façade, which holds my favorite element: a whimsical *trompe l'oeil* mural of a classical building by Richard Haas. The firm of Ashley, Meyer & Associates won a national competition to design 320 Newbury Street, which opened in 1966. Founded in 1889, the BAC is a lively institution that offers undergrad and graduate degrees as well as continuing-ed programs. It exhibits work of interest to the design community (not just student and faculty shows) in two public spaces: the McCormick Gallery, in the lobby, and the fourth-floor Stankowicz Gallery. *320 Newbury St. (Hereford St.).* ☎ *617/ 262-5000. www.the-bac.edu. Mon– Thurs 8am–10:30pm, Fri 8am–5pm, Sat 9am–5pm, Sun noon–5pm. T: Green Line B, C, or D to Hynes/ICA.*

11 ★★ Trident Booksellers & Cafe. This is the perfect place to wind down—it offers good food, drink, books, and people-watching. The menu is hospitable to vegetarians and the atmosphere conducive to lingering. *338 Newbury St. (Mass. Ave.).* ☎ *617/267-8688. www.trident bookscafe.com. $.*

Hidden Cambridge

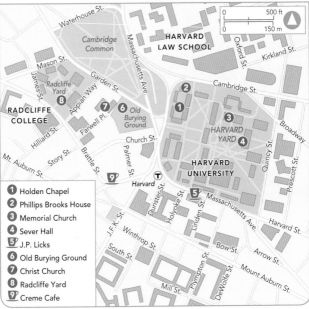

1 Holden Chapel
2 Phillips Brooks House
3 Memorial Church
4 Sever Hall
5 J.P. Licks
6 Old Burying Ground
7 Christ Church
8 Radcliffe Yard
9 Creme Cafe

The beaten track in and around Harvard Square is beaten indeed—for example, eager photographers wore down the lawn across from the John Harvard Statue in Harvard Yard so thoroughly that the university finally paved over the bare earth of the shutterbugs' favorite spot. But even this frenzied neighborhood offers some pockets of peace and (relative) quiet. START: **Red Line to Harvard**

1 ★ **Holden Chapel.** Between the main part of busy Harvard Yard and Massachusetts Avenue (on the other side of the wall) sits this tiny Georgian building. Completed in 1744, it was a chapel for only about the first 20 years of its existence. It has also been a garage, a store-room, office space, barracks for Revolutionary War troops serving under George Washington, and an anatomy lab. Today it's a classroom and a rehearsal space for under-graduate choral groups. *Harvard*

Yard, off Massachusetts Ave. near Peabody and Cambridge sts.

2 ★ **Phillips Brooks House.** The quietest corner of the Yard is home to Phillips Brooks House (1899), the name of both the build-ing (designed by Alexander Wad-sworth Longfellow, Jr., the poet's nephew) and the public-service association headquartered here. *Harvard Yard, off Cambridge St.*

3 ★★ **Memorial Church.** The university's church was dedicated in 1932 in memory of those who had

died in what was then optimistically called the Great War. Sculptures and plaques commemorate them; the south wall, to the right as you enter, lists their names. (They include Joseph P. Kennedy, Jr., the president's brother, class of 1938.) Nondenominational Protestant services (including morning prayer, Mon–Sat 8:45–9am during the academic year) are open to the public. ⏱ *30 min.* ☎ *617/495-5508. www.memorial church.harvard.edu. Harvard Yard, near Broadway and Cambridge sts.*

④ ★★★ **Sever Hall.** H. H. Richardson, the architect of Boston's Trinity Church, designed Sever (rhymes with "fever"), a classroom building that opened in 1880 and drives architects wild. They rave about the brickwork, the chimneys, the roof, and even the window openings. Not being an architect, I love it because if you stand to one side of the front door and whisper into the archway, someone standing next to you can't hear a thing, but someone at the other end of the arch can hear you loud and clear. Try it! ⏱ *10 min. Harvard Yard, off Quincy St.*

⑤ ★ **J. P. Licks.** The local ice cream chain, launched in 1981, is known for its huge variety of flavors. *1312 Mass. Ave. (Linden St.).* ☎ *617/ 492-1001. www.jplicks.com. $.*

⑥ ★★ **Old Burying Ground.** This cemetery, sometimes called the Cambridge Burying Ground, has been here since 1635, a year before the founding of the university. As you explore the compact area, some 2 centuries' worth of examples can help you trace evolving fashions in gravestones. ⏱ *30 min. Massachusetts Ave. (Garden St.).*

⑦ **Christ Church.** This is the oldest standing church building in Cambridge; designed by Peter

Holden Chapel.

Harrison, it opened in 1761. It's wood, with a square tower and some longstanding war wounds: British muskets made the bullet holes in the vestibule during the Revolution. ⏱ *10 min. Zero Garden St.* ☎ *617/876-0200. www.cc cambridge.org.*

⑧ **Radcliffe Yard.** Founded as the Harvard Annex in 1879 and chartered as Radcliffe College in 1894, Harvard's "sister school" existed until 1999. The creation of the Radcliffe Institute for Advanced Study ended its independent status, completing a process that began in 1943, when Radcliffe students first gained admission to Harvard classrooms. Busy Harvard Yard is large and dramatic; Radcliffe Yard is an enclave of serenity. It consists of red-brick buildings executed in typical New England college style (Greek Revival and Federal). *Appian Way (Garden and Brattle sts.).*

⑨ **Crema Cafe.** The inventive coffee and tea offerings and the tasty food (savory and sweet) make Crema wildly popular. In fine weather, you can sit outside. *27 Brattle St. (Mount Auburn St.).* ☎ *617/876-2700. www.crema cambridge.com. $–$$.*

Romantic Boston

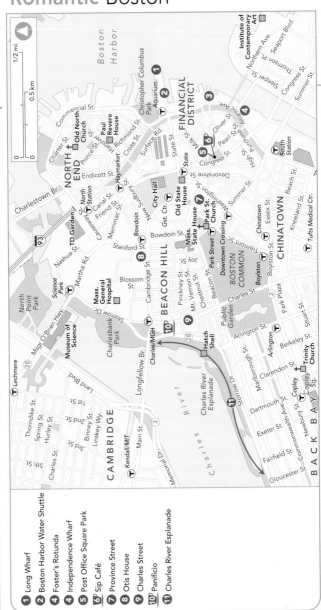

You and your sweetie are in an unfamiliar city, and I'm sending you on an unfamiliar route, across town from one body of water to another. It's fun no matter when you set out, as long as you get to the Otis House in time for the last tour, at 4:30pm. You're rebels, traveling roughly perpendicular to the Freedom Trail, off the beaten path. It's you against the world. See? Bonding already. START: **Blue Line to Aquarium**

1 ★★ **Long Wharf.** Surrounded by water on three sides, in view of the airport and most of the harbor ferry and sightseeing-boat routes, the little plaza at the end of the wharf is a perfect front-row seat for a busy seaport. The lovely design on the ground next to the flagpole is a useful decoration known as a compass rose. If the wharf is crowded, seek out the boardwalk behind the granite building across from the sightseeing boats for some peace and (relative) quiet. ⏱ *at least 10 min. Long Wharf (end of State St.).*

2 ★★★ **Boston Harbor Water Shuttle.** Some commuter boats go to distant suburbs; the smaller ones are local. Getting out on the water is the best part of the experience of taking a narrated cruise, and riding to Charlestown and back on your own costs far less than a formal tour. If you didn't have time to visit the plaza on Long Wharf before jumping on the water shuttle, allow time when you return. ⏱ *1 hr. See p 9, bullet* **10**.

3 ★ **Foster's Rotunda.** The ninth-floor balcony provides an awe-inspiring perspective on Boston Harbor, Logan Airport, and the Seaport District. Be prepared to skip this stop in favor of Independence Wharf on weekends and when there's a private function in the rotunda (the lobby security staff will turn you away). ⏱ *30 min. You may have to show ID, sign in, or both. 30 Rowes Wharf (Atlantic Ave. between High St. and Old Northern Ave.), in the Boston Harbor Hotel complex. Mon–Fri 11am–4pm. T: Blue Line to Aquarium or Red Line to South Station.*

4 ★ **Independence Wharf.** Independence Wharf is more likely to be open when you visit than Foster's Rotunda, but the view isn't quite as amazing. If you've already been there, you can skip this stop. If not, the 14th-floor vistas of

Boston Harbor Water Shuttle.

The winding streets of Beacon Hill are the perfect place for a romantic stroll.

Boston Harbor and the Fort Point Channel from here are worth your time. ⏱ *30 min. You may have to show ID, sign in, or both. 470 Atlantic Ave. (Moakley Bridge at Seaport Blvd.). Daily 10am–5pm. T: Red Line to South Station or Blue Line to Aquarium.*

⑤ ★ Post Office Square Park. This gorgeous patch of green occupies land that once held an ugly municipal garage. A visionary redevelopment project moved the parking into a new underground facility (aka the "Garage Mahal") and created an arrangement under which the revenues from below help support the green space above. The beautifully groomed park has free Wi-Fi and a fountain for dogs, with water flowing at their mouth level. The 1.7-acre (.7 hectare) space, formally Norman B. Leventhal Park, sits at the heart of the Financial District and enjoys the distinction of being one of the busiest warm-weather pickup joints around. What's romantic about that? You and your honey get to feel like chaperons at the junior high school dance. No gloating, please. ⏱ at

least 10 min. Zero Post Office Sq. ☎ 617-423-1500. www.normanb leventhalpark.org. T: Blue or Orange Line to State.

⑥ ★★ Sip Café. Post Office Square Park is home to this top-notch purveyor of salads, sandwiches, and sweets. Many ingredients are local, organic, or both. George Howell Coffee, a local artisan roaster, provides the caffeine. Closed weekends. *Post Office Square Park.* ☎ 617-338-3080. www.sipboston.com. $–$$.

⑦ ★ Province Street. A side street in a downtown business district might not seem promising for romance, but push on. In the 1820s, this was a posh residential neighborhood. On the same side of the street as the luxe 45 Province high-rise is a short stone wall topped by a metal fence with a fancy gate in the middle. The gate sits at the bottom of a short flight of stone stairs—a perfect place to steal a kiss. *Province St. at Bosworth St. (between Bromfield and School sts.).*

⑧ ★★★ Otis House. One of New England's most famous architects, Charles Bulfinch, made his name by popularizing the Federal style in residences as well as public spaces that survive to this day (including the Massachusetts State House). This magnificent home, completed in 1796, was the first of three he designed for his friend Harrison Gray Otis. The engrossing tour touches on the history of the neighborhood, discusses historic preservation, and, most important, shows off the house and its furnishings. As interesting as the architectural details are, they share the spotlight with the story of an appealing young family bound for bigger things. Otis, a real estate developer who was later a congressman and mayor of Boston, and his wife, Sally Foster Otis, appointed their home in grand style and enjoyed a reputation for entertaining lavishly. They were married for nearly 50 years—what an inspiration. ⏱ *1 hr. 141 Cambridge St. (Staniford St.); enter from Lynde St.* ☎ *617/227-3956. www. historicnewengland.org. Tours $8 adults, $7 seniors, $4 students. Tours on the hour and half-hour Wed–Sun 11am–4:30pm. T: Green or Blue Line to Government Center (or Blue Line to Bowdoin, on weekdays only).*

⑨ ★★ Charles Street. One of the best streets in the entire city for aimless strolling, Charles Street abounds with gift and antiques shops. It's also the heart of this little residential area, with such nontouristy businesses as a pharmacy, hardware store, and convenience store (the 7-Eleven at 66 Charles St., with hilariously low-key signage that follows the street's strict zoning rules). See chapter 4 for shopping tips, or just wander around. *Cambridge St. to Beacon St. T: Red Line to Charles/MGH.*

⑩ ★ Panificio. Superb fresh breads, pastries, sandwiches, and pizza will draw you to this little storefront restaurant. The cozy atmosphere will keep you here for a while. *144 Charles St. (Revere and Cambridge sts.).* ☎ *617/227-4340. www.panificioboston.com. $–$$.*

⑪ ★★ Charles River Esplanade. Created from the smelly mud flats that once lined the river, the Esplanade (say es-pluh-*nahd*) is one of Boston's busiest parks. Its 64 acres are home to the Hatch Shell—the amphitheater where the Boston Pops Orchestra puts on its famous July 4th concert—and much more. Walk in at the east end, or cross Storrow Drive on one of the eight footbridges. You can stroll, picnic, or just enjoy quiet time under a tree. If you're feeling energetic, there's a signposted exercise course, and the walkway is part of the 18-mile bike and pedestrian path that connects Boston to suburban Watertown. *From Charles Circle (near the Museum of Science) to the Boston University Bridge. www. esplanadeassociation.org. T: Red Line to Charles/MGH or Green Line to Arlington or one of six other stops (see website).*

The Salt and Pepper Bridge (aka Longfellow Bridge), with its namesake towers.

Tying the **Freedom Trail** Together

1. Boston Common
2. Robert Gould Shaw Memorial
3. Massachusetts State House
4. Park Street Church
5. Granary Burying Ground
6. King's Chapel & Burying Ground
7. First Public School / Benjamin Franklin Statue
8. Old Corner Bookstore Building
9. Old South Meeting House
10. Old State House Museum
11. Boston Massacre Site
12. Faneuil Hall
13. Faneuil Hall Marketplace
14. The New England Holocaust Memorial
15. Paul Revere House
16. Mike's Pastry
17. James Rego Square (Paul Revere Mall)
18. Old North Church
19. Copp's Hill Burying Ground
20. USS *Constitution*
21. USS *Constitution* Museum
22. Bunker Hill Monument
23. Sorelle

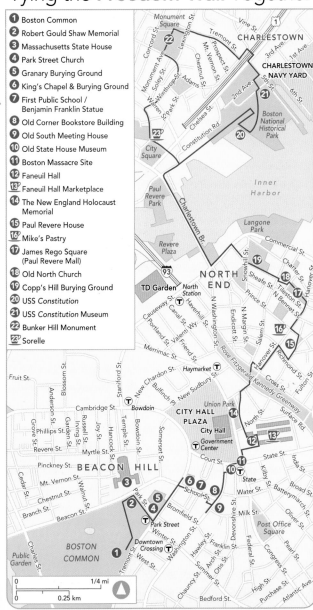

A reminder: The Freedom Trail is a suggested route. People constantly tell me they're curious about the rest of downtown Boston, but they don't want to get lost. They're afraid to start at the end of the trail, skip a stop or two, and generally personalize the experience. But Boston is tiny. No matter how far you wander, you can't get very lost. To emphasize how modular the trail can be—if you're willing to approach it that way—I've scattered the descriptions of many of the stops throughout the rest of this book. If you're determined to "do" the trail in order, allow at least 4 hours and be prepared to incorporate a serendipitous detour or two. This itinerary follows the usual order. START: **Red or Green Line to Park St.**

Freedom Trail marker.

1 ★ Boston Common.
Near the T stop, check out the Brewer Fountain, 22 feet tall and lavishly decorated with mythological sea creatures. See p 7, bullet **1**.

2 ★★★ Robert Gould Shaw Memorial. See p 7, bullet **2**.

3 ★ Massachusetts State House. At the back of the building (off Bowdoin St.), check out the column topped by an eagle. It's 60 feet (18m) tall, representing the original height of Beacon Hill before earth from the top went into 19th-century landfill projects. See p 47, bullet **1**.

4 Park Street Church. The plaques across the front of this striking building describe significant events in its history. Most Bostonians know the church for its 217-foot (66m) clock tower and steeple, which chimes on the quarter-hour. *1 Park St. (Tremont St.)* ☎ *617/523-3383. www.parkstreet.org/tours. Tours mid-June to Aug Tues–Sat 9am–3pm. T: Red or Green Line to Park St.*

5 ★★ Granary Burying Ground. See p 97, bullet **1**.

6 ★ King's Chapel and Burying Ground. My favorite thing about this church is the method of construction: The granite building went up around its wooden predecessor, which remained in use. See p 97, bullet **2**.

7 First Public School/ Benjamin Franklin Statue. The Benjamin Franklin statue sits behind the fence that surrounds Old City Hall. The colorful sidewalk mosaic out front marks the site of the first public school in the United States. See p 8, bullet **6**.

8 Old Corner Bookstore Building. This land once belonged to religious reformer Anne Hutchinson, who was excommunicated and banished from Massachusetts for heresy in 1638. The current structure dates to around 1712. It's best known today as the onetime home of Ticknor & Fields, publisher of some such authors as Longfellow, Emerson, Thoreau, Alcott, and Stowe. Step across the street and take a moment to appreciate the scale and the very existence of this building, which was already old when the American Revolution was just breaking out. *285 Washington St. (School St.).*

⑨ ★ kids Old South Meeting House. The Boston Tea Party, one of the pivotal political demonstrations of the pre-Revolutionary era, started here in 1773. The displays and exhibits in the former house of worship—now used for lectures, concerts, and other events—tell the story in a low-key yet compelling fashion. *A tip:* As you leave, look across the street at 1 Milk Street, an office building standing roughly where 17 Milk Street was in 1706, when Benjamin Franklin was born there. The facade incorporates a bust of Ben and the words BIRTHPLACE OF FRANKLIN. *310 Washington St. (Milk St.).* ☎ *617/482-6439. www.oldsouthmeetinghouse. org. Admission $6 adults, $5 seniors and students, $1 kids 6–18, free for kids under 6. Freedom Trail ticket (with Old State House Museum and Paul Revere House) $13 adults, $2 children. Daily Apr–Oct 9:30am–5pm; Nov–Mar 10am–4pm. T: Blue or Orange Line to State.*

⑩ ★ kids Old State House. See p 8, bullet ⑦.

⑪ Boston Massacre Site. A circle of cobblestones honors the five men killed by British troops on March 5, 1770. *State St. at Devonshire St.*

⑫ ★ kids Faneuil Hall. See p 9, bullet ⑧.

⑬ ★★ kids Faneuil Hall Marketplace. See p 9, bullet ⑨.

Six million numbers are etched into the Holocaust memorial's six glass towers, representing the six million Jews who died.

⑭ ★★ kids The New England Holocaust Memorial. This memorial isn't formally on the Freedom Trail. I always include it, though—when we think about freedom, it's important to contemplate the consequences of not having it. *Union St. (North and Hanover sts.)* ☎ *617/457-8755. www.nehm.org. T: Orange or Green Line to Haymarket.*

⑮ ★★★ kids Paul Revere House. See p 10, bullet ⑪

⑯ ★★ Mike's Pastry. Italian pastries are always a good idea. So are all-American treats such as brownies and chocolate chip cookies. *300 Hanover St. (Prince St.)* ☎ *617/742-3050. www.mikespastry.com. $.*

⑰ ★ James Rego Square (Paul Revere Mall). Be sure to check out the left-hand wall of this square, which holds tablets that describe important people and places in the history of the North End. *Off Hanover St. (Clark St.).*

⑱ ★★ Old North Church. See p 52, bullet ⑥.

⑲ ★ Copp's Hill Burying Ground. See p 98, bullet ⑤.

⑳ ★★ kids USS Constitution. See p 57, bullet ②.

㉑ ★ kids USS Constitution Museum. See p 58, bullet ③.

㉒ ★ Bunker Hill Monument. See p 59, bullet ⑥.

㉓ ★ Sorelle. Pastries, sandwiches, and salads served in a sleek contemporary space make a good transition from your colonial excursion back to real life. *100 City Sq. (Chelsea St.).* ☎ *617/242-5980. www.sorellecafe.com. $–$$.* ●

Beacon Hill

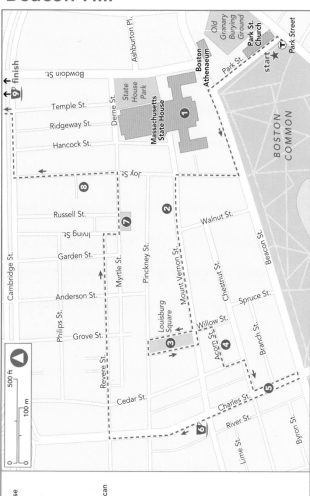

1 Massachusetts State House
2 Nichols House Museum
3 Louisburg Square
4 Acorn Street
5 Charles Street
6' Café Vanille
7 Myrtle Street Playground
8 Museum of African American History
9' Viva Burrito

Previous page: Acorn Street in Beacon Hill.

The views are better from the waterfront and the real estate is more expensive in the Back Bay, but the most prestigious addresses in Boston are on beautiful Beacon Hill, as they have been for most of the past 2 centuries. Post-Revolution prosperity created Boston's most prominent (in all senses of the word) neighborhood, which is a visual treat from every angle. Wear comfortable shoes. START: **Red or Green Line to Park Street**

❶ ★ **Massachusetts State House.**

The construction of the state capitol, which opened in 1798, coincided with the emergence of Beacon Hill as a fashionable neighborhood. Before the Revolution, most Bostonians lived in the area around what are now Faneuil Hall Marketplace and the North End; with peace and increasing prosperity, the population ballooned and construction boomed. The prototypical Boston building, of red brick with white marble trim, owes its iconic status to one man: Charles Bulfinch. The best-known architect of the Federal era (1780–1820), Bulfinch designed the golden-domed central building of the State House as well as many of the graceful residences you'll see on this tour. *See p 7, bullet ❸.*

❷ ★ **Nichols House Museum.**

In contrast to the adjacent Back Bay, where many historic structures hold offices, schools, condos, and apartments, Beacon Hill retains a fair number of one-family homes (along with plenty of condos and apartments). Almost all of the private residences on the narrow streets of "the Hill" are tantalizingly close yet inaccessible to visitors. This 1804 building, which is attributed to Charles Bulfinch, is a welcome exception. It permits a glimpse of Boston during the lifetime of the house's most famous occupant, Rose Standish Nichols (1872–1960). "Miss Rose" was a suffragist, feminist, pacifist, and pioneering landscape designer. She traveled the world, returning

home with much of the art and artifacts that decorate her house, which became a museum after her death. Most of the furnishings in the four-story building are gorgeous antiques collected by several generations of the Nichols family. They moved here in 1885, not long before the novelist Henry James called Mount Vernon "the only respectable street in America." ⏱ *45 min. 55 Mount Vernon St. (Joy and Walnut sts.).* ☎ *617/227-6993. www.nichols housemuseum.org. Admission $8, free for kids 12 and under. Apr–Oct Tues–Sat 11am–4pm, Nov–Mar Thurs–Sat 11am–4pm; tours every 30 min. T: Red or Green Line to Park St.*

❸ ★★★ **Louisburg Square.**

The fanciest addresses in Boston's fanciest neighborhood surround the namesake park—pronounced "lewis-burg"—which sits within a daunting iron fence. The architecture is consistent yet random, employing the same materials in a pleasing variety of styles. Take some time to circle the square. ⏱ *20 min. Between Mount Vernon St. (at Willow St.) and Pinckney St. (at Grove St.).*

The Massachusetts State House.

Louisburg Square

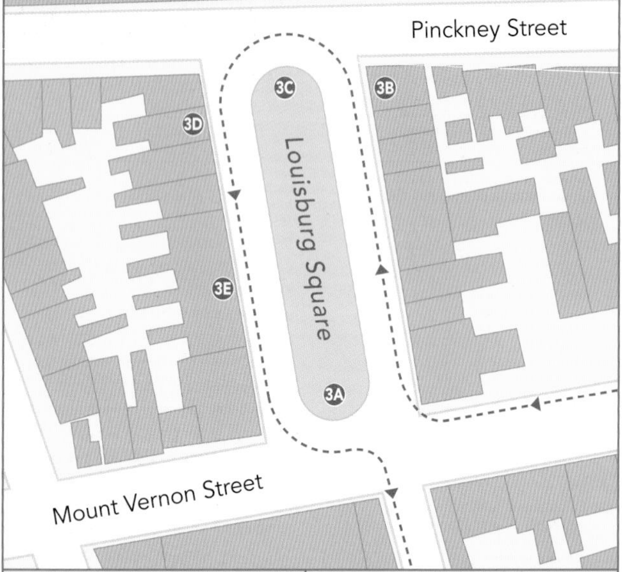

Pinckney Street

Louisburg Square

Mount Vernon Street

An Italian marble likeness of Athenian statesman **3A Aristides** anchors one end of the private park, which is the common property of the Louisburg Square Proprietors. The organization is believed to be the oldest homeowners' association in the country. The 22 houses that surround the graceful patch of grass and trees were built between 1834 and 1848; Aristides landed here in 1850. Not so long ago, lingering in front of **3B 19 Louisburg Square** would have earned you a chat with a Secret Service agent. Secretary of State John Kerry, the 2004 Democratic presidential candidate, lives here (and in a number of other swanky places). The rendering of **3C Christopher Columbus** in the square is believed to be the first American statue honoring Columbus. Use him as an excuse to peer inside the fence. The celebrated 19th-century singer Jenny Lind—promoted as the "Swedish Nightingale" by impresario P. T. Barnum—married her accompanist in the parlor of the house at **3D 20 Louisburg Square** in 1852. Beloved author Louisa May Alcott bought the house at **3E 10 Louisburg Square** in 1885, but she lived here for only about 3 years. She had contracted mercury poisoning while serving as a nurse during the Civil War, and her health was failing. In 1888, on the day after her father's funeral, Alcott died here.

4 Acorn Street. This adorable cobblestone thoroughfare feels like a surprise. It's something of an open secret to Bostonians—and no secret at all to postcard photographers. You'll see why when you get there. *Between Willow and W. Cedar sts.*

5 ★★ Charles Street. Look past the signs and merchandise to appreciate the structural details of the 19th-century buildings that line Beacon Hill's main commercial street. This might be the most enjoyable area in the city in which to wander. ⓘ *At least 30 min. See p 41, bullet* **9**.

6 ★★ Café Vanille. One of the best French bakeries in the city, Café Vanille is a perfect place to relax with a pastry or sandwich and a cup of strong coffee. In fine weather, try to snag a table in the outdoor seating area. *70 Charles St.* ☎ *617-523-9200. www.cafevanille boston.com. $.*

7 Myrtle Street Playground. Climbing all over Beacon Hill is no holiday for your legs; give them a rest at this delightful little oasis. *Myrtle and Irving sts. www.myrtlestreetplayground.org.*

8 ★★ Museum of African American History. This

Indulge in a decadent French pastry at Café Vanille.

fascinating museum offers visitors a comprehensive look at the history and contributions of blacks in Boston and Massachusetts. It occupies the Abiel Smith School (1834), the first American public grammar school for African-American children, and the African Meeting House (1806), one of the oldest black churches in the country. Changing and permanent exhibits use art, artifacts, documents, historic photographs, and other objects to explore an important era that often takes a back seat in Revolutionary War–obsessed New England. Don't leave without venturing down Holmes Alley, off Smith Court—the narrow passageway is believed to have been a hiding place for fugitive slaves traveling the Underground Railroad. ⓘ *1 hr. 46 Joy St. (Myrtle and Cambridge sts.).* ☎ *617/725-0022. www.maah. org. Admission $5 adults, $3 seniors and kids 13–17, free for kids 12 and under. Mon–Sat 10am–4pm. T: Red or Green Line to Park St.*

9 ★ Viva Burrito. Some of Boston's best Mexican food (an exceptionally competitive category) comes from this off-the-beaten-path cafe. If you're looking to wind down but not dine, the smoothies and flan are excellent. *66 Staniford St. (Cambridge St.).* ☎ *617/523-5390. www.vivaburrito.com. $.*

Homes in Beacon Hill's exclusive Louisburg Square.

The North End

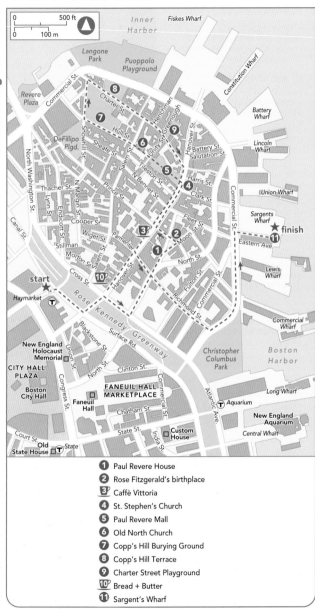

1 Paul Revere House

2 Rose Fitzgerald's birthplace

3 Caffè Vittoria

4 St. Stephen's Church

5 Paul Revere Mall

6 Old North Church

7 Copp's Hill Burying Ground

8 Copp's Hill Terrace

9 Charter Street Playground

10 Bread + Butter

11 Sargent's Wharf

Boston's best-known Italian-American neighborhood is in transition, but it's still the area's top destination for pasta, cappuccino, pastries, and the lively street life that makes this crowded, friendly area endlessly appealing. As you wander around, remember to look up—among the architectural flourishes executed by the talented craftsmen who worked on many of the buildings, you may spy a *nonna* (grandma) looking out the window, keeping track of the action on her street. START: **Green or Orange Line to Haymarket**

1 ★★★ kids Paul Revere House. With its good water supply and easy access to the harbor, the North End was one of the first areas of Boston settled by Europeans. The Paul Revere House, the oldest surviving house downtown, was built around 1680, in the wake of a huge fire in 1676. *See p 10, bullet* **11**.

2 Rose Fitzgerald's birthplace. A plaque marks the modest tenement building where President John Fitzgerald Kennedy's mother came into the world in 1890. It recalls the days when the North End was an Irish and Jewish neighborhood. For much of the 20th century, the North End was Boston's best-known Italian-American area. Today the neighborhood is less than half Italian-American; it's popular with young professionals who walk to work downtown and, more recently,

empty nesters fleeing the suburbs. *4 Garden Court at Prince St.*

3 ★★ Caffè Vittoria. Locals and out-of-towners alike come here for the extensive selection of coffee drinks, Italian baked goods, and peerless people-watching. *290–296 Hanover St. (Parmenter and Prince sts.).* ☎ *617/227-7606. www.vittoria caffe.com. $.*

4 ★ St. Stephen's Church. St. Stephen's, one of three Roman Catholic houses of worship in the tiny North End, is the only standing church building in Boston designed by Charles Bulfinch. The design bears the hallmarks of the architect's iconic style, including the symmetry that makes Federal architecture so pleasing to the eye— step across the street to appreciate

Paul Revere made his living as a silversmith, but he made his reputation as an equestrian.

You can snap your own version of this shot, one of Boston's best photo ops, on the Paul Revere Mall.

it fully. At its dedication in 1804, St. Stephen's was Congregational; it changed with the neighborhood's population and became Catholic in 1862. A refurbishment in 1965 restored the building's original austere details, including clear (not stained) glass windows. The bell, installed in 1805, came from Paul Revere's foundry and cost $800. Rose Fitzgerald (later Rose Kennedy) was baptized here in 1890, and her funeral took place here in 1995. ⏱ *10 min. 401 Hanover St. (Clark St.).*

⑤ ★ Paul Revere Mall. Also known as James Rego Square but usually just called the Prado, this tree-shaded plaza links the

The Old North Church, the oldest church building in Boston, dates to 1723.

commotion of Hanover Street and the serenity of the Old North Church. One of the best photo ops in the city is here: With the church steeple in the background, focus on the equestrian statue of Paul Revere. The sculptor was Cyrus Dallin, who also created the Indian on horseback in front of the Museum of Fine Arts. Wander slowly here, taking time to peruse the plaques that line the left-hand wall; they commemorate important people and places in the history of the neighborhood. *Hanover St. (Clark and Harris sts.).*

⑥ ★ Old North Church (Christ Church). This beautifully proportioned brick church, designed in the style of Sir Christopher Wren, fairly overflows with historic associations. It contains the oldest American church bells (cast in Gloucester, England, and installed in 1745), the Revere family's pew, and a bust of George Washington that's believed to be the first memorial to the first president. The strongest link is with Paul Revere, who arranged for sexton Robert Newman to hang two lanterns in the steeple on the night of April 18, 1775, signaling to the rebellious colonists that British troops were leaving Boston by water ("two if by sea"), bound for Lexington and Concord. The original weather vane tops the current steeple, the church's third, which is a replica of the original. The 30-minute behind-the-scenes tour takes visitors up into the spire and down to the crypt. It's definitely not

for the claustrophobic, but is irresistible for those who are curious about colonial times. My favorite feature of Christ Church (its formal name) isn't actually in the church—it's the tranquil gardens on the north side of the building (to the left as you face the main entrance from the street). 🕐 *40 min. 193 Salem St.* ☎ *617/523-6676 or* ☎ *617/523-4848 for tour information. www.oldnorth.com. Donation requested. Free tours every 15 min. Behind-the-scenes tour $8 adults, $6 seniors, $5 kids 16 and under; available Mar–Dec, by appointment Jan–Feb. Reservations recommended. March–May daily 9am–5pm, June–Oct daily 9am–6pm, Nov–Dec daily 10am–5pm, Jan–Feb Tues–Sun 10am–4pm. T: Orange or Green Line to Haymarket.*

➐ ★ Copp's Hill Burying Ground.

The highest point in the North End affords a panoramic view across the Inner Harbor to the Charlestown Navy Yard, where the three masts of USS *Constitution* poke into view. "Old Ironsides" was built near here, at Hartt's Shipyard at what's now 409 Commercial Street, and launched in 1797. *See p 98, bullet* ➎.

➑ ★★ Copp's Hill Terrace.

Because the back gate of the burying ground is always locked, you'll have to walk all the way around to get to this little park, designed by legendary landscape architect Frederick Law Olmsted. The seating area, on a patch of concrete that overlooks a terraced lawn, has a great view of the action on the athletic fields across the street and the harbor and Charlestown Navy Yard beyond. Commercial Street, directly below, was the location of one of the weirdest disasters ever, in this or any other city: the molasses flood of January 1919. A 2.3-million-gallon (8.7-million-liter)

industrial storage tank blew apart, sending thousands of tons of molasses pouring through the streets. The flood killed 21 people and injured dozens more. *Charter St. (Snowhill and Foster sts.).*

➒ ★ Charter Street Playground.

Seek out this pocket park tucked between the tourist tracks of the Freedom Trail and Hanover Street, and you'll be the only out-of-towner who's here intentionally. The little patch of greenery and cobblestones is home to a sweet sculpture of a seal. *Greenough Lane, off Charter St. at Unity St.*

➓ ★ Bread + Butter.

Any feelings that you're missing a chance to enjoy Italian pastries will vanish the instant you sink your teeth into one of Lee Napoli's sweet or savory concoctions. The view of the Greenway from the indoor and outdoor tables is appealing, but ask for your treats to go. *64 Cross St. (Salem St.).* ☎ *617/248-6900. www.breadbutterboston.com. $.*

⑪ ★ Sargent's Wharf.

The little park at the end of the wharf behind the parking lot is a neighborhood secret—it's not visible from the street, but it hums with activity. The free binoculars allow views of the maritime traffic on the Inner Harbor and the action at the airport, which feels close enough to touch. *Off Commercial St. at Eastern Ave. (north side of 2 Atlantic Ave.).*

Copp's Hill Burying Ground.

The Waterfront

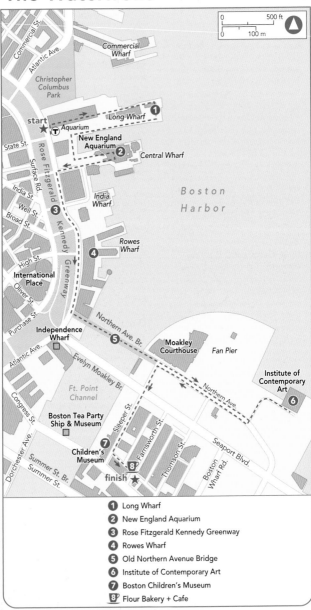

1 Long Wharf
2 New England Aquarium
3 Rose Fitzgerald Kennedy Greenway
4 Rowes Wharf
5 Old Northern Avenue Bridge
6 Institute of Contemporary Art
7 Boston Children's Museum
8 Flour Bakery + Cafe

Boston is a thoroughly modern city, and its commerce and conveniences sometimes make it feel interchangeable with any other good-sized municipality. Then the wind shifts and tangy sea air pours in from the coast, a powerful reminder that you're visiting a legendary port. The Seaport District on the South Boston waterfront is growing like a weed, making a visit an ever-changing experience. Stroll along the harbor to explore Boston's shoreline. START: **Blue Line to Aquarium**

1 ★★ **Long Wharf.** Though hardly a famous attraction, the plaza at the end of this peninsula is one of my favorite places in Boston. *Tip:* In the summer, check the time the full moon rises, and be here to watch—you'll never forget it. *See p 39, bullet* **1**.

2 ★ kids **New England Aquarium.** See p 22, bullet **4**.

3 ★★ **Rose Kennedy Greenway.** The Greenway offers numerous active and passive activities. A fun stop is the Boston Harbor Islands Pavilion, near State Street. A visit to the islands takes at least half a day; if you can't manage that, the information center (staffed May–Oct) makes a good introduction. *See p 23, bullet* **6**.

4 ★★ **Rowes Wharf.** This hotel-office-retail-residential complex centers on a landmark archway. Walk along the water to fully appreciate Rowes Wharf's brilliant combination of private development and public access. *Atlantic Ave. at High St., near Northern Ave.*

5 ★ **Old Northern Avenue Bridge.** When it was in use, this 1908 iron-turntable or "swing" bridge opened by rotating on a pivot rather than by lifting up like a drawbridge. It's now pedestrian only. *Old Northern Ave. (Atlantic Ave. and Sleeper St.).*

6 ★★ **Institute of Contemporary Art.** Boston's first new art museum in almost a century opened in 2006 (the institution dates to 1936) and just gets more popular. The ICA's horizon-broadening definition of art encompasses everything from painting and sculpture to film and dance. The building juts out over the harbor, allowing breathtaking views. ⏱ *2 hr. 100 Northern Ave. (Seaport Blvd.).* ☎ *617/478-3100. www.ica boston.org. Admission $15 adults, $13 seniors, $10 students, free for kids under 18; free to all Thurs after 5pm. Tues–Sun and some Mon holidays 10am–5pm (until 9pm Thurs–Fri). T: Waterfront Silver Line bus to World Trade Center.*

7 ★★ kids **Boston Children's Museum.** See p 23, bullet **5**.

8 ★★ kids **Flour Bakery + Cafe.** Sublime baked goods—from sticky buns to fancy cakes—are the headliner; breakfast, lunch, and dinner are great, too. *12 Farnsworth St. (Congress St.).* ☎ *617/338-4333. www.flourbakery.com. $–$$.*

The Institute of Contemporary Art graces the waterfront.

Charlestown

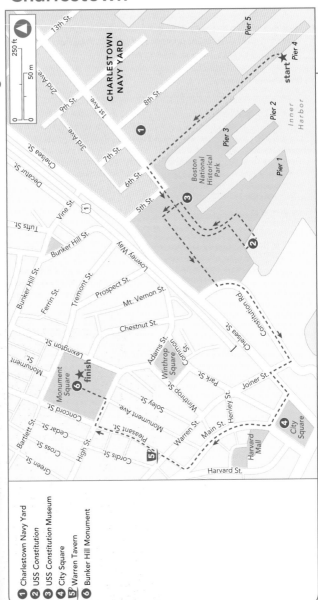

1 Charlestown Navy Yard
2 USS Constitution
3 USS Constitution Museum
4 City Square
5 Warren Tavern
6 Bunker Hill Monument

Charlestown, the neighborhood across the Inner Harbor from the North End, was originally settled as a separate town in 1629 (a year before Boston proper). It became part of the city in 1874 but retains an air of individuality—and a reputation for insularity that's slowly yielding to gentrification. START: **Ferry from Long Wharf (Blue Line T to Aquarium) to Charlestown Navy Yard**

① Charlestown Navy Yard.

The shipyard built, supplied, and maintained U.S. Navy vessels from 1800 to 1974. At its height, during World War II, the facility employed more than 40,000 people. Although it's no longer an active base, it's home to one of the most famous ships in American history, USS *Constitution*. The navy yard combines residential, office, and lab space with military monuments, explanatory plaques galore, and a 30-acre (12 hectare) piece of the Boston National Historical Park. Take a ranger-guided tour if you wish; thanks to all the plaques, you can do almost as well wandering on your own. ⏱ *15 min. to explore independently; 1 hr. for ranger tour. Building 5, off Chelsea St.; enter through Gate 1, at Constitution Rd.* ☎ *617/242-5601. www.nps.gov/ bost. Daily 9am–5pm. Free admission. T: Ferry from Long Wharf, or Green or Orange Line to North Station and 10-min. walk.*

② ★★ kids USS Constitution.

The frigate's three masts loom over the navy yard, and its gorgeous black hull is one of the most eye-catching sights on the harbor. On August 19, 1812, in an engagement with HMS *Guerriere* during the War of 1812, the British vessel's cannonballs bounced off the *Constitution*'s thick oak hull as if it were metal, and the nickname "Old Ironsides" was born. The oldest commissioned floating warship in the world (launched in 1797 and retired in 1815), Old Ironsides never lost a

battle, but narrowly escaped destruction several times in its first 2 centuries. Today the 204-foot-long (62m) ship is a beloved symbol of Boston. This is an active-duty posting for the sailors who lead the tours (wearing replicas of 1812 uniforms), and visiting means clearing security. The tour—a fascinating overview as well as a great opportunity to mingle with people from all over the country and around the world—is worth the slight inconvenience. ⏱ *1 hr., including security screening; arrive as early as possible to beat the tour groups. Charlestown Navy Yard.* ☎ *617/242-7511. www. history.navy.mil/ussconstitution. Free*

"Old Ironsides."

Quincy Market architect Alexander Parris also designed the USS Constitution Museum building.

admission. Apr–Sept Tue–Sun 10am–6pm, Oct Tues–Sun 10am–4pm, Nov–Mar Thu–Sun 10am–4pm. Tours year-round every 30 min. until 30 min. before closing time. T: Ferry from Long Wharf, or Green or Orange Line to North Station and 10-min. walk.

3 ★ kids USS Constitution Museum. The Constitution is, for the most part, a hands-off experience; its engaging museum is exactly the opposite. Children (and adults) push buttons, open doors, pull ropes, study artifacts, watch demonstrations of maritime crafts, and enjoy the interactive exhibits. The granite building was originally the navy yard's wood and metal shop. ⓘ 30 min. Building 22, off First Ave. ☎ 617/426-1812. www.ussconstitutionmuseum.org. Suggested donation $5 adults, $3 seniors, $2 kids. Daily Apr–Oct 9am–6pm; Nov–Mar 10am–5pm. T: Ferry from Long Wharf, or Green or Orange Line to North Station and 10-min. walk.

4 ★ City Square. Not so long ago, this was a grim patch of asphalt beneath a hideous highway overpass. Today it's one of the most pleasant side effects of the Big Dig, the highway-construction project that took over Boston in the 1990s. The centerpiece is City Square Park, a 1-acre (.4 hectare) oasis of lawns, trees, shrubs, flowers, and benches, dotted with plaques, memorials, and a fountain. After the highway moved underground, the park opened in 1996, foreshadowing the explosion of public outdoor space that followed the completion of the Big Dig, notably the Rose Kennedy Greenway. Note the sculptures of creatures around the park; they include a crane at the top of the fountain (the Three Cranes Tavern once stood on this site) and numerous cod, honoring the integral role the fish once played in Boston's economy. Rutherford Ave. and Chelsea St.

5 ★ **Warren Tavern.** The British torched Charlestown as they withdrew in 1775, destroying most of its pre-Revolutionary buildings. This wooden structure, completed around 1780, was part of the wave of construction that followed. It's a pleasant, if touristy, place for a bite and a break. *2 Pleasant St. (Main St.).* ☎ *617/241-8142. www.warren tavern.com. $–$$.*

6 ★ **Bunker Hill Monument.** The narrow streets of Charlestown all seem to lead to this elegant square. The 221-foot (67m) granite obelisk at the center, designed by the prolific Solomon Willard, commemorates the Battle of Bunker Hill on June 17, 1775; June 17 is now Bunker Hill Day, a holiday in Suffolk County. The British won that battle, but nearly half of their troops were killed or wounded. Partly as a consequence of the carnage, royal forces abandoned Boston 9 months later. The exhibits in the small but fascinating museum across the street (43 Monument Sq.) tell the story of the battle. Think hard before attempting the 294 stairs to the top of the monument; the climb is tough, and it ends at a small space with frustratingly tiny windows. I've done it, but when I find myself here with people who insist on heading up, I opt to wander the perimeter of the square and check out the pleasantly diverse architecture. A bit of trivia: The Battle of Bunker Hill was actually fought on Breed's Hill; you're there. ⏱ *30 min. if you stay on the ground; 1 hr. if you climb the stairs. Monument Sq. at Monument Ave.* ☎ *617/242-5641. www.nps.gov/bost. Free admission. Museum daily 9am–5pm (until 6pm July–Aug); monument daily 9am–4:30pm (until 5:30pm July–Aug). T: Orange Line to Community College.*

Statue of William Prescott, who gave the legendary command: "Don't fire until you see the whites of their eyes."

Harvard Square

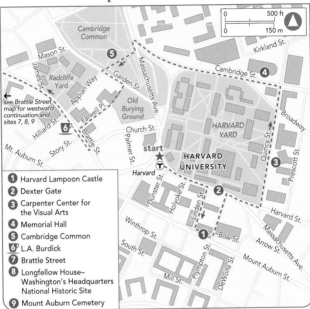

0   500 ft
0   150 m

Cambridge Common

Kirkland St.

Mason St.

James St.

Radcliffe Yard

Appian Way

Garden St.

Massachusetts Ave.

Cambridge St.

Farwell Pl.

see Brattle Street map for westward continuation and sites 7, 8, 9

Old Burying Ground

Hilliard St.

Story St.

Brattle St.

Church St.

Palmer St.

HARVARD YARD

Broadway

Mt. Auburn St.

start

Harvard

HARVARD UNIVERSITY

Quincy St.

Prescott St.

Dunster St.

Holyoke St.

Linden St.

Harvard St.

Winthrop St.

South St.

Bow St.

Arrow St.

Massachusetts Ave.

Plympton St.

DeWolfe St.

Mount Auburn St.

Mill St.

1 Harvard Lampoon Castle
2 Dexter Gate
3 Carpenter Center for the Visual Arts
4 Memorial Hall
5 Cambridge Common
6 L.A. Burdick
7 Brattle Street
8 Longfellow House– Washington's Headquarters National Historic Site
9 Mount Auburn Cemetery

Much of the interesting architecture in and around Harvard Square is on the main Harvard University campus, and a great deal of it isn't. This tour touches on both. The school and "the Square" have been inextricably linked since they were just starting out—in the 1630s. Neither would be what it is today without the other. START: Red Line to Harvard

1 ★ Harvard Lampoon Castle. A peerless blend of form and function, the castle is the home of the university's best-known undergraduate humor magazine, the *Harvard Lampoon*. The triangular building is suitably madcap, with colorful trim all around and a "face" of three windows and a door on the Linden Street end. The 1909 structure is the work of Edmund Wheelwright of the Boston firm of Wheelwright & Haven, also the architect of the Longfellow Bridge and numerous cultural venues. The *Lampoon* is a

legendary launching pad—the founders of the *National Lampoon* and dozens of writers for *Saturday Night Live, The Simpsons,* Conan O'Brien's various efforts, and other TV hits (and misses) got their start here. *57 Mount Auburn St. and 44 Bow St. (Linden and Plympton sts.).*

2 Dexter Gate. Facing the street, the engraving on this portal to Harvard Yard reads ENTER TO GROW IN WISDOM. On the other side, the inscription says DEPART TO SERVE BETTER THY COUNTRY AND THY KIND. *Massachusetts Ave. at Plympton St.*

3 ★★ Carpenter Center for the Visual Arts. Completed in 1963, the Carpenter Center is the only North American building designed by the Swiss-French architect Le Corbusier. The concrete building's dynamic design encourages visitors to circulate on ramps that allow views of studio space from the public areas. The two gallery spaces are open to the public. Purists deplore the way the Carpenter Center relates to its surroundings; pause across the street to contemplate the site, which does seem to cramp the building's style, even to the amateur's eye. *24 Quincy St. (Harvard St. and Broadway).* ☎ *617/495-3251. www.ves.fas.harvard.edu/ccva.html. Sept–May Mon–Sat 9am–11:30pm, Sun noon–11:30pm.*

4 ★ Memorial Hall. The architects of "Mem Hall," the firm of Ware & Van Brunt, won a design competition that was open only to Harvard graduates (who wonder why people think they're snobs). The cornerstone was laid in 1870 and construction completed in 1875. *See p 18, bullet 6.*

5 ★ Cambridge Common. Set aside as public land in 1631, just a year after the founding of Cambridge (then called Newtowne), the Common sometimes feels like one of the only quiet parts of Harvard Square. Legend has it that George Washington took control of the Continental Army here in July 1775, but historians have debunked the specifics. Nevertheless, a memorial surrounded by three cannons commemorates the event. A more

John Harvard statue in Harvard Yard.

interesting marker is on the edge of the Common. While Paul Revere was leaving Boston by boat on April 18, 1775, William Dawes slipped out of town on horseback, following what's now Washington Street. Both headed for Lexington and Concord, and Dawes rode through the heart of Cambridge. On Massachusetts Avenue north of Garden Street, horseshoes embedded in the sidewalk illustrate his path. *Massachusetts Ave. and Garden St.*

6 ★★ L. A. Burdick Chocolate Shop & Café. The cafe serves pastries and drinks (hot and cold) and sells high-end chocolates created by the New Hampshire–based confectioner. *52 Brattle St.* ☎ *617/491-4340. www.burdickchocolate.com. $.*

Memorial Hall.

7 ★★★ Brattle Street. One of the most beautiful residential streets in the country, Brattle Street has been an exclusive address since colonial times. It gained fame—and the nickname "Tory Row"—around the time of the Revolution because of its association with British sympathizers. The loyalists later evacuated, but some of their lovely homes survive.

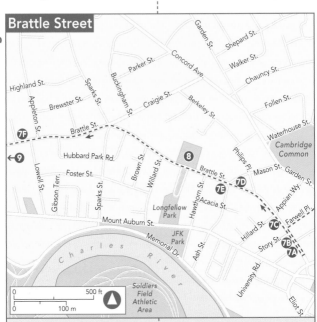

Brattle Street

The 1727 **7A William Brattle House** (no. 42) is the property of the nonprofit Cambridge Center for Adult Education. A splash of modern design in Colonial Cambridge, the 1969 **7B Design Research Building** (no. 48) is the work of Benjamin Thompson and Associates. The Cambridge Center for Adult Ed also owns the **7C Hancock-Dexter-Pratt House** (no. 54), constructed in 1811 and immortalized by Longfellow, who saw the village blacksmith working here in the late 1830s, in his words, "under a spreading chestnut tree." The 1847 Gothic Revival **7D Burleigh House** is also known as the Norton-Johnson-Burleigh House (no. 85). Our old friend H. H. Richardson, architect of Boston's Trinity Church, designed the **7E Stoughton House** (no. 90), which was completed in 1883. The Cambridge Historical Society (☎ 617/547-4252; www.cambridge history.org) makes its home in the striking **7F Hooper-Lee-Nichols House** (no. 159), built around 1685 and substantially modified since then. It's open to the public but was closed for renovations at press time; check ahead to see whether tours (offered only a couple of times a week) have resumed.

The former home of Henry Wadsworth Longfellow on Brattle Street.

❽ ★★ Longfellow House–Washington's Headquarters National Historic Site. Henry Wadsworth Longfellow lived here from 1843 until his death, in 1882. He first lived here as a boarder in 1837; after he married Fanny Appleton, her father made the house a wedding present. The current furnishings and books belonged to the poet and his descendants. Built in 1759, the Vassall-Craigie-Longfellow House was George Washington's headquarters in 1775 and 1776, during the siege of Boston. The 45-minute guided tour is the only way to see the house, but the lovely grounds and gardens are open year-round during daylight hours. ⏱ *1 hr. 105 Brattle St. (Longfellow Park).* ☎ *617/491-1054. www.nps.gov/long. Late May to Oct Wed–Sun 9:30am–4:30pm; always check ahead. Admission & tour free. T: Red Line to Harvard, 10-min. walk on Brattle St.*

❾ ★★ Mount Auburn Cemetery. Consecrated in 1831, Mount Auburn was the first of the "garden cemeteries" that gained popularity as urban centers became too congested to support the expansion of downtown burying grounds. I find all cemeteries interesting; this one is a particularly fascinating combination of landscaping, statuary, sculpture, architecture, and, most important, history. You can tour on foot or in a car, using several routes available through the website. The notable people buried here range from Charles Bulfinch, who died in 1844, to Bernard Malamud, who died in 1986. They include Mary Baker Eddy, Isabella Stewart Gardner, Oliver Wendell Holmes, Julia Ward Howe, Winslow Homer, Henry Wadsworth Longfellow, and abolitionist Charles Sumner, among many others—and their numbers continue to grow. Bear in mind that Mount Auburn is an active cemetery: Animals and recreational activities (including picnicking and jogging) are forbidden. ⏱ *2 hr. 580 Mount Auburn St. (Brattle St. and Aberdeen Ave.).* ☎ *617/547-7105 (info) or* ☎ *617/607-1981 (events). www.mountauburn.org. Daily summer 8am–8pm, winter 8am–5pm; visitor center daily 9am–4:30pm. Admission & self-guided tours free; fees for guided group tours vary. T: Red Line to Harvard; then bus no. 71 or 73.*

Mount Auburn's 175 acres (71ha) hold some 5,000 trees representing 700-plus species.

The South End

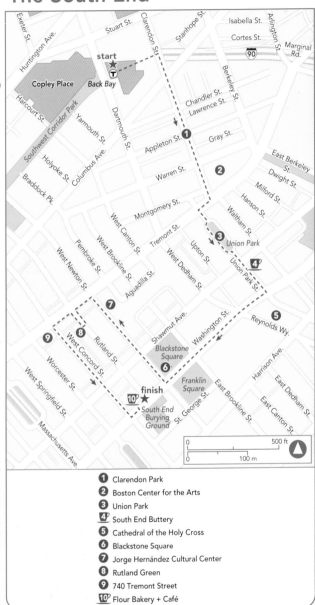

1 Clarendon Park
2 Boston Center for the Arts
3 Union Park
4 South End Buttery
5 Cathedral of the Holy Cross
6 Blackstone Square
7 Jorge Hernández Cultural Center
8 Rutland Green
9 740 Tremont Street
10 Flour Bakery + Café

Long known as one of the city's most culturally and economically diverse neighborhoods, with a large gay community and an exciting restaurant scene, the sprawling South End gets more gentrified by the day. Despite a lack of museums or other prominent attractions, its rewards are considerable for visitors who don't mind a fair amount of walking. Note that neither church on this route keeps regular open hours—though both are quite engaging from the outside—and remember that they don't admit sightseers during religious services. START: **Orange Line to Back Bay**

① ★ **Clarendon Park.** Narrow, picturesque streets make up the tiny enclave known as Clarendon Park. In either direction from Clarendon Street south of Columbus Avenue, little brick row houses with modest entrances and black-painted shutters line streets just wide enough to hold one lane of parking (a perennial scarcity in Boston) and one lane of traffic. The housing stock here recalls the mansions of Beacon Hill, but on a scale more accessible to the working people who made their homes in the South End before late-20th-century gentrification swept through. Today this is prime real estate. *Chandler, Lawrence, Appleton, and Gray sts. and Warren Ave. between Berkeley and Dartmouth sts.*

② ★★ **Boston Center for the Arts.** The Boston Center for the Arts, or BCA, is a 4-acre (7-hectare) complex of multiple performance spaces that centers on the Cyclorama. Regrettably not visible from the street, the circular Cyclorama—a huge enclosed space beneath a graceful 127-foot-wide (39m) dome—represents a popular form of 19th-century entertainment. Designed by Cummings and Sears and opened to the public in 1884, it originally held a panoramic painting, *The Battle of Gettysburg*, which was 50 feet (15m) tall and 400 feet (122m) long. As the popularity of cycloramas faded, the building became an entertainment venue, a boxing ring, an industrial site, and eventually the city's flower market. Redevelopment in the 1970s resulted in the return of the 23,000-square-foot (2,137 sq. m) Cyclorama to its roots as an exhibition and performance space. If it's open to the public during your visit— I've been there for everything from a poetry reading to an antiques show—check it out. *539 Tremont St. (Clarendon and Berkeley sts.).* ☎ 617/426-5000. www.bcaonline.org.

Modern performances take place in the 19th-century Boston Center for the Arts.

Union Park dates from the late 1850s.

Cyclorama Mon–Fri 9am–5pm except during events.

③ ★★ Union Park. One of the most beautiful spots in the city is this 1-block stretch of brick row houses surrounding an oval park. Appealing architectural details abound, and an iron fence encloses the namesake park, which holds trees, flowers, lawns, and bubbling fountains. This was the first completed square in the rapidly developing neighborhood, which was then considered a rival to the newly created Back Bay. The South End never quite gained the same cachet, however, and to this day—partly because public-transit access is better there—the Back Bay is ever so slightly pricier. *Tremont St. to Shawmut Ave.*

④ South End Buttery. Sit inside or out, sip a drink, enjoy a snack or meal, and take in the neighborhood scene. *314 Shawmut Ave. (Union Park St.).* ☎ *617/482-1015. www.southendbuttery.com. $–$$.*

⑤ ★ Cathedral of the Holy Cross. In Boston's early years, this land held the town gallows. The Puritan settlement wasn't exactly a magnet for Roman Catholics, but by the mid-19th century, the city's social and political climate had changed dramatically. The decade following the Civil War saw the construction of this edifice, which rivals Westminster Abbey in size. The building is 364 feet (111m) long and seats more than 1,700. The Gothic Revival design, executed in Roxbury puddingstone and limestone, is by the prolific Patrick Keely, an Irish immigrant who was reputedly the architect of more than 600 American houses of worship. The plan originally called for a spire on each of the two towers, but they were never built. An unsightly elevated railway ran along Washington Street for most of the 20th century, literally overshadowing the cathedral; the building and its stained-glass windows benefited considerably from the demolition of the "El," in 1987, and the resulting increased illumination. Most of the windows date to 1880, but my favorite is from 1940—a triptych in the south nave that depicts St. Fortunatus. It has so much going on that it almost appears to be

When it was consecrated in 1875, Holy Cross was the largest Catholic church in the United States.

moving. ⏱ *20 min. 1400 Washington St. (Union Park).* ☎ *617/542-5682. www.holycrossboston.com.*

❻ ★★ Blackstone Square. The little park on your right is Blackstone Square; its sibling across Washington Street is Franklin Square. Charles Bulfinch planned this intersection in 1801, but his vision wasn't executed until the 1860s, when development was sweeping across the South End. Imagine this area as Bulfinch would have seen it, when Washington Street was the primary land route to downtown Boston. Today, the twin green spaces break up the man-made landscape of this built-up area; at the turn of the 19th century, they would have formed a stately entranceway to the city. *Washington St. (W. Brookline and W. Newton sts.).*

❼ Jorge Hernández Cultural Center. A skillful restoration of a historic building, the cultural center occupies the former All Saints Lutheran Church. The German Gothic facade encloses a performance and event space that often books Latin musical artists and groups—in a place where Albert Schweitzer once played the organ. The 1898 church was falling apart when it was rehabbed in 1986, retaining a gorgeous stained-glass window. The renovated parish house is home to the Latino-focused Villa Victoria Center for the Arts, which has an art gallery and studio space. *85 W. Newton St. (Tremont St.).* ☎ *617/927-1737. www.villa victoriaarts.org. La Galería art gallery Thurs–Fri 3–6pm, Sat 1–4pm.*

❽ ★★ Rutland Green. A neighborhood resident tipped me off to this delightful pocket park, which holds the seating you probably want by now and abundant greenery to admire while you recharge. *Rutland St. (Aguadilla St.).*

Fountain in Blackstone Square.

❾ ★ 740 Tremont Street. Originally the Tremont Street Methodist Church and later New Hope Baptist, this 1862 Gothic Revival edifice is distinguished by the presence of two full-blown towers, one on either end. Now divided into luxury condos, the building was the first church in the Boston area constructed of Roxbury puddingstone, which later became a popular building material. The architect was Hammatt Billings, who earned his greatest fame as an illustrator. Now little known, he was one of the best-known designers in Boston in the mid-19th century, when he created everything from fireworks displays to the original illustrations for *Uncle Tom's Cabin.* *740 Tremont St. (W. Concord St.).*

❿ ★ Flour Bakery + Café. Flour is a homey destination for all sorts of culinary delights, from a single superb cookie to a full meal. If they're available, don't miss the doughnuts. *1595 Washington St. (Rutland St.).* ☎ *617/267-4300. www.flourbakery.com. $–$$.*

The Best Neighborhood Tours

The Back Bay

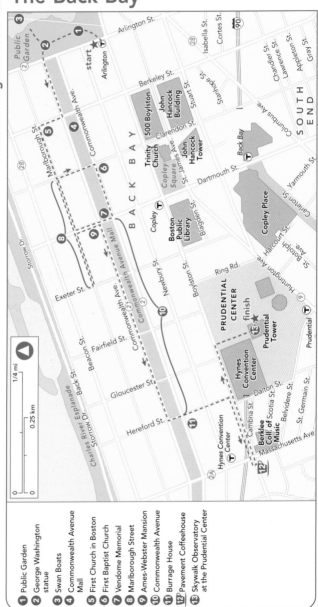

1 Public Garden
2 George Washington statue
3 Swan Boats
4 Commonwealth Avenue Mall
5 First Church in Boston
6 First Baptist Church
7 Vendome Memorial
8 Marlborough Street
9 Ames-Webster Mansion
10 Commonwealth Avenue
11 Burrage House
12 Pavement Coffeehouse
13 Skywalk Observatory at the Prudential Center

Landfill projects executed between 1835 and 1882 created this area, which replaced a marshy body of water. The street pattern is a grid, a nice contrast with the crazy-quilt geography of the city's older neighborhoods. The streets here go in alphabetical order, starting at the Public Garden with Arlington Street and continuing across Massachusetts Avenue. You may not be able to gain entrance to both churches on this route—and there's no sightseeing during religious services—but the exteriors are fascinating in their own right. This is mostly an outdoor excursion; in the heat of summer, try to get an early start. START: **Green Line to Arlington**

① ★★★ Kids Public Garden.
Today, Charles Street separates Boston Common from the Public Garden; in colonial times, it was the shore of the Charles River. On the night of April 18, 1775, British troops bound for Lexington and Concord boarded boats to Cambridge ("two if by sea") at the foot of the Common and set off across what's now the Public Garden. *See p 15, bullet* ⑥.

② ★★ George Washington statue. Boston's first equestrian statue guards the most dramatic entrance to the city's loveliest park. The 38-foot-tall (12m) statue is considered an excellent likeness of the first president, an outstanding horseman. The artist, Thomas Ball, was a Charlestown native who worked in Italy. Among his students was noted sculptor Daniel Chester French (he created the Abraham Lincoln statue in Washington, D.C.'s Lincoln Memorial, among many other works). *Off Arlington St. at Commonwealth Ave.*

③ ★★ Swan Boats. A beloved symbol of Boston, the Swan Boats are a low-tech delight in a high-tech world. Pedaling one of these things looks like brutally hard work—for the attendants at the back of each boat who do the pedaling. Meanwhile, the passengers relax on benches, taking in the passing scene of ducks, swans,

George Washington statue in the Public Garden.

pigeons, dogs, and humans lazing on the shores of the little lagoon. The swan-drawn boat in the opera *Lohengrin* inspired the design of the vessels, which have been the Paget family business since 1877; the current fleet consists of larger versions of the originals. If you're a fiend for planning, make sure your family is familiar with E. B. White's charming novel *The Trumpet of the Swan* before you even see a Swan Boat—you won't be sorry. ① *15 min. for the ride; allow 1 hr., including a little down time before or after.*

First Baptist Church. The trumpeters on the corners of this frieze are sometimes called "the bean blowers."

The Public Garden is bordered by Arlington, Boylston, Charles, and Beacon sts.; the boats operate on the lagoon in the middle. ☎ *617/522-1966. www.swanboats.com. Tickets $3 adults, $2 seniors, $1.50 kids 2–15, free for kids 1 and under. Sat before Patriots Day to mid-June daily 10am–4pm; mid-June to Labor Day daily 10am–5pm; day after Labor Day to mid-Sept Mon–Fri noon–4pm, Sat–Sun 10am–4pm. Closed mid-Sept to mid-Apr. T: Green Line to Arlington.*

④ ★★ Commonwealth Avenue Mall. The centerpiece of architect Arthur Gilman's French-inspired design of the Back Bay is this dramatic boulevard, 240 feet (73m) wide with a 100-foot-wide (30m) mall down the center. Construction began in 1858, and by the late 1870s, the mall was important enough for landscape architect Frederick Law Olmsted to include it in his system of Boston parks known as the Emerald Necklace. Beautiful buildings line both sides of the street, and a curious collection of statuary embellishes the mall; it begins with Alexander Hamilton (across Arlington St. from George Washington) and extends to Leif Eriksson (at the west end, not far from Kenmore Square). *Arlington St. to Charlesgate.*

⑤ ★ First Church in Boston. First Church in Boston is a direct successor of *the* first church in Boston. John Winthrop and his followers had barely landed when they adopted the covenant that launched the congregation in 1630. This building dates to 1867, when the institution was known as the First and Second Church. The original architects, Ware and Van Brunt (who designed Harvard's Memorial Hall), intended the edifice to resemble an English country church. A fire in 1968 destroyed much of that building; Paul Rudolph's 1971 renovation preserves much of the remaining structure. Now Unitarian Universalist, the congregation voted to revert to the current name in 2005. ⏱ *15 min. 66 Marlborough St. (Berkeley St.).*

☎ 617/267-6730. www.firstchurch boston.org. T: Green Line to Arlington.

6 ★ First Baptist Church. The legendary architect H. H. Richardson was just starting out when he designed this church, a Roxbury puddingstone structure with a 176-foot (54m) tower. This is the first church in the style now known as Richardsonian Romanesque (the best-known example is Trinity Church in Copley Square). Completed in 1872, it originally belonged to the Brattle Square Unitarian Society, which sold it in 1882. It's notable not just for Richardson's work, but for the contribution of another genius who went on to a better-known project: The frieze at the top of the tower is the work of Frédéric Auguste Bartholdi, designer of the Statue of Liberty. Louis Comfort Tiffany designed the stained-glass window depicting Jesus' baptism, but the three rose windows are the real treasures here. Almost every guidebook I've ever seen says this building's nickname is the "Church of the Holy Bean Blowers," but I've never heard an actual person call it that. ⏱ 15 min. 110 Commonwealth Ave.

(Clarendon St.). ☎ 617/267-3148. www.firstbaptistchurchofboston.org. T: Green Line to Arlington.

7 ★★ Vendome Memorial. On June 17, 1972, fire devastated the former Hotel Vendome—and the Boston Fire Department. A blaze in the lovely building at 160 Commonwealth Avenue had been extinguished and cleanup operations were under way when the southeast section of the structure unexpectedly collapsed. Nine firefighters were killed—the worst tragedy in the history of the department. The dramatic memorial, unveiled in 1997, is a low, curving black granite wall. The feature that pushes Ted Clausen's design from dramatic to heartbreaking is the bronze rendering of a firefighter's helmet and coat draped over the wall. *Commonwealth Ave. at Dartmouth St.*

8 ★★ Marlborough Street. In contrast to the grandeur of Commonwealth Avenue, the commerce of Newbury Street, and the traffic of Beacon Street, Marlborough Street is a gracious residential thoroughfare. I'm sending you on a somewhat meandering route that includes a 2-block stretch of

The Vendome Memorial.

Burrage Mansion.

Marlborough Street to ensure that you appreciate the contrast. If you like what you see, take some extra time to go farther. *Clarendon St. to Exeter St.*

9 ★ **Ames-Webster Mansion.** Constructed in 1872 and enlarged in 1882, this French Academic–style landmark boasts some of the most elaborate exterior decoration in the Back Bay—which is really saying something. The 50-room property holds offices; you can probably slip into the lobby and check out the interior ornamentation. *306 Dartmouth St. (Commonwealth Ave.). T: Green Line to Copley.*

10 ★★★ **Commonwealth Avenue.** The buildings that line "Comm. Ave." proceed in roughly chronological order. As the landfill that created the Back Bay neighborhood marched west, architectural styles grew wilder, leaving behind a few stretches where it hardly seems possible that the building facades could hold more ornamentation. Take your time as you explore this 4-block stretch,

which abounds with gables, archways, medallions, fanciful wrought iron, and ornamental brickwork. *Dartmouth St. to Hereford St.*

11 **Burrage House.** Inspired by the Château de Chenonceau in France's Loire Valley, the 1899 mansion designed by Charles Brigham is a rare Boston example of over-the-top French Renaissance architecture. The roof of the limestone building, now divided into four huge condos, is especially ornate—check out the turrets. *314 Commonwealth Ave. (Hereford St.).*

12 ★ **Pavement Coffeehouse.** A welcoming space that's usually crawling with students, Pavement is part of a small local chain known for terrific coffee and almost-as-good food. *1096 Boylston St. (Mass. Ave.).* ☎ *617/236-1500. www.pavement coffeehouse.com. $.*

13 ★★ **Skywalk Observatory at the Prudential Center.** Having seen the Back Bay from street level, you'll get a new perspective when you study it from above. The Skywalk, on the 50th floor of the Prudential Tower, affords views of far more than just the Back Bay—the 360-degree panorama extends as far as New Hampshire and Cape Cod when the sky is clear. Interactive audiovisual displays, including exhibits about immigration, trace Boston's history. ⏱ *1 hr. 800 Boylston St. (Fairfield St.).* ☎ *617/ 859-0648. www.topofthehub.net/ skywalk.php. Daily 10am–8pm (until 10pm mid-March to early Nov); always call first, because the space sometimes closes for private events. Admission $15 adults, $13 seniors and students, $10 kids in 6th grade and younger. T: Green Line E to Prudential, or B, C, or D to Hynes Convention Center.* ●

Shopping Best Bets

Most **Fun Gifts**
★★★ Joie de Vivre, *1792 Massachusetts Ave., Cambridge (p 86)*

Most **Socially Conscious Gifts**
★★★ Ten Thousand Villages, *252 Washington St. and branches (p 87)*

Most **Unusual Souvenirs**
★★ Lannan Ship Model Gallery, *99 High St. (p 86)*

Best **Sweet Spot**
★★ Beacon Hill Chocolates, *91 Charles St. (p 85)*

Best **Fancy Jewelry**
★★ John Lewis, Inc., *97 Newbury St. (p 87)*

Best **Antiques**
★★★ Upstairs Downstairs Antiques, *93 Charles St. (p 78)*

Best **Craft Supplies**
★★ Paper Source, *338 Boylston St. and branches (p 82)*

Most **Unexpected**
★★★ International Poster Gallery, *205 Newbury St. (p 79)*

Best **Home Decor**
★ Simon Pearce, *103 Newbury St. (p 86)*

Best **Reason to Visit Harvard Square**
★★ Colonial Drug, *49 Brattle St., Cambridge (p 88)*

Best **Wedding Gifts**
★★ Jonathan Adler, *129 Newbury St. (p 86)*

Best **Toys for Adults**
★ Black Ink, *101 Charles St. and 5 Brattle St., Cambridge (p 85)*

Best **Toys for Kids**
★★ Magic Beans, *800 Boylston St. (p 81)*

Best **Children's Clothing**
★★ The Red Wagon, *69 Charles St. (p 81)*

Most **Teen-Friendly**
★ Newbury Comics, *North Market Building, Faneuil Hall Marketplace, and branches (p 88)*

Best **Salute to Texas**
★ Helen's Leather Shop, *110 Charles St. (p 84)*

There's some good shopping around Harvard Square. Previous page: Antique store window.

Downtown Boston Shopping

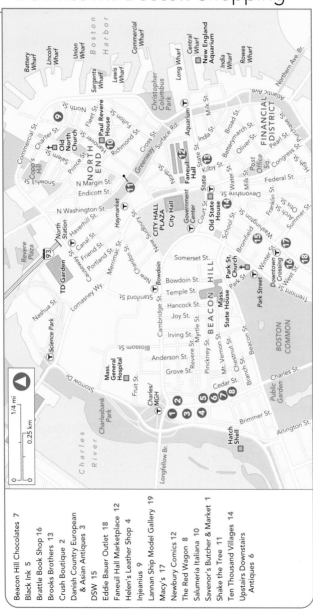

Back Bay Shopping

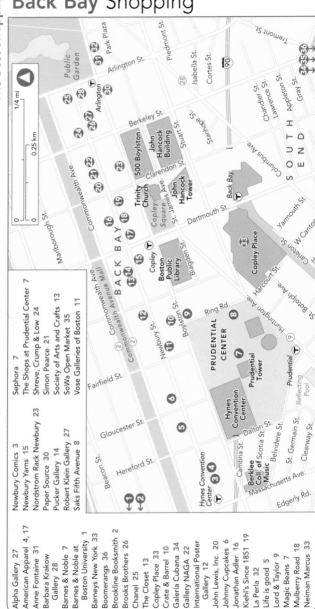

Harvard Square Shopping

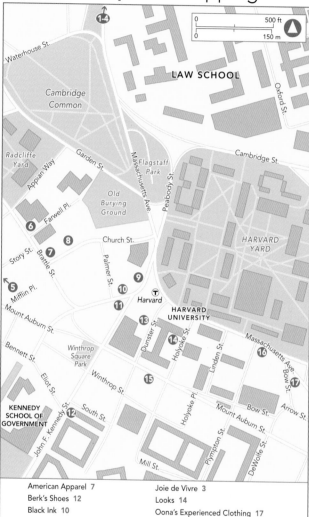

American Apparel 7

Berk's Shoes 12

Black Ink 10

Cambridge Artists' Cooperative Craft Gallery 8

Colonial Drug 6

Crate & Barrel 19

The Games People Play 18

Harvard Book Store 16

The Harvard Coop 9

Joie de Vivre 3

Looks 14

Oona's Experienced Clothing 17

Paper Source 2

Planet Records 5

Porter Square Books 1

Schoenhof's Foreign Books 15

Topaz 13

WardMaps LLC 4

The World's Only Curious George Store 11

Cambridge Shopping

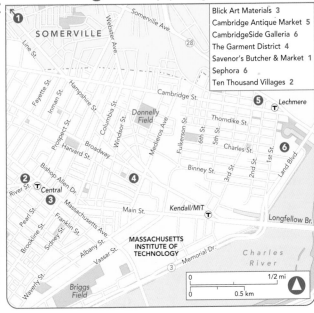

Blick Art Materials 3
Cambridge Antique Market 5
CambridgeSide Galleria 6
The Garment District 4
Savenor's Butcher & Market 1
Sephora 6
Ten Thousand Villages 2

Boston Shopping A to Z

Antiques & Collectibles
★★ Cambridge Antique Market CAMBRIDGE Five floors and more than 100 dealers make a hit-or-miss experience—with more hits than misses. Many of the merchants accept credit cards. *201 Msgr. O'Brien Hwy. (Third St.).* ☎ *617/868-9655. www.marketantique.com. T: Green Line to Lechmere. Map above.*

★ Danish Country European & Asian Antiques BEACON HILL The specialty here is the unexpected but delightful combo of Scandinavian and Asian antiques and furnishings. *138 Charles St. (Revere St.).* ☎ *617/227-1804. www.europeanstyle antiques.com. AE, MC, V. T: Red Line to Charles/MGH. Map p 75.*

★★★ Upstairs Downstairs Antiques BEACON HILL Arranged as a series of tastefully appointed rooms, this subterranean shop reflects its owners' discerning eye and nose for value. *93 Charles St. (Pinckney St.).* ☎ *617/367-1950. MC, V. T: Red Line to Charles/MGH. Map p 75.*

Art
★ Alpha Gallery BACK BAY Contemporary paintings, sculpture, and works on paper are the focus. *37 Newbury St., 4th floor (Arlington and Berkeley sts.).* ☎ *617/536-4465. www.alphagallery.com. MC, V. T: Green Line to Arlington. Map p 76.*

★★★ Barbara Krakow Gallery

BACK BAY   This venerable gallery is an important destination for post-1945 paintings, sculptures, drawings, and prints. *10 Newbury St. (Arlington St.).* ☎ *617/262-4490. www.barbarakrakowgallery.com. No credit cards. T: Green Line to Arlington. Map p 76.*

★★ Galería Cubana

SOUTH END   Cuban art direct from the island, in a huge variety of styles and media, makes this a can't-miss destination. *460 Harrison Ave. (Thayer St.).* ☎ *617/292-2822. www.lagaleriacubana.com. AE, MC, V. T: Orange Line to New England Medical Center or Silver Line SL4/SL5 to E. Berkeley St. Map p 76.*

★★ Gallery NAGA

BACK BAY   Inside the Church of the Covenant, Gallery NAGA focuses on contemporary painting, photography, studio furniture, and (so cool!) holography. *67 Newbury St. (Berkeley St.).* ☎ *617/267-9060. www.gallerynaga.com. AE. T: Green Line to Arlington. Map p 76.*

★★★ International Poster Gallery

BACK BAY   The huge stock of French, Swiss, Italian, Soviet, and other international vintage posters here is always worth a look. *205 Newbury St. (Exeter and Fairfield sts.).* ☎ *617/375-0076. www.internationalposter.com. AE, MC, V. T: Green Line to Copley. Map p 76.*

★ Pucker Gallery

BACK BAY   Five floors of gallery space encompass African, Asian, Israeli, and Inuit work, an impressive variety of contemporary art, photographs, and more. *171 Newbury St. (Dartmouth and Exeter sts.).* ☎ *617/267-9473. www.puckergallery.com. MC, V. T: Green Line to Copley. Map p 76.*

★★★ Robert Klein Gallery

BACK BAY   This prestigious gallery represents fine-art photographers from the 19th through 21st centuries. *38 Newbury St. (Arlington and Berkeley sts.).* ☎ *617/267-7997. www.robertkleingallery.com. AE, MC, V. T: Green Line to Arlington. Map p 76.*

★ Vose Galleries of Boston

BACK BAY   The specialty here is American paintings from the 18th through the early 20th century. *238 Newbury St. (Fairfield St.).* ☎ *866/862-4871 or 617/536-6176. www.vosegalleries.com. AE, MC, V. T: Green Line to Copley or Green Line*

The International Poster Gallery.

B, C, or D to Hynes Convention Center. Map p 76.

Books

★ kids Barnes & Noble BACK BAY

This branch of the national chain is almost always busy; check ahead for kids' events, especially on weekends. There's also a Barnes & Noble at Boston University. *Shops at Prudential Center, 800 Boylston St. (Fairfield St.).* ☎ 617/247-6959. www.barnesandnoble.com. AE, DISC, MC, V. T: Green Line E to Prudential. Also at 660 Beacon St. (Commonwealth Ave.), Kenmore Sq. ☎ 617/267-8484. www.bu.bncollege.com. T: Green Line B, C, or D to Kenmore. Map p 76.

★★ Brattle Book Shop DOWNTOWN CROSSING

One of the best used-book dealers around, the Brattle Book Shop also sells rare and out-of-print titles. *9 West St. (Washington and Tremont sts.).* ☎ 800/447-9595 or 617/338-1467. www.brattlebookshop.com. AE, MC, V. T: Red or Orange Line to Downtown Crossing. Map p 75.

★★★ kids Brookline Booksmith COOLIDGE CORNER

Great selections of new and used books, tons of gifts, and an enthusiastic staff make this one of the Boston area's best bookstores. *279 Harvard St. (Beacon St.), Brookline.* ☎ 617/566-6660. www.brooklinebooksmith.com. AE, DISC, MC, V. T: Green Line C to Coolidge Corner. Map p 76.

★★ Harvard Book Store CAMBRIDGE

Great selections of new books upstairs, remainders and used books downstairs, and bookworms everywhere. Be sure to check out the machine that prints books on demand. *1256 Massachusetts Ave. (Plympton St.).* ☎ 800/542-READ or 617/661-1515. www.harvard.com. AE, DISC, MC, V. T: Red Line to Harvard. Map p 77.

★ The Harvard Coop CAMBRIDGE

At the heart of Harvard Square is this excellent bookstore and logo-merchandise shop. It is *not* true that everyone looks smarter in a Harvard T-shirt. *1400 Massachusetts Ave. (Brattle St.).* ☎ 617/499-2000. www.thecoop.com. AE, MC, V. T: Red Line to Harvard. Map p 77.

★★ kids Porter Square Books CAMBRIDGE

This is a classic independent neighborhood bookstore—in a super-literate neighborhood. *Porter Square Shopping Center, 25 White St. (off Mass. Ave.).* ☎ 617/491-2220. www.portersquarebooks.com. AE, DISC, MC, V. T: Red Line to Porter. Map p 77.

There are plenty of bargains to be found at the Brattle Book Shop.

★ **Schoenhof's Foreign Books**
CAMBRIDGE If it's printed,
bound, and in a language other
than English, Schoenhof's likely
stocks it or can order it. *76A Mount
Auburn St. (Holyoke St.).* ☎ *617/547-
8855. www.schoenhofs.com. AE, MC,
V. T: Red Line to Harvard. Map p 77.*

★ **kids The World's Only Curious George Store** CAMBRIDGE
The children's books and toys here
include a huge selection of items
that feature the famous inquisitive
monkey—and plenty of things
that don't. *1 John F. Kennedy St.
(Brattle St.).* ☎ *617/547-4500. www.
thecuriousgeorgestore.com. AE,
DISC, MC, V. T: Red Line to Harvard.
Map p 77.*

Children: Fashion & Toys
★ **kids Magic Beans** BACK BAY
The city location of this small local
chain carries wonderful toys and
gifts as well as plenty of baby gear.
*Shops at Prudential Center, 776
Boylston St. (Fairfield St.).* ☎ *617/383-
8296. www.mbeans.com. AE, DISC,
MC, V. T: Green Line to Copley. Map
p 76. Check website for other
locations.*

★ **kids Mulberry Road** BACK
BAY Chic yet cozy, Mulberry Road
focuses on clothes and gifts for the
fashionable under-5 set. *128 Newbury St. (Clarendon St.).* ☎ *617/859-
5861. www.mulberryroad.com. DISC,
MC, V. T: Green Line to Copley. Map
p 76.*

★ **kids The Red Wagon** BEA-
CON HILL This welcoming space
overflows with toys and gorgeous,
pricey clothing and shoes for infants
to preteens. *69 Charles St. (Mount
Vernon St.).* ☎ *617/523-9402. www.
theredwagon.com. AE, DISC, MC, V.
T: Red Line to Charles/MGH. Map
p 75.*

*The Harvard Coop, a Harvard Square
mainstay.*

**Craft Galleries & Craft
Supplies**
★ **Blick Art Materials** CAM-
BRIDGE The Central Square
branch of the national chain carries
gift items as well as a limited but
well-organized stock of paint, pen-
cils, easels, canvas, and more. *619
Massachusetts Ave. (Pearl St.).*
☎ *617/441-6360. www.dickblick.
com. AE, DISC, MC, V. T: Red Line to
Central. Map p 78. Check website for
other locations.*

★★ **Cambridge Artists' Cooperative Craft Gallery** CAM-
BRIDGE The three-level gallery
spotlights top-notch American artisans; ask the savvy staff for point-
ers. *59A Church St. (Brattle St.).*
☎ *617/868-4434. www.cambridge
artistscoop.com. AE, MC, V. T: Red
Line to Harvard. Map p 77.*

★ **Newbury Yarns** BACK BAY
The merchandise and prices at this
little shop suit the tony neighborhood—and the welcoming attitude
is a nice contrast. *166 Newbury St.
(Dartmouth and Exeter sts.).* ☎ *617/
572-3733. www.newburyyarns.com.
AE, MC, V. T: Green Line to Copley.
Map p 76.*

There's beautiful work on display and for sale at the Society of Arts and Crafts.

★★ **Paper Source** BACK BAY
Gorgeous wrapping, writing, and
craft papers accompany an exten-
sive selection of gifts, books, pens,
stickers, stamps, and more. *338
Boylston St. (Arlington St.).* ☎ *617/
536-3444. www.paper-source.com.
AE, DISC, MC, V. T: Green Line to
Arlington. Map p 76. Also at 1810
Massachusetts Ave. (Arlington St.),
Cambridge.* ☎ *617/497-1077. T:
Red Line to Porter. Map p 77. Check
website for other locations.*

★★ **Society of Arts and Crafts**
BACK BAY   The nonprofit organization specializes in contemporary
American work. The sales floor is
downstairs, the gallery on the
second floor. *175 Newbury St. (Dartmouth and Exeter sts.).* ☎ *617/266-
1810. www.societyofcrafts.org. AE,
MC, V. T: Green Line to Copley. Map
p 76.*

Department Stores
★★ **Lord & Taylor** BACK BAY
An excellent destination for wom-
en's special-occasion finery, Lord &
Taylor also has terrific men's and
cosmetics departments and great
sales. *760 Boylston St. (Ring Rd.).*
☎ *617/262-6000. www.lordand
taylor.com. AE, DISC, MC, V. T:
Green Line to Copley. Map p 76.*

Macy's DOWNTOWN CROSSING
The anchor store of Downtown
Crossing, Macy's carries a wide
selection of men's and women's

fashion, cosmetics, housewares,
and more. *450 Washington St. (Summer St.).* ☎ *617/357-3000. www.
macys.com. AE, DISC, MC, V. T: Red
or Orange Line to Downtown Crossing. Map p 75. Check website for
other locations.*

★ **Neiman Marcus** BACK BAY
When you're shopping for the person who has everything and money
is no object, this is the place. *5
Copley Place, 100 Huntington Ave.
(Dartmouth St.).* ☎ *877/563-4626 or
617/536-3660. www.neimanmarcus.
com. AE, DISC, MC, V. T: Orange
Line to Back Bay. Map p 76.*

Saks Fifth Avenue BACK BAY
Fashion, cosmetics, and shoes
galore make Saks one of the New
York names Bostonians have
embraced without any complaints.
*Shops at Prudential Center, 800
Boylston St. (Ring Rd.).* ☎ *617/262-
8500. www.saksfifthavenue.com. AE,
DISC, MC, V. T: Green Line E to Pru-
dential. Map p 76.*

Discount Shopping
★ **DSW** DOWNTOWN CROSS-
ING   Discounted men's and wom-
en's shoes cram two floors of DSW
(formerly Designer Shoe Ware-
house). Leave time to check the
clearance racks. *385 Washington St.
(Bromfield St.).* ☎ *617/556-0052.
www.dswshoe.com. AE, DISC, MC, V.
T: Red or Orange Line to Downtown
Crossing. Map p 75.*

★ **Eddie Bauer Outlet** DOWN-TOWN CROSSING The sportswear specialist nicks some prices and slashes others at this large, well-maintained store. *500 Washington St. (Temple Place).* ☎ *617-423-4722. www.eddiebauer.com. AE, DISC, MC, V. T: Red or Orange Line to Downtown Crossing. Map p 75.*

★★ **Nordstrom Rack Newbury** BACK BAY What's better than high-quality women's and men's fashion and that legendary Nordstrom service? Getting it all at a discount. *497 Boylston St. (Clarendon St.).* ☎ *857/300-2300. www.nordstromrack.com. AE, DISC, MC, V. T: Green Line to Copley. Map p 76.*

Fashion

★ **American Apparel** BACK BAY The anti-sweatshop pioneer creates fun T-shirts, sexy tanks, and other comfy knits, all made in downtown Los Angeles. *138 Newbury St. (Dartmouth St.).* ☎ *617/536-4768. www.americanapparel.net. AE, DISC, MC, V. T: Green Line to Copley. Map p 76. Also at 330 Newbury St. (Hereford St.).* ☎ *617/236-1636. T: Green Line B, C, or D to Hynes Convention Center. Also at 47 Brattle St. (Church St.), Cambridge.* ☎ *617/661-2770. T: Red Line to Harvard. Map p 77.*

★ **Anne Fontaine** BACK BAY The French designer's specialty is perfect white blouses. Pastels sometimes sneak in (I've even seen black!), but it's really all about the white blouses. *318 Boylston St. (Arlington St.).* ☎ *617/423-0366. www.annefontaine.com. AE, MC, V. T: Green Line to Arlington. Map p 76.*

★ **Barneys New York** BACK BAY The New York–based luxury store specializes in men's and women's designer fashions and cosmetics. The women's shoe department is gigantic. *Copley Place, 100 Huntington Ave. (Dartmouth St.).* ☎ *617/385-3300. www.barneys.com. AE, MC, V. T: Orange Line to Back Bay. Map p 76.*

★★ **Berk's Shoes** CAMBRIDGE A Harvard Square standby, Berk's stocks the latest trends in footwear plus classic lines like Birkenstock and Converse. *50 John F. Kennedy St. (Winthrop St.).* ☎ *800/362-8386 or 617/492-9511. www.berkshoes.com. AE, DISC, MC, V. T: Red Line to Harvard. Map p 77.*

★ **Brooks Brothers** BACK BAY A mainstay of traditional New England "fashion." Lawyers and bankers predominate at the downtown branch. *46 Newbury St. (Berkeley St.).* ☎ *617/267-2600. www.brooksbrothers.com. AE, DISC, MC, V. T: Green Line to Arlington. Map p 76.*

Black Ink in Boston.

Also at 75 State St. (Merchants Row), 1 block from Faneuil Hall Marketplace. ☎ 617/261-9990. T: Blue or Orange Line to State. Map p 75.

★★ **Chanel** BACK BAY The Taj Boston hotel is home to the French fashion legend's only freestanding Boston boutique. 5 Newbury St. (Arlington St.). ☎ 617/859-0055. www.chanel.com. AE, MC, V. T: Green Line to Arlington. Map p 76.

★★ **Boomerangs** SOUTH END The "Special Edition" is the most fashionable outlet in a mini-chain of resale shops whose proceeds benefit the AIDS Action Committee. 1407 Washington St. (Union Park St.). ☎ 617/456-0996. www.shop boomerangs.com. AE, MC, V. T: Silver Line SL4/SL5 to Union Park. Map p 76.

★★★ **The Closet** BACK BAY Gorgeous merchandise for women and men at great prices makes The Closet the consignment shop to put at the top of your list. 175 Newbury St. (Dartmouth and Exeter sts.). ☎ 617/536-1919. www.closetboston. com. AE, DISC, MC, V. T: Green Line to Copley. Map p 76.

★★ **Crush Boutique** BEACON HILL A home run: Choice women's fashions, often by young designers, a good range of prices, and terrific service. 131 Charles St. (Revere St.). ☎ 617/720-0010. www. shopcrushboutique.com. AE, MC, V. T: Red Line to Charles/MGH. Map p 75. Also at 264 Newbury St. (Fairfield and Gloucester sts.), Back Bay. ☎ 617/424-0010. T: Green Line B, C, or D to Hynes Convention Center.

★ **The Garment District** CAMBRIDGE Fantastic deals on vintage clothing and accessories for men, women, and kids—plus costumes (to buy or rent). First-floor merchandise costs $1.50 a pound.

200 Broadway (Davis St.). ☎ 617/876-5230. www.garmentdistrict.com. AE, DISC, MC, V. T: Red Line to Kendall/MIT. Map p 78.

★ **Helen's Leather Shop** BEACON HILL Western boots and shirts, leather jackets and coats, and beautiful accessories make Helen's a particular favorite with displaced Texans. 110 Charles St. (Pinckney St.). ☎ 617/742-2077. www.helensleather.com. AE, DISC, MC, V. T: Red Line to Charles/MGH. Map p 75.

★★ **Injeanius** NORTH END Jeans by well-known and up-and-coming designers, plus gorgeous tops and accessories. Selection and service are excellent. 441 Hanover St. (Salutation St.). ☎ 617/523-5326. www.injeanius.com. AE, MC, V. T: Green or Orange Line to Haymarket. Map p 75.

★★ **Johnny Cupcakes** BACK BAY The limited-edition T-shirts mark you as a member of a club that verges on a graphics-obsessed cult. 279 Newbury St. (Gloucester St.). ☎ 617/375-0100. www.johnny cupcakes.com. AE, MC, V. T: Green Line B, C, or D to Hynes Convention Center. Map p 76.

★ **La Perla** BACK BAY If my lingerie wardrobe contained these gorgeous Italian concoctions, I might never get dressed. And not just because I wouldn't be able to afford clothes. 250 Boylston St. (Arlington St.). ☎ 617/423-5709. www.laperla.com. AE, MC, V. T: Green Line to Arlington. Map p 76.

★★ **Life is good.** BACK BAY Comfy, colorful cotton T-shirts with hand-drawn designs were just the start for this popular brand of adults' and kids' clothing and accessories. 285 Newbury St. (Fairfield and Gloucester sts.). ☎ 617/262-5068. www.lifeisgood.com. AE,

MC, V. T: Green Line B, C, or D to Hynes Convention Center. Map p 76.

★★ Looks. CAMBRIDGE The exceptional selection of women's clothing and accessories makes Looks a can't-miss stop in Harvard Square. *11–13 Holyoke St. (Mass. Ave.).* ☎ 617/491-4251. www.looks-clothing.com. AE, MC, V. T: Red Line to Harvard. Map p 77.

★★ Oona's Experienced Clothing HARVARD SQUARE Oona's carries a huge but choice stock of vintage and modern clothing, accessories, and jewelry. *1210 Massachusetts Ave. (Bow St.).* ☎ 617/491-2654. www.oonas boston.com. AE, MC, V. T: Red Line to Harvard. Map p 77.

Food & Candy

★★ Beacon Hill Chocolates BEACON HILL High-end indulgence, whether you want a single sweet or a big box of deliciousness. *91 Charles St. (Pinckney St.).* ☎ 617/725-1900. www.beaconhillchocolates. com. AE, MC, V. T: Red Line to Charles/MGH. Map p 75.

★★ Salumeria Italiana NORTH END The best Italian grocery store in town carries cheeses,

Oona's can dress you for Halloween or for your wedding.

meats, pastas, olives, olive oils, vinegars, fresh bread, and more. Picnic, anyone? *151 Richmond St. (Hanover St.).* ☎ 617/523-8743. www.salumeriaitaliana.com. MC, V. T: Green or Orange Line to Haymarket. Map p 75.

★ Savenor's Butcher & Market BEACON HILL An excellent gourmet market with an intriguing specialty (exotic meat, like buffalo and rattlesnake), Savenor's is a perfect picnic launching pad. *160 Charles St. (Cambridge St.).* ☎ 617/723-6328. www.savenorsmarket.com. AE, MC, V. T: Red Line to Charles/MGH. Map p 75. Also at 92 Kirkland St. (Line St.), Cambridge. ☎ 617/576-6328. T: Red Line to Harvard, 20-min. walk. Map p 78.

Gifts & Home Accessories

★★ kids Black Ink BEACON HILL The constantly changing stock of funky gifts and household items, games, toys, and office accessories means Black Ink is never the same twice. The Harvard Square branch is equally delightful. *101 Charles St. (Revere and Pinckney sts.).* ☎ 617/723-3883. www.black inkboston.squarespace.com. AE, DC, MC, V. T: Red Line to Charles/MGH. Map p 75. Also at 5 Brattle St. (John F. Kennedy St.), Cambridge. ☎ 866/497-1221. T: Red Line to Harvard. Map p 77.

★★ Crate & Barrel BACK BAY Top-quality housewares, classic furniture and home accessories, and kitchen items for every budget make this national chain my personal happy place. *777 Boylston St. (Exeter and Fairfield sts.).* ☎ 617/262-8700. www.crateandbarrel.com. AE, DISC, MC, V. T: Green Line to Copley. Map p 76. Also at 1045 Massachusetts Ave. (Trowbridge St.), Cambridge. ☎ 617/547-3994. T: Red Line to Harvard. Map p 77.

★ **kids The Games People Play** CAMBRIDGE Come here for board games, puzzles, chess and backgammon sets, and anything else you need to turn a coffee table into a playground. *1100 Massachusetts Ave. (Mount Auburn St.).* ☎ 888/492-0711 or ☎ 617/492-0711. www.thegamespeopleplay cambridge.com. AE, DISC, MC, V. T: Red Line to Harvard. Map p 77.

★★★ **Joie de Vivre** CAMBRIDGE My favorite gift shop carries an incredible selection of sophisticated and retro toys, jewelry, note cards, puzzles, and novelty items. *1792 Massachusetts Ave. (Arlington St.).* ☎ 617/864-8188. www.joiede vivre.net. AE, MC, V. T: Red Line to Porter. Map p 77.

★★ **Jonathan Adler** BACK BAY Inventive home accessories, quirky gifts, and lovely furniture are helping to make the "happy chic" designer a household name. *129 Newbury St. (Clarendon and Dartmouth sts.).* ☎ 617/437-0018. www.jonathanadler.com. AE, MC, V. T: Green Line to Copley. Map p 76.

★★ **Lannan Ship Model Gallery** WATERFRONT Alongside the models, this jam-packed space sells nautical charts, maritime paintings and memorabilia, and even home decor. *On the Rose Kennedy Greenway, 99 High St.; enter at 185 Purchase St. (Congress St.).* ☎ 617/451-2650. www.lannangallery.com. AE, MC, V. T: Red Line to South Station. Map p 75.

★★ **Shake the Tree** NORTH END Just off the Freedom Trail, Shake the Tree carries a constantly changing selection of irresistible jewelry, crafts, clothing, home accessories, candles, and ceramics. *67 Salem St. (Cross St.).* ☎ 617/742-0484. www.shaketheetreeboston.com. MC, V. T: Green or Orange Line to Haymarket. Map p 75.

★★ **Simon Pearce** BACK BAY The Vermont-based brand specializes in ultra-high-quality handmade pottery, hand-blown glass, and home accessories. *103 Newbury St. (Clarendon St.).* ☎ 617/450-8388. www.simonpearce.com. AE, MC, V. T: Green Line to Copley. Map p 76.

If you can't afford the real thing, shop for prints, art books, and more at the Museum of Fine Arts Gift Shop. See p. 13.

Faneuil Hall Marketplace.

★ **Ten Thousand Villages**
DOWNTOWN CROSSING The fair-trade chain specializes in folk art, home accessories, and other items handcrafted by international artisans. *252 Washington St. (Water St.).* ☎ *617/372-8743. www.tenthousandvillages.com. AE, DISC, MC, V. T: Orange or Blue Line to State. Map p 75, 78. Check website for other locations.*

★★ **WardMaps LLC** CAMBRIDGE Vintage maps—the real things, and the designs printed on everything from coasters to tote bags—make up the stock here. *1735 Massachusetts Ave. (Prentiss St.).* ☎ *617/497-0737. www.wardmaps.com. AE, DISC, MC, V. T: Red Line to Porter. Map p 77.*

Jewelry

★★★ **John Lewis, Inc.** BACK BAY Unique designs crafted on the premises in platinum, gold, and silver are both lovely and imaginative. *97 Newbury St. (Clarendon St.).* ☎ *617/266-6665. www.johnlewisinc.com. MC, V. T: Green Line to Arlington. Map p 76.*

★ **Shreve, Crump & Low** BACK BAY Boston's answer to Tiffany's features fine jewelry as well as unique items like gurgling cod pitchers. *39 Newbury St. (Berkeley St.).* ☎ *800/225-7088 or* ☎ *617/267-9100. www.shrevecrumpandlow.com. AE, MC, V. T: Green Line to Arlington. Map p 76.*

★ **Topaz** CAMBRIDGE Beautiful jewelry that won't break the bank dominates; also check out the accessories and unusual gift items. *11 Dunster St. (Mass. Ave.), Cambridge.* ☎ *617/492-3700. www.topazcambridge.com. AE, MC, V. T: Red Line to Harvard. Map p 77.*

Malls & Shopping Centers
CambridgeSide Galleria
CAMBRIDGE The mall at home probably has one of every store here. Kids may enjoy that comfort level—or the canal-side seating outside the food court. *100 CambridgeSide Place (First St. and Land Blvd.).* ☎ *617/621-8666. www.shopcambridgeside.com. T: Green Line to Lechmere, or Red Line to Kendall/MIT and mall shuttle. Map p 78.*

★★ **Copley Place** BACK BAY This sleek enclave of boutiques and luxury mall brands adjoins the Shops at Prudential Center (see below). *100 Huntington Ave. (Dartmouth St.).* ☎ *617/262-6600. www.shopcopleyplace.com. T: Orange Line to Back Bay. Map p 76.*

★ **Faneuil Hall Marketplace** DOWNTOWN The generic retail selection doesn't keep shoppers from flocking to the five-building marketplace. Check the pushcarts for more creative items. *North, Congress, and State sts. and Atlantic Ave.* ☎ *617/523-1300. www.faneuilhallmarketplace.com. T: Green or Blue Line to Government Center. Map p 75.*

★ **kids The Shops at Prudential Center** BACK BAY "The Pru" mixes high-end chain shops and boutiques with pushcarts holding crafts and novelty items. *800 Boylston St. (Fairfield St.).* ☎ *800/ SHOP-PRU. www.prudentialcenter. com. T: Green Line E to Prudential or Green Line to Copley. Map p 76.*

Markets

★ **kids SoWa Open Market** SOUTH END This funky market offers crafts, jewelry, antiques, produce, flowers, and baked goods. Many but not all vendors accept credit cards. Open Sundays May through October from 10am to 5pm. *460 Harrison Ave. (Randolph St.).* ☎ *617/481-2257. www.sowa openmarket.com. T: Orange Line to Back Bay, 10-min walk. Or Silver Line SL4/SL5 to Union Park St. Map p 76.*

Music

★ **Newbury Comics** BACK BAY Novelty items, T-shirts, posters, and comics dominate at this local chain, which also carries new and used CDs, including imports and independent labels. *North Market Building, Faneuil Hall Marketplace.* ☎ *617/248-9992. www.newbury comics.com. AE, DISC, MC, V. T: Green Line to Government Center or Orange Line to Haymarket. Map p 75. Check website for other locations.*

★ **Planet Records** CAMBRIDGE One of the Harvard Square area's few remaining record stores has survived thanks to two things: the constantly changing selection and the exceptional staff. *144 Mount Auburn St. (Brewer St.).* ☎ *617/492-0693. www.planet-records.com. MC, V. T: Red Line to Harvard. Map p 77.*

Perfume & Cosmetics

★★ **Colonial Drug** HARVARD SQUARE My favorite fragrance— so obscure that department stores haven't stocked it in years—is one of the 1,000 options here (along with numerous body-care products). *49 Brattle St. (Church St. and Appian Way).* ☎ *617/864-2222. www. colonialdrug.com. No credit cards. T: Red Line to Harvard. Map p 77.*

★ **Kiehl's Since 1851** BACK BAY The skin, hair, and body preparations here have a (deservedly) cult-like following. *112 Newbury St. (Clarendon St.).* ☎ *617/247-1777. www.kiehls.com. AE, DC, MC, V. T: Green Line to Copley. Map p 76.*

★ **Sephora** BACK BAY The large self-service boutiques carry a vast assortment of cosmetics and fragrances, with plenty of testers and helpful staff members. *Shops at Prudential Center, 800 Boylston St. (Fairfield St.).* ☎ *617/262-4200. www. sephora.com. AE, DISC, MC, V. T: Green Line to Copley. Map p 76. Check website for other locations.* ●

Galeria Cubana.

5

The Best of the
Outdoors

The Public Garden & Boston Common

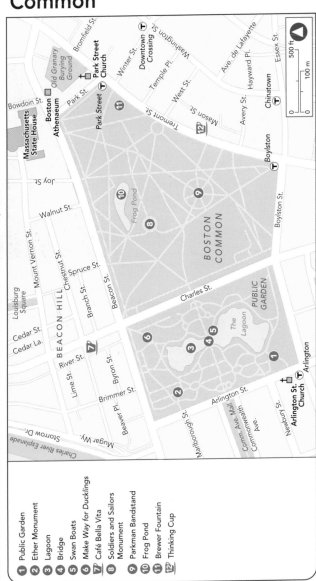

1 Public Garden
2 Ether Monument
3 Lagoon
4 Bridge
5 Swan Boats
6 Make Way for Ducklings
7 Café Bella Vita
8 Soldiers and Sailors Monument
9 Parkman Bandstand
10 Frog Pond
11 Brewer Fountain
12 Thinking Cup

Previous page: Boats on Boston Harbor at sunset.

Asked to explain the difference between the Public Garden and the Common, I usually go for the easy analogy. The Public Garden is Boston's front yard, where anyone passing by can see how beautiful this year's flowers are; Boston Common is the backyard, where the kids play ball and that one dusty patch just won't go away. START: **Green Line to Arlington**

1 ★★★ Public Garden. The 19th century left an indelible mark on Boston, and nowhere is that mark more permanent or more pleasant than in the Public Garden. The city set aside this land in the 1820s, the institution was formally established in 1837, and creating the nation's first public botanical garden out of a marshy riverbank and tons of landfill took over 2 decades. By the late 1850s, the Public Garden had assumed roughly the form you see today—but there's nothing rough about it. These 24 acres (10 ha) crisscrossed with walkways hold hundreds of formally arranged trees and shrubs, five fountains, and dozens of statues and memorials. The gardens of Versailles inspired the original plan. The exquisite flowerbeds change regularly, complementing the perennial plantings and giving the staid design a dynamic component. Besides walking and resting, the actual activities here—other than taking a ride on a Swan Boat—aren't much. Let the low-tech atmosphere set the pace, and before long you'll realize that you can't remember why you were feeling so stressed when you arrived. Was that really half an hour ago? We just sat down for a minute. . . *See p 15, bullet* **6**.

2 ★ Ether Monument. The oldest statue in the Public Garden, erected in 1868, celebrates the first use of general anesthesia in an operation. The procedure, the removal of a jaw tumor, took place at Massachusetts General Hospital

Lagoon.

in 1846, and the monument was commissioned a mere 20 years later. In Boston, a city that does nothing quickly, this was clearly a big deal. The sculpture atop the monument—an elaborate confection, in keeping with the fashion of the time—is John Quincy Adams Ward's depiction of the Good Samaritan. At the base, the streams of water that issue from the lions' heads represent healing.

3 ★★ Lagoon. The 3-acre (1 ha) lagoon is a triumph of optical illusion—viewed from above, it's tiny, but from anywhere along the curving shore, it looks huge. With the completion of the signature water feature in 1861, George F. Meacham's design of the Public Garden was substantially complete. Today the murky water is home to the Swan Boats (see below), two pairs of live swans (Romeo, Juliet, Castor, and Pollux), and numerous ducks, that nest on the islands. Designed to resemble an English pond, the lagoon is temptingly cool in the heat of summer, but I strongly suggest that you play by the rules and stay out—I've seen the basin drained, and it's not pretty.

4 ★★ Bridge. The word "adorable" has no place in a discussion of landscape architecture, but this thing is seriously cute. It sits at the heart of the Public Garden, surrounded by flowerbeds and swarming with pedestrians. Step away, perhaps to the lagoon shore, to appreciate the bridge's graceful proportions.

5 ★★ Swan Boats. In keeping with the Victorian atmosphere of the rest of the Public Garden, the main attraction is a fancy version of something simple. Each pedal-powered vessel (the employees do the work) has an elaborate swan at the back, concealing the pedaling mechanism and transforming a humble boat ride into an operatic fantasy. Robert Paget, who founded the Swan Boats in 1877, got the idea from the swan-drawn boat in the Wagner opera *Lohengrin*. Your family may associate it with *The Trumpet of the Swan*, a children's book by E. B. White (who wrote *Charlotte's Web* and *Stuart Little*). Outside of Swan Boat

The Make Way for Ducklings *sculpture is a popular photo op for visitors with kids.*

hours, the dock is still worth a look—the boats tied up at dusk are one of the city's best photo ops. *See p 69, bullet* **3**.

6 ★★★ Make Way for Ducklings. Do you know the story of Mrs. Mallard and her eight babies, Jack, Kack, Lack, Mack, Nack, Ouack, Pack, and Quack? You will soon. Robert McCloskey's beloved 1941 book introduces young readers to Boston, where the Mallard family goes in search of a new place to live. After perilous adventures, they arrive at the Public Garden. Sculptor Nancy Schön's graceful rendering of McCloskey's charcoal drawings was unveiled in 1987, the 150th anniversary of the Public Garden. Her sculptures, created using the lost-wax process, capture the imagination of just about everyone who encounters the row of bronze waterfowl waddling in the direction of the water.

7 Café Bella Vita. Try to snag a window seat so you can take in the action on Beacon Hill's main street as you sip coffee and snack on gelato or a pastry. *30 Charles St. (Chestnut St.).* ☎ *617/720-4505. $.*

8 ★ Soldiers and Sailors Monument. Set aside as public land in 1634, Boston Common has been in constant use ever since—no wonder parts of it look so tired. Over the years, these 45 acres (18 ha) have held pasture, barracks, gallows, a cemetery, parade grounds, ball fields, and more. Today the Common sits atop a parking garage and two subway stations. Almost everywhere, you'll see plaques, statues, fountains, memorials, and monuments. The most prominent sits atop the highest point on the Common, Flagstaff Hill. Also known as the Soldiers'

The Public Garden's bridge is one of the smallest suspension bridges in the world.

Monument, it's the work of Martin Milmore, an Irish immigrant who apprenticed under Thomas Ball, the sculptor of the equestrian George Washington in the Public Garden (see p 69, bullet ❷). Dedicated in 1877—when the gold standard in public art was over-the-top ornate—it commemorates Boston residents who died in the Civil War.

❾ ★ **Parkman Bandstand.** The Classical Revival bandstand sits at the center of a particularly lovely network of paths surrounded by stately trees. The bandstand bears the name of George Francis Parkman, who died in 1908, leaving the city $5.5 million to be used for the maintenance of the Common.

❿ ★★ **Frog Pond.** In Colonial times, real frogs lived in the pond here. Today the Frog Pond is a skating rink in the winter, a wading pool in the summer, and a reflecting pool in the spring and fall. Look up for an unusual perspective on the dome of the State House. *www. bostonfrogpond.org.*

⓫ ★★ **Brewer Fountain.** The ornate bronze fountain is an exact replica of an installation at the 1855 Paris World's Fair. The figures frolicking in the water include Poseidon, the Greek god of the sea, and

his wife, Amphitrite. The humans frolicking on the plaza might be playing chess or checkers, listening to piano music (live at midday on weekdays), or just people watching. *www.friendsofthepublicgarden.org.*

⓬ ★★ **Thinking Cup.** One of the only places in New England to get Stumptown Coffee, this is a good place to unwind after exploring with a drink and a delicious pastry. *165 Tremont St. (Avery St.).* ☎ *617/482-5555. www.thinkingcup.com. $.*

The Public Garden is particularly lovely when the flowers bloom in spring and summer.

The Esplanade

1 Community Boating
2 Hatch Shell
3 Arthur Fiedler Memorial
4 Storrow Lagoon
5 Sweet

Charles/MGH

Charles River

Charles River Esplanade

Storrow Lagoon

PUBLIC GARDEN
The Lagoon

Revere St.
Pinckney St.
Mt. Vernon St.
Lime St.
Chestnut St.
Beaver Pl.
Byron St.
Back St.
Beacon St.
Cedar St.
Charles St.
River St.
Brimmer St.
Arlington St.
Berkeley St.
Storrow Dr.
Mugar Wy.

0   500 ft
0   100 m

Everyone has a place that they take for granted until out-of-towners start raving about it. For many Bostonians, the Esplanade is that place—it's where we meet friends to go walking (or running, biking, or skating) on the weekend or after work. We don't really think about it. Then someone reminds us that it's gorgeous and interesting, and we take another look. Visit www.esplanadeassociation.org for an overview. START: **Red Line to Charles/MGH. Cross the footbridge over Storrow Drive and turn left (keeping the river on your right).**

1 Community Boating. The first building you'll pass is this lovely boathouse. The oldest public sailing program in the country, Community Boating was established in 1936 and moved here in 1941. Thousands of people have learned to sail under its cooperative structure, initially designed to keep local youth off the streets of Depression-era Boston. To this day, kids 10 to 18 can sail all summer for as little as $1. It's a decent deal for experienced visitors, too—$79 for a day of sailing on the Charles River basin, or $40 for a day of kayaking. *21 David G. Mugar Way.* ☎ *617/523-1038. www.community-boating.org.*

2 ★★ Hatch Shell. The Charles River Esplanade evolved slowly into the pleasant park you see today, which rests on landfill. The river originally ended in a tidal basin rimmed with reeking mud flats; before the Charles River Dam

Hatch Shell.

opened in 1910, what's now the Charles River basin was an outrage to both eyes and noses (which is why the magnificent old residences on Beacon Street face the land, not the water). By 1929, the Esplanade was home to a temporary venue for the Boston Pops. Landscape architect Arthur Shurcliff's design of the Esplanade, which involved creating new land from fill pumped off the river bottom, took 5 unsightly years to execute. The permanent Hatch Shell (formally the Edward Hatch Memorial Shell) was built in 1940 using a graceful design by Richard Shaw. The amphitheater bears the names of 86 composers—including Sousa and Tchaikovsky, the stars of the Pops' annual Fourth of July concert (www.july4th.org). Stroll around the shell, an Art Deco confection with a rustic terrazzo exterior; if you arrive at the right time, you can plunk down on the lawn to listen to some music. Free events take over the stage at least twice a week in the summer, making this one of Boston's most popular cultural venues. ☎ *617/626-4970. State Department of Conservation and Recreation: www.mass.gov/eea/ agencies/dcr/massparks/programs-and- events/hatch-shell-events.html.*

❸ ★★★ **The Arthur Fiedler Memorial.** Sculptor Ralph Helmick created this unforgettable memorial to the legendary conductor of the Boston Pops. Installed in 1985, it consists of stacked plates of sand-blasted aluminum that blend into an uncanny likeness of the head of Fiedler (1894–1979), who presided over the Pops from 1930 until his death. To appreciate the full impact, note that, in Helmick's words, the sculpture "reads most coherently from afar"—a commentary on the contrast between Fiedler's public face and private persona.

❹ ★ **Storrow Lagoon.** An important feature of the Esplanade's design, the lagoon stretches more or less from Exeter Street to Fairfield Street (the actual streets don't extend this far). I especially love the little bridges at either end of the narrow lagoon, surrounded by elaborate plantings and shady trees. The busy parkway to your left is Storrow Drive. Construction began in 1949, encroaching on the Esplanade. Rather than allow the parkland to shrink permanently, the state created islands offshore.

❺ ★ **Sweet.** The cupcake craze came late to Boston, but this place (part of a small local chain) was worth waiting for. Seasonal flavors complement excellent renditions of the classics. *49 Massachusetts Ave. (Marlborough).* ☎ *617/247-2253. www.sweetcupcakes.com. $.*

Storrow Lagoon.

Boston's **Colonial Cemeteries**

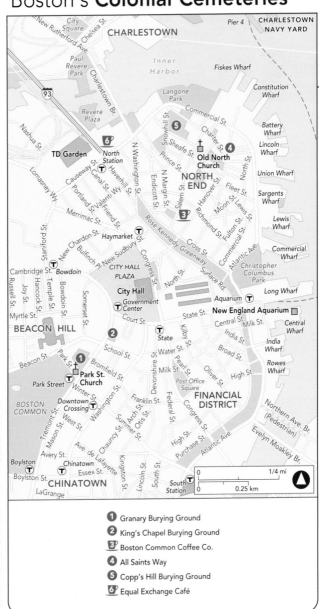

1 Granary Burying Ground
2 King's Chapel Burying Ground
3 Boston Common Coffee Co.
4 All Saints Way
5 Copp's Hill Burying Ground
6 Equal Exchange Café

olonial Boston was about a third the size of the present-day city. Its residents clustered in what's now the downtown area, where they lived, worked, worshiped, and even buried their dead. Boston was more than 2 centuries old when Mount Auburn Cemetery (see p 63, bullet ❾) opened in Cambridge in 1831, heralding the new custom of establishing cemeteries outside of population centers. START: Red or Green Line to Park St.

❶ ★★ Granary Burying Ground.

Originally a section of Boston Common, this graveyard was laid out in 1660. It got its name from the granary, or grain-storage building, that once stood on the site of Park Street Church. Solomon Willard, architect of the Bunker Hill Monument, designed the granite entrance. Wander the walkways, learn a bit about the people buried here, and take in the diversity of markers and ornamental carvings. When the King's Chapel Burying Ground (see below) was established, life in the New World was daunting, and the skulls, bones, and scary animals that dominate its headstone decorations reflect that. By the time this graveyard opened, life seemed more stable, and the afterlife a bit less intimidating. You'll see the graves of Paul Revere, Samuel Adams, Peter Faneuil (who donated Faneuil Hall to Boston; his monument says "FUNAL"), the victims of the Boston Massacre, Benjamin Franklin's parents, and the wife of Isaac Vergoose. Also known as Elizabeth Foster Goose, she's believed to be "Mother Goose" of nursery-rhyme fame. Even in death, John Hancock has a little more style than everyone else: The carving on his monument is a rebus. Look for the hand above the three birds, or cocks; "hand-cocks," get it? *See p 7, bullet* ❹.

❷ ★ King's Chapel Burying Ground.

The oldest cemetery in Boston, this little graveyard was established shortly after the

Paul Revere's grave, Granary Burying Ground.

settlement of Boston, in 1630. Buried here are the first colonial governor, John Winthrop, and Mary Chilton, the first woman to come ashore in Plymouth in 1620. You can also see the graves of William Dawes—Paul Revere's counterpart who rode to Lexington and Concord on the night of April 18, 1775—and Elizabeth Pain, reputedly the model for Hester Prynne in *The Scarlet Letter*. The Puritan burying ground gained an Anglican neighbor in 1686, when King's Chapel was established for British officers; it became Unitarian after the Revolution. The current chapel (1749) is the country's oldest church in continuous use as well as its oldest major stone building. Designed by Peter Harrison, the architect of

King's Chapel interior.

Christ Church in Cambridge, King's Chapel was constructed by erecting the granite building around its wooden predecessor, then removing the old chapel. *58 Tremont St. (School St.).* ☎ *617/523-1749. www. kings-chapel.org. Donation suggested. Chapel year-round Mon–Sat from 10am, Sun from 1:30pm; call or check website for closing time. Burying ground daily 8am–5:30pm (until 3pm in winter). T: Green or Blue Line to Government Center.*

3 ★★ **Boston Common Coffee Co.** A homey contrast to the North End's espresso bars, this is a lively cafe with yummy food, comfy seating, and, yes, excellent coffee. *97 Salem St. (Wiget St., near Parmenter St.).* ☎ *617/725-0040. www.boston commoncoffee.com. $.*

4 ★★ **All Saints Way.** A delightful surprise: Thousands of images of saints adorn the brick walls of this alleyway shrine. Local resident Peter Baldassari assembled and maintains the folk-art collection. If the door is locked, some images are visible above the gate. *4–8 Battery St. (Hanover St.). Daily by chance. T: Green or Orange Line to North Station.*

5 ★ **Copp's Hill Burying Ground.** Boston didn't set aside a second cemetery until 1659, when it established this graveyard. The neighborhood is still residential, and the location, at the crest of Copp's Hill, translates to lovely views of Charlestown and the harbor. As in Boston's other colonial cemeteries, the grave markers alone are worth a trip. The family plot of the prominent Puritan ministers Increase Mather (who was also president of Harvard) and Cotton Mather (Increase's son) is here, as is the grave of Robert Newman, sexton of the Old North Church in 1775 (he hung the lanterns that signified "two if by sea" in the steeple). Phillis Wheatley, a poet and freed slave who was America's first published black author, is believed to lie in an unmarked grave. Many slaves and free blacks were buried here; Boston's first black neighborhood was nearby, and an estimated 1,000 of the 10,000 or so people buried here over the years were black. The best known is Prince Hall, who fought at Bunker Hill and later founded the first black Masonic lodge. *Fun fact:* The 10-foot-wide (3m) private home at 44 Hull St., across from the graveyard entrance, is the narrowest house in Boston. *Hull St. (Salem and Snowhill sts.). Daily 9am–5pm (until 3pm in winter). T: Green or Orange Line to North Station.*

6 ★ **Equal Exchange Café.** Just outside the North End, you'll find organic coffee, tea, and even chocolate at the fair-trade pioneer's retail outlet. Dairy products, snacks, and sweets come from local purveyors. *226 Causeway St. (Beverly St.).* ☎ *617/372-8777. www.equal exchangecafe.com. $.* ●

The Best Dining

Dining Best Bets

Best Seafood
★★★ Legal Sea Foods $$$ 255 State St. and branches (p 109)

Best Raw Bar
★ Union Oyster House $$$ 41 Union St. (p 112)

Best Clam Shack
★★ Jasper White's Summer Shack $$$ 50 Dalton St. (p 109)

Best Pizza
★★ Pizzeria Regina $ 11½ Thacher St. (p 110)

Best for Business
★★ Sultan's Kitchen $–$$ 116 State St. (p 111)

Most Romantic
★★ UpStairs on the Square $$$$ 91 Winthrop St., Cambridge (p 112)

Best Fancy Italian
★★★ Mamma Maria $$$$ 3 North Square (p 110)

Best Down-Home Italian
★ La Summa $$ 30 Fleet St. (p 109)

Best North End Hangout
★★ Volle Nolle $–$$ 351 Hanover St. (p 112)

Best Mediterranean
★★ Oleana $$$ 134 Hampshire St., Cambridge (p 110)

Best Barbecue
★★ Sweet Cheeks $$ 1381 Boylston St. (p 111)

Best Sushi
★ Sakurabana $$ 57 Broad St. (p 111)

Best Dim Sum
★★ Hei La Moon $ 88 Beach St. (p 108)

Most Unusual Combo
★ The Elephant Walk $$ 900 Beacon St. (p 107)

Most Unusual Transatlantic Combo
★ Taranta Cucina Meridionale $$$$ 210 Hanover St. (p 112)

Durgin-Park serves oysters, Boston baked beans, and other New England classics. Previous page: Union Oyster House.

Cambridge Dining

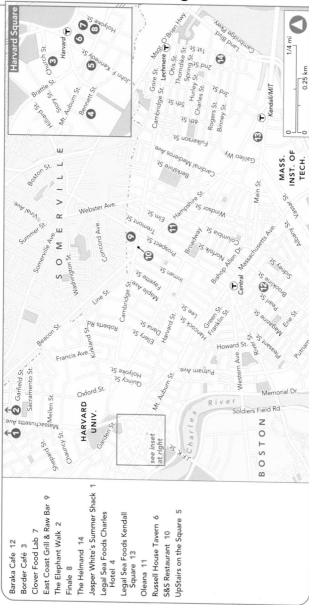

Baraka Cafe 12

Border Café 3

Clover Food Lab 7

East Coast Grill & Raw Bar 9

The Elephant Walk 2

Finale 8

The Helmand 14

Jasper White's Summer Shack 1

Legal Sea Foods Charles Hotel 4

Legal Sea Foods Kendall Square 13

Oleana 11

Russell House Tavern 6

S&S Restaurant 10

UpStairs on the Square 5

Boston Dining

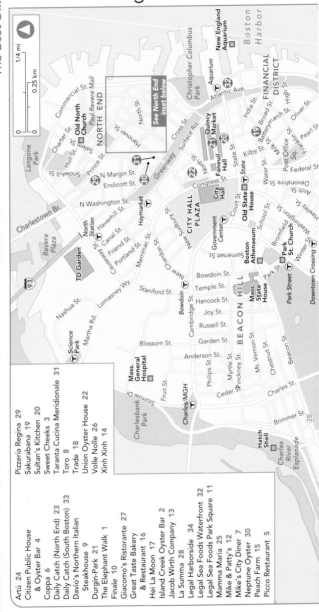

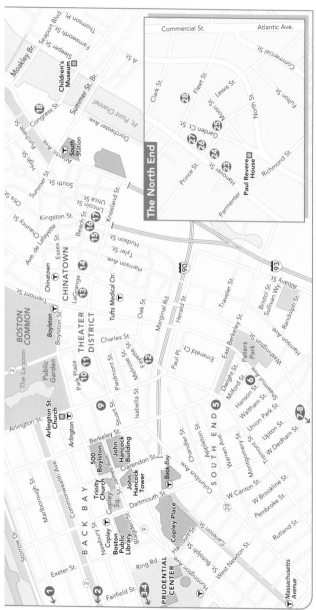

The North End

Commercial St.

Atlantic Ave.

Paul Revere House

The Best Dining

Back Bay Dining

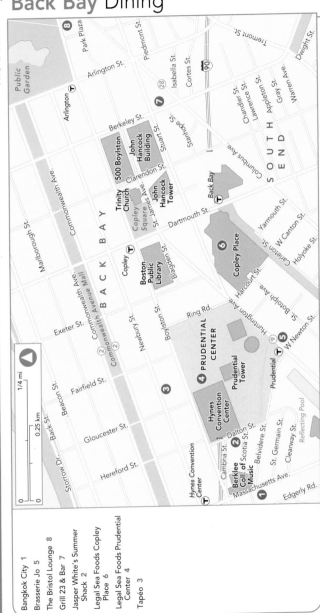

Bangkok City 1
Brasserie Jo 5
The Bristol Lounge 8
Grill 23 & Bar 7
Jasper White's Summer Shack 2
Legal Sea Foods Copley Place 6
Legal Sea Foods Prudential Center 4
Tapéo 3

Boston Dining A to Z

★ **kids Artú** NORTH END *ITALIAN* Though it's right on the Freedom Trail, Artú is a neighborhood favorite that serves terrific pastas, sandwiches, and roasted meats to both visitors and locals. *6 Prince St. (Hanover St. and North Sq.).* ☎ *617/742-4336. www.artuboston.com. Entrees $7–$24. AE, MC, V. Lunch & dinner daily. T: Green or Orange Line to Haymarket. Map p 102.*

★ **Bangkok City** BACK BAY *THAI* The best Thai restaurant in town serves excellent takes on the usual noodle dishes as well as a huge variety of curries. *167 Massachusetts Ave. (Haviland St.).* ☎ *617/266-8884. www.bangkokcityrestaurant boston.com. Entrees $10–$19. AE, DISC, MC, V. Lunch & dinner Mon–Sat, dinner Sun. T: Green Line B, C, or D to Hynes Convention Center. Map p 104.*

★★ **Baraka Cafe** CAMBRIDGE *ALGERIAN/TUNISIAN* The location, on a dreary side street, belies

Plenty of Boston restaurants serve fresh seafood. Try Legal Sea Foods or Union Oyster House for some of the best.

the wonderful, unusual cuisine and colorful, welcoming atmosphere. No alcohol. *80½ Pearl St. St. (William St.).* ☎ *617/868-3951. www. barakacafe.com. Entrees $9–$16. No credit cards. Lunch Tues–Sat, dinner Tues–Sun. T: Red Line to Central. Map p 101.*

★ **kids Border Café** CAMBRIDGE *TEX-MEX* The nonstop party, lubricated with margaritas and beer, overshadows tasty enchiladas, fajitas, tacos, and such at this longtime Harvard hangout. *32 Church St. (Palmer St.).* ☎ *617/864-6100. www.bordercafe.com. Entrees $7–$18. AE, MC, V. Lunch & dinner daily. T: Red Line to Harvard. Map p 101.*

★ **Brasserie Jo** BACK BAY *FRENCH* A classic brasserie, with long hours and a wide-ranging menu, this lively place hops until midnight (until 11pm Sun). *120 Huntington Ave. (W. Newton and Garrison sts.), in the Colonnade Hotel Boston.* ☎ *617/425-3240. www. brasseriejoboston.com. Entrees $18–$39. AE, DISC, MC, V. Breakfast, lunch & dinner daily. T: Green Line E to Prudential. Map p 104.*

★★ **The Bristol Lounge** BACK BAY *AMERICAN* The luxury hotel's restaurant serves astounding comfort food—including superb desserts—and Boston's best afternoon tea. *200 Boylston St. (Hadassah Way), in the Four Seasons Hotel.* ☎ *617/351-2037. www.fourseasons. com/boston. Entrees $21–$49. AE, DISC, MC, V. Breakfast, lunch, afternoon tea & dinner daily. T: Green Line to Arlington. Map p 104.*

★ **Citizen Public House & Oyster Bar** FENWAY *AMERICAN* Lively and crowded, this inventive gastropub (ask about the pig roast)

Davio's.

is a standout in a restaurant-choked neighborhood. *1310 Boylston St. (Jersey St.).* ☎ *617/450-9000. www.citizenpub.com. Entrees $17–$23. AE, DISC, MC, V. Dinner daily, brunch Sun. T: Green Line to Fenway. Map p 102.*

★ **Clover Food Lab** CAMBRIDGE VEGETARIAN/VEGAN Good food served fast, not "fast food." Originally a trendy food truck, Clover serves great sandwiches, soups, salads, coffee, and beer, all local and organic when possible. *7 Holyoke St. (Mass. Ave.).* ☎ *617/640-1884. www.cloverfoodlab.com. All items $7 or less. MC, V. Breakfast, lunch & dinner daily. T: Red Line to Harvard. Map p 101. Check website for other locations, including multiple trucks.*

★★ **Coppa** SOUTH END ITALIAN Phenomenal bar snacks and cured meats, amazing pizza and pasta, and delectable main courses draw huge crowds to this little storefront. Portions are modest—sample away, and worry about the bill later. *253 Shawmut Ave. (Milford St.).* ☎ *617/ 391-0902. www.coppaboston.com. Menu items $8–$27. AE, MC, V. Lunch weekdays, dinner daily, brunch Sun. T: Silver Line SL4/SL5 to E. Berkeley St. Map p 102.*

★ **Daily Catch** NORTH END SEA-FOOD/SOUTHERN ITALIAN Follow the aroma of garlic to this tiny

storefront, where the specialty is calamari (squid) and everything is delicious. The Seaport District location takes credit cards. *323 Hanover St. (Prince St.).* ☎ *617/523-8567. www.dailycatch.com. Entrees $17–$27. No credit cards. Lunch & dinner daily. T: Green or Orange Line to Haymarket. Map p 102. Also at 2 Northern Ave. (Sleeper St.)., in the Moakley Courthouse, South Boston.* ☎ *617/772-4400. T: Silver Line SL1/SL2 to Courthouse.*

★★ **Davio's Northern Italian Steakhouse** BACK BAY NORTH-ERN ITALIAN/STEAK Northern Italian classics, including the best lobster risotto around, share the menu with steakhouse favorites and inventive starters (like cheesesteak spring rolls) and sides. Somehow, it works beautifully. *75 Arlington St. (Stuart St.).* ☎ *617/357-4810. www.davios.com. Entrees $18–$55. AE, DISC, MC, V. Lunch weekdays, dinner daily. T: Green Line to Arlington. Map p 102.*

★★ kids **Durgin-Park** FANEUIL HALL MARKETPLACE NEW ENG-LAND Communal tables give the tourist-choked dining rooms a boardinghouse feel, but they're not terribly noisy—everyone's mouth is full of tasty home-style food. *340 Faneuil Hall Marketplace (Clinton St.).* ☎ *617/227-2038. www.durgin-park. com. Entrees $11–$47 (most*

$15—$27), specials market price. AE, DISC, MC, V. Lunch & dinner daily. T: Green or Blue Line to Government Center. Map p 102.

★★★ kids East Coast Grill & Raw Bar CAMBRIDGE SEAFOOD/ BARBECUE

This place is a riot— of colors, flavors, and fun. It's been one of the best seafood restaurants in New England for nearly 3 decades. 1271 Cambridge St. (Prospect St.). ☎ 617/491-6568. www.east coastgrill.net. Entrees $18–$30. AE, MC, V. Dinner daily, lunch Sat, brunch Sun. T: Red Line to Central, 10-min. walk. Map p 101.

★★ The Elephant Walk BACK BAY FRENCH/CAMBODIAN

French on one side, Cambodian on the other, this is the most interesting menu in Boston—with all the tastiest food. 900 Beacon St. (Park Dr.). ☎ 617/247-1500. www. elephantwalk.com. Entrees $18–$24. AE, DISC, MC, V. Lunch weekdays, brunch Sun, dinner daily. T: Green Line C to St. Mary's St. Map p 101. Also at 2067 Massachusetts Ave. (Walden St.), Cambridge.

Daily Catch.

Durgin-Park is the best place in the city to try Boston baked beans.

☎ 617/492-6900. T: Red Line to Porter. Map p 102.

★ Finale THEATER DISTRICT DESSERT/LIGHT FARE

Finale isn't a restaurant; it's a "desserterie." It serves appetizer-size portions of savories—including soup, pizza, and sandwiches—but it exists to answer the prayers of anyone who's ever wanted to eat dessert first. 1 Columbus Ave. (Park Plaza). ☎ 617/ 423-3184. www.finaledesserts.com. Entrees $6–$15. AE, MC, V. Lunch & dinner daily. T: Green Line to Arlington. Map p 102. Also at 30 Dunster St. (Mount Auburn St.), Cambridge. ☎ 617/441-9797. Map p 101.

★★ Giacomo's Ristorante NORTH END ITALIAN/SEAFOOD

The line is long, the dining room small, and the food worth the trouble. Be sure to check the specials board. 355 Hanover St. (Fleet St.). ☎ 617/523-9026. Entrees $14–$21. No credit cards. Dinner daily. T: Green or Orange Line to Haymarket. Map p 102.

Jacob Wirth Company has been serving Bostonians since 1868.

★★ Great Taste Bakery & Restaurant CHINATOWN *CANTONESE*

The perfect combination of authentic Chinese and Chinese-American food would seem like enough—but there's also a la carte dim sum *and* a bakery. *61–63 Beach St. (Hudson St.).* ☎ *617-426-6688. www.bostongreattastebakery.com. Entrees $28–$62. AE, DISC, MC, V. Breakfast, lunch & dinner daily. T: Orange Line to Chinatown. Map p 102.*

★ Grill 23 & Bar BACK BAY *STEAKS*

The city's top steakhouse is a magnet for the high-rolling, deal-making set. I could make a meal of the toothsome a la carte side dishes. *161 Berkeley St. (Stuart St.).* ☎ *617/542-2255. www.grill23. com. Entrees $25–$59. AE, DISC, MC, V. Dinner daily. T: Green Line to Arlington. Map p 104.*

★★ Hei La Moon CHINATOWN *DIM SUM/CHINESE*

The best dim sum in the city—the variety is largest on weekends—brings huge crowds to this cavernous restaurant. It's worth the wait. *88 Beach St. (Surface Artery).* ☎ *617/338-8813. Entrees $7–$15. MC, V. Dim sum, lunch & dinner daily. T: Red Line to South Station. Map p 102.*

★ The Helmand CAMBRIDGE *AFGHAN*

The cuisine at this elegant restaurant combines elements of Indian, Pakistani, and Middle Eastern food to good effect. It's flavorful, filling (but not heavy), and vegetarian friendly. *143 First St. (Bent St.).* ☎ *617/492-4646. www. helmandrestaurant.com. Entrees $13–$27. AE, MC, V. Dinner daily. T: Green Line to Lechmere. Map p 101.*

★★ Island Creek Oyster Bar KENMORE SQUARE *SEAFOOD*

The specials change daily; the

Jasper White's Summer Shack prepares lobster in both humble (rolls) and gourmet (pan-roasted with herbs) style.

constant is sparkling-fresh seafood in an elegant but loud dining room. Even the burger is fantastic. *500 Commonwealth Ave. (Kenmore St.), in the Commonwealth Hotel.* ☎ *617/532-5300. www.islandcreekoysterbar.com. Entrees $13–$38. AE, DC, DISC, MC, V. Dinner daily, Sun brunch. T: Green Line B, C, or D to Kenmore. Map p 102.*

★ **Jacob Wirth Company** THEATER DISTRICT *GERMAN/AMERICAN* The decor suggests a vintage saloon, and rib-sticking specialties like wursts and Wiener schnitzel share the menu with salads, burgers, and comfort food like chicken potpie. *31–37 Stuart St. (Tremont St.).* ☎ *617/338-8586. www.jacobwirth.com. Entrees $9–$23. AE, DISC, MC, V. Lunch & dinner daily. T: Green Line to Boylston. Map p 102.*

★★ kids **Jasper White's Summer Shack** BACK BAY *SEAFOOD* The Summer Shack feels like a casual seaside place (think corn dogs, lobster rolls, fried clams) and tastes like the brainchild of a gourmet chef (think pan-roasted lobster with chervil and chives). *50 Dalton St. (Scotia St.).* ☎ *617/867-9955. www.summershackrestaurant.com. Entrees $6–$36. AE, DISC, MC, V. Lunch weekdays (except Nov–Mar), brunch weekends, dinner daily. T:*

Green Line B, C, or D to Hynes Convention Center. Map p 104. Also at 149 Alewife Brook Pkwy. (Rindge Ave.), Cambridge. ☎ *617/520-9500. Lunch & dinner daily. T: Red Line to Alewife. Map p 101.*

★ **La Summa** NORTH END *ITALIAN* A neighborhood native owns and runs La Summa, a friendly place where many specialties are family recipes; try the handmade pasta. *30 Fleet St. (Hanover and North sts.).* ☎ *617/523-9503. www.lasumma.com. Entrees $13–$24. AE, DISC, MC, V. Dinner daily. T: Green or Orange Line to Haymarket. Map p 102.*

★★★ kids **Legal Sea Foods** WATERFRONT *SEAFOOD* I'd love to point you to a hole-in-the-wall and say, "There's the secret place that only the locals know about—it's the best seafood restaurant in the Boston area." I can't, though. Legal is no secret, but it is the best. *255 State St. (Atlantic Ave.).* ☎ *617/742-5300. www.legalseafoods.com. Entrees $14–$35. AE, DISC, MC, V. Lunch & dinner daily. T: Blue Line to Aquarium. Also at Prudential Center, 800 Boylston St. (Fairfield St.),* ☎ *617/266-6800, T: Green Line to Copley; Park Sq., 26 Park Plaza (Columbus Ave. and Stuart St.),* ☎ *617/426-4444, T: Green Line to Arlington; Copley Place, 100*

Sweet Cheeks BBQ.

Huntington Ave. (Dartmouth St.), 2nd level, ☎ 617/266-7775, T: Orange Line to Back Bay; Legal Harborside, 270 Northern Ave. (D St.), ☎ 617/477-2900. T: Silver Line SL1/SL2 to Silver Line Way; 20 University Rd. (Bennett St.), in the Charles Hotel, Cambridge, ☎ 617/491-9400, T: Red Line to Harvard; 5 Cambridge Center (Main and Ames sts.), ☎ 617/864-3400, T: Red Line to Kendall/MIT. Maps p 101, 102, and 104.

★★★ Mamma Maria NORTH END *NORTHERN ITALIAN* My favorite North End restaurant serves creative cuisine in a romantic town house. The best dish is osso buco, and anything with seafood is wonderful. *3 North Square (Prince and Garden Court sts.).* ☎ *617/523-0077. www.mammamaria.com. Entrees $27–$40. AE, DISC, MC, V. Dinner daily. T: Green or Orange Line to Haymarket. Map p 102.*

★ Mike & Patty's BAY VILLAGE *AMERICAN* This closet-size, mostly takeout place almost defies description; I'll say "gourmet diner." Breakfast options are sublime; at lunch, try a *torta* (Mexican-style sandwich). *12 Church St. (Fayette St.).* ☎ *617/423-3447. www.mikeandpattys.com. Entrees $3–$9. MC, V. Breakfast & lunch Wed–Sun. T: Orange Line to Tufts Medical Center. Map p 102.*

★★ kids Mike's City Diner SOUTH END *AMERICAN* A neighborhood stalwart that serves huge portions of yummy diner classics, Mike's often has a line out the door on weekends—and with good reason. *1714 Washington St. (E. Springfield St.).* ☎ *617/267-9393. www.mikescitydiner.com. Entrees $4–$12. No credit cards. Breakfast & lunch daily. T: Silver Line SL4/SL5 to Worcester Sq. Map p 102.*

★★ Neptune Oyster NORTH END *SEAFOOD* Tiny and crammed full of hungry diners, Neptune is an open secret: The busy little kitchen produces some of the best seafood in the city. Be ready to wait. *63 Salem St. (Cross St.).* ☎ *617/742-3474. www.neptune oyster.com. Entrees $19–$35. AE, MC, V. Lunch & dinner daily. T: Green or Orange Line to Haymarket. Map p 102.*

★★ Oleana CAMBRIDGE *MEDITERRANEAN* The emphatic flavors, seasonal ingredients, and cozy atmosphere make Oleana my top choice for a shot of summer on a frosty winter night. In fine weather, try for a table on the delightful patio. *134 Hampshire St. (Elm St.).* ☎ *617/661-0505. www.oleana restaurant.com. Entrees $24–$30. AE, MC, V. Dinner daily. T: Red Line to Central, 10-min. walk. Map p 101.*

★ Peach Farm CHINATOWN *SEAFOOD/CANTONESE* One of Chinatown's top seafood destinations, Peach Farm is the place to go for ultra-fresh fish and shellfish prepared at lightning speed. *4 Tyler St. (Beach St.).* ☎ *617/482-3332. www. peachfarmboston.com. Entrees $5–$35 (most $20 or less). AE, MC, V. Lunch & dinner daily. T: Orange Line to Chinatown. Map p 102.*

★ kids Picco Restaurant SOUTH END *PIZZA* The name is short for "Pizza and Ice Cream Company"; salads, sandwiches, and great fish tacos complement the excellent pizza. Ice cream makes a perfect chaser. *513 Tremont St. (E. Berkeley and Clarendon sts.).* ☎ *617/927-0066. www.piccorestaurant.com. Pizza $12 and up. MC, V. Lunch & dinner daily. T: Orange Line to Back Bay. Map p 102.*

★★ kids Pizzeria Regina NORTH END *PIZZA* That picture you have in your head of a neighborhood pizza place in an old-time Italian neighborhood? This is it.

11½ Thacher St. (North Margin St.). ☎ 617/227-0765. www.pizzeria regina.com. Pizza $11 and up. AE, DISC, MC, V. Lunch & dinner daily. T: Green or Orange Line to Haymarket. Map p 102.

★★ Russell House Tavern

CAMBRIDGE *NEW AMERICAN* The gastropub is a Harvard hotspot with a diverse menu—everything from gourmet pizza to heirloom pork—and three comfy seating areas (including a patio). *14 John F. Kennedy St. (Brattle St.).* ☎ 617/500-3055. www.russellhouse-cambridge.com. Entrees $12–$35. AE, DISC, MC, V. Lunch & dinner daily, brunch weekends. T: Red Line to Harvard. Map p 101.

★★ kids S&S Restaurant CAM-

BRIDGE *DELI* The best weekend-brunch restaurant in the Boston area serves classic deli food all week. *1334 Cambridge St. (Prospect and Hampshire sts.).* ☎ 617/354-0777. www.sandsrestaurant.com. Entrees $6–$20. AE, MC, V. Breakfast, lunch & dinner daily; brunch weekends. T: Red Line to Central, 10-min. walk. Map p 101.

★ Sakurabana FINANCIAL DIS-

TRICT *SUSHI/JAPANESE* An unassuming destination for top-notch sushi, Sakurabana is a madhouse at midday (lunch boxes and specials are good deals) and calmer after work. *57 Broad St. (Milk St.).* ☎ 617/542-4311. www.sakurabanaboston. com. Entrees $14–$40; sushi $2 and up. AE, DISC, MC, V. Lunch weekdays, dinner Mon–Sat. T: Blue Line to Aquarium. Map p 102.

★★ Sultan's Kitchen FINAN-

CIAL DISTRICT *TURKISH* Mostly a takeout operation, the Sultan's Kitchen is perfect for a picnic. It also has enough tables to allow for

You'll find some of Boston's best pizza at Pizzeria Regina.

a business lunch over delectable Middle Eastern specialties and a rainbow of salads. *116 State St. (Broad St.).* ☎ 617/570-9009. www.sultans-kitchen.com. Entrees $6–$12. AE, MC, V. Lunch & dinner weekdays, lunch Sat. T: Blue Line to Aquarium. Map p 102.

★★ Sweet Cheeks

FENWAY *BARBECUE* Almost everything about this upscale joint near Fenway park is perfect—succulent barbecue, fantastic side dishes, hospitable service, biscuits so good you'll forsake your Southern grandma. But it's so loud! Eat outside if you can. *1381 Boylston St. (Brookline Ave.).* ☎ 617/266-1300. www. sweetcheeksq.com. Entrees $11–$28. AE, DISC, MC, V. Lunch & dinner daily, weekend brunch. T: Green Line D to Fenway. Map p 102.

★★ Tapéo BACK BAY *SPANISH*

A perfect place for a celebration, Tapéo specializes in flavorful tapas that go well with sangria. *266 Newbury St. (Fairfield and Gloucester sts.).* ☎ 617/267-4799. www.tapeo. com. Entrees $25–$40, tapas $6–$13. AE, MC, V. Lunch weekends, dinner daily. T: Green Line B, C, or D to Hynes Convention Center. Map p 104.

★★ Taranta Cucina Meridio-

nale NORTH END *ITALIAN/ PERUVIAN* The flavors of the owner-chef's native Peru jazz up Taranta's menu, which deftly combines neighborhood favorites and culinary adventure. *210 Hanover St. (Cross St.).* ☎ 617/720-0052. www. tarantarist.com. Entrees $19–$36. AE, MC, V. Dinner daily. T: Green or Orange Line to Haymarket. Map p 102.

Ye Olde Union Oyster House is the perfect place to try clam chowder or oyster stew.

★ **Toro** SOUTH END *SPANISH* The draw here is authentic tapas, with luscious additions like Mexican-style grilled corn. Toro is just busy enough at lunch, noisy and crowded at dinner. *1704 Washington St. (E. Springfield St.).* ☎ *617/536-4300. www.toro-restaurant.com. Entrees $17–$38; tapas $5–$16. AE, DC, DISC, MC, V. Lunch weekdays, brunch Sun, dinner daily. T: Silver Line SL4/SL5 to Worcester Sq. Map p 102.*

★★ **Trade** WATERFRONT *MEDITERRANEAN* Come for the bar scene, stay for the delectable, shareable flatbreads, salads, pasta, and more. Business travelers and foodies are equally happy here—and yelling about it. *540 Atlantic Ave. (Congress St.).* ☎ *617/451-1234. www.trade-boston.com. Menu items $8–$28. AE, MC, V. Lunch weekdays, dinner daily. T: Red Line to South Station. Map p 102.*

★ kids **Union Oyster House** FANEUIL HALL MARKETPLACE *SEAFOOD* The country's oldest restaurant (since 1826) is on the Freedom Trail—tourist central—but popular with locals. *41 Union St. (North and Hanover sts.).* ☎ *617/227-2750. www.unionoysterhouse.com. Entrees $21–$34. AE, DISC, MC, V. Lunch & dinner daily. T: Orange or Green Line to Haymarket. Map p 102.*

★★ **UpStairs on the Square** CAMBRIDGE *AMERICAN* The second-floor dining room, the Monday Club Bar, is a cozy destination for upscale comfort food. *91 Winthrop St. (Kennedy and Eliot sts.).* ☎ *617/864-1933. www.upstairson thesquare.com. Entrees $13–$38. AE, DISC, MC, V. Lunch Mon–Sat, brunch Sun, dinner daily. T: Red Line to Harvard. Map p 101.*

★★ **Volle Nolle** NORTH END *WINE BAR* At dinnertime, North Enders often hide from the tourist hordes. Cozy little Volle Nolle draws them out with savory small plates and well-chosen wine and beer. *351 Hanover St. (Fleet St.).* ☎ *617/523-0003. Menu items $4–$12. No credit cards. Dinner Tues–Sat. T: Orange or Green Line to Haymarket. Map p 102.*

★ **Xinh Xinh** CHINATOWN *VIETNAMESE* The best Vietnamese food in town comes from this little storefront, where the friendly staff can help you navigate the mile-long menu. *7 Beach St. (Knapp St.).* ☎ *617/422-0501. www.facebook. com/XinhXinhRestaurant. Entrees $8–$17. DISC, MC, V. Lunch & dinner daily. T: Orange Line to Chinatown. Map p 102.* ●

Nightlife Best Bets

Best Views
★★★ Top of the Hub, *Prudential Center, 800 Boylston St.* (p 122)

Best Alfresco Pickup Joint
★ Tia's, *200 Atlantic Ave.* (p 119)

Best Martinis
★★ The Bar at Taj Boston, *15 Arlington St.* (p 118)

Best Upscale Pool Hall
★★ Flat Top Johnny's, *1 Kendall Sq., Cambridge* (p 123)

Best Irish Pub
★★ Mr. Dooley's Boston Tavern, *77 Broad St.* (p 123)

Best Gay Scene
★★ Club Café, *209 Columbus Ave.* (p 120)

Best Deal
★★ Toad, *1912 Massachusetts Ave., Cambridge* (p 122)

Best Scorpion Bowls
★ The Hong Kong, *1238 Massachusetts Ave., Cambridge* (p 118)

Most Worth the Trip
★★★ Johnny D's Uptown Restaurant & Music Club, *17 Holland St., Somerville* (p 121)

Best Location
★ Bleacher Bar, *82A Lansdowne St.* (p 118)

Best Folk Club
★★★ Club Passim, *47 Palmer St., Cambridge* (p 121)

Best Rock Club
★★★ The Middle East, *472–480 Massachusetts Ave., Cambridge* (p 122)

Best Blues Club
★★★ House of Blues, *15 Lansdowne St.* (p 121)

Best Comedy Club
★★ The Comedy Studio, *1238 Massachusetts Ave., Cambridge* (p 119)

Best Old-School Jazz Club
★ Wally's Cafe, *427 Massachusetts Ave.* (p 121)

Best Upscale Jazz Club
★★★ Scullers Jazz Club, *400 Soldiers Field Rd.* (p 120)

Best Old-School Sports Bar
★★ The Fours, *166 Canal St.* (p 123)

Best Yuppie Sports Bar
★ Game On! Sports Café, *82 Lansdowne St.* (p 124)

Soak in the skyline at Top of the Hub. Previous page: Fireworks behind Massachusetts State House.

Cambridge Nightlife

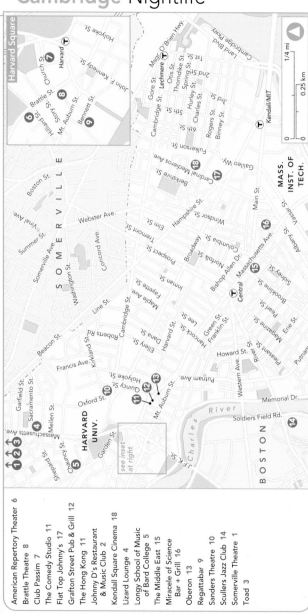

American Repertory Theater 6
Brattle Theatre 8
Club Passim 7
The Comedy Studio 11
Flat Top Johnny's 17
Grafton Street Pub & Grill 12
The Hong Kong 11
Johnny D's Restaurant & Music Club 2
Kendall Square Cinema 18
Lizard Lounge 4
Longy School of Music of Bard College 5
The Middle East 15
Miracele of Science Bar + Grill 16
Oberon 9
Regattabar 9
Sanders Theatre 10
Scullers Jazz Club 14
Somerville Theatre 1
Toad 3

Boston Nightlife

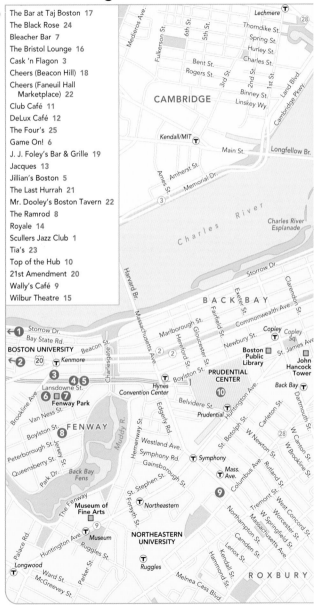

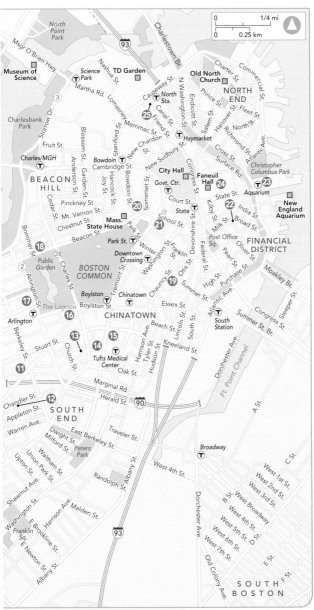

North Point Park

Msgr O'Brien Hwy.

Museum of Science

Science Park Ⓣ

TD Garden

Nashua St.

Charlestown Br.

Charter St.

Commercial St.

Old North Church

NORTH END

Martha Rd. Lomasney Way

Causeway St.

25 North Sta. Ⓣ

Canal St.

Friend St.

Merrimac St.

Prince St.

Fleet St.

Salem St.

Hanover St.

N. Washington St.

Endicott St.

Richmond St.

North St.

Atlantic Ave.

3

Charlesbank Park

Storrow Dr.

Fruit St.

Charles/MGH Ⓣ

Blossom St.

Garden St.

Anderson St.

New Chardon St.

Staniford St.

New Sudbury St.

Haymarket Ⓣ

Cross St.

Surface Rd.

Christopher Columbus Park

BEACON HILL

Bowdoin Ⓣ

Cambridge St.

Hancock St.

Joy St.

Bowdoin St.

Somerset St.

City Hall

Congress St.

Govt. Ctr. Ⓣ

Faneuil Hall 24

Aquarium Ⓣ 23

New England Aquarium

Cedar St.

Pinckney St.

Mt. Vernon St.

Chestnut St.

Beacon St.

20

Court St.

School St.

State Ⓣ 21

State St.

Kilby St.

India St.

Broad St.

22

Mass. State House

Park St.

Park St. Ⓣ

Winter St.

Franklin St.

Devonshire St.

Milk St.

Post Office Sq.

Oliver St.

FINANCIAL DISTRICT

Pearl St.

Pearl St.

Purchase St.

Federal St.

Moakley Br.

18

Public Garden

28

Charles St.

BOSTON COMMON

Tremont St.

Washington St.

Chauncy St.

Otis St.

Summer St.

High St.

Atlantic Ave.

2

Arlington Ⓣ

17

The Lagoon

16

Boylston Ⓣ

Boylston St.

Chinatown Ⓣ

CHINATOWN

Essex St.

Beach St.

Lincoln St.

South St.

South Station

Congress St.

Summer St. Br.

Sleeper St.

Arlington

Berkeley St.

11

Stuart St.

Church St.

13

14

15

Harrison Ave.

Tyler St.

Hudson St.

Kneeland St.

Dorchester Ave.

Ft. Point Channel

Tufts Medical Center Ⓣ

Oak St.

Chandler St.

12

Appleton St.

SOUTH END

Marginal Rd.

Herald St.

90

A St.

Warren Ave.

Dwight St.

Milford St.

East Berkeley St.

Peters Park

Traveler St.

Broadway Ⓣ

West 1st St.

West 2nd St.

West 3rd St.

C. St.

Waltham St.

Union Park St.

Upton St.

West St.

West 4th St.

B. St.

West Broadway

West 5th St. D. St.

Shawmut Ave.

Washington St.

E. Brookline St.

Harrison Ave.

Malden St.

Randolph St.

Albany St.

West 4th St.

West 6th St.

Franklin Sq.

E. Newton St.

Albany St.

93

Dorchester Ave.

Old Colony Ave.

West 7th St.

SOUTH BOSTON

E. St.

F. St.

0   1/4 mi

0   0.25 km

Boston Nightlife A to Z

Bars

★★ The Bar at Taj Boston

BACK BAY   This classic aristocratic watering hole is a cozy, paneled room with a power-broker clientele, a baronial fireplace, a view of the Public Garden, and killer martinis. *15 Arlington St. (Newbury St.), in the Taj Boston hotel.* ☎ *617/598-5255. T: Green Line to Arlington. Map p 116.*

★★ Bleacher Bar FENWAY

Under—under!—the Fenway Park bleachers is a standard-issue bar with a unique feature: a picture window that faces the outfield. The prime tables, which enjoy a smashing view through one-way glass, have a time limit on game days. *82A Lansdowne St. (Brookline Ave. and Ipswich St.).* ☎ *617/262-2424. www.bleacherbarboston.com. T: Green Line B, C, or D to Kenmore. Map p 116.*

Cheers BEACON HILL & FANEUIL

HALL MARKETPLACE   The bar that inspired the TV show was a fun neighborhood place called the Bull & Finch. Now it's called Cheers (bring a camera—the sign is outside), and although it's still fun, the neighborhood atmosphere is gone. There's another Cheers at Faneuil Hall that faithfully replicates the set of the TV show. *84 Beacon St. (Brimmer St.).* ☎ *617/227-9605. www. cheersboston.com. T: Green Line to Arlington. Map p 116. Also at Quincy Market, South Canopy.* ☎ *617/227-0150. T: Green or Blue Line to Government Center. Map p 116.*

★★ DeLux Café SOUTH END

The awesome decor—posters, postcards, album covers (from LPs!), and such—makes a perfect backdrop for the cool neighborhood crowd, microbrew selection, and veggie-friendly food. *100 Chandler St. (Clarendon St.).* ☎ *617/338-5258. T: Orange Line to Back Bay. Map p 116.*

★ The Hong Kong CAMBRIDGE

The upstairs bar at this retro Chinese restaurant is a Harvard

Cheers at Faneuil Hall.

There's a lot to do at Long Wharf at night after the sun goes down.

hangout that inspires the question: How do these kids suck down so many Scorpion Bowls and stay so smart? *1238 Massachusetts Ave. (Bow St.).* ☎ *617/864-5311. www. hongkongharvard.com. T: Red Line to Harvard. Map p 115.*

★ J. J. Foley's Bar & Grille
DOWNTOWN   The epitome of a divey after-work bar, Foley's is a big, noisy place with a topnotch beer menu and an excellent juke-box. Plan to eat somewhere else. *21 Kingston St. (Summer and Bedford sts.).* ☎ *617/695-2529. www. jjfoleysbarandgrill.com. T: Red or Orange Line to Downtown Crossing. Map p 116.*

★★ The Last Hurrah
DOWNTOWN CROSSING   The Parker House's 19th-century atmosphere extends to the lobby bar, which is popular with the after-work crowd as well as Beacon Hill political types. *60 School St. (Tremont St.), in the Omni Parker House hotel.* ☎ *617/227-8600. T: Green or Blue Line to Government Center. Map p 116.*

★★ Miracle of Science Bar + Grill
CAMBRIDGE   Near MIT and Kendall Square, Miracle of Science draws a techie crowd. It has an 8am liquor license and serves veggie-friendly food all day—the menu is the drawing on the wall that looks like the periodic table. *321 Massachusetts Ave. (State St.).* ☎ *617/686-2866. www.miracleof science.us. T: Red Line to Central. Map p 115.*

Tia's
WATERFRONT   In warm weather, the huge patio a stone's throw from the Financial District attracts what looks like every 20-something in town. *200 Atlantic Ave. (State St.), next to the Boston Marriott Long Wharf Hotel.* ☎ *617/ 227-0828. www.tiaswaterfront.com. T: Blue Line to Aquarium. Map p 116.*

★ 21st Amendment
BEACON HILL   Across the street from the State House, the 21st Amendment is a neighborhood bar in a politico-infested neighborhood. (The 21st Amendment repealed Prohibition— get it?) *150 Bowdoin St. (Beacon St.).* ☎ *617/227-7100. www.21stboston. com. T: Red or Green Line to Park St. Map p 116.*

Comedy Clubs
★★★ The Comedy Studio
CAMBRIDGE   A hilarious proving ground for up-and-coming comics, who complement stand-up with sketches and improv, the Comedy Studio is no secret to network

scouts. *1238 Massachusetts Ave. (Bow St.), 3rd floor of the Hong Kong.* ☎ *617/661-6507. www.the-comedystudio.com. Tickets $10–$12. T: Red Line to Harvard. Map p 115.*

★ **Wilbur Theatre** THEATER DISTRICT   The historic theater is Boston's highest-profile comedy venue; the space also books musical acts when national and local comics aren't in the spotlight. *246 Tremont St. (Stuart St.).* ☎ *617/248-9700. www.thewilburtheatre.com. Tickets $20–$75. T: Green Line to Boylston. Map p 116.*

Dance Club

★★★ **Royale** THEATER DISTRICT A former hotel ballroom with a stage and a balcony (great for watching the crowd), Royale books concerts as well as top local and national DJs. *279 Tremont St. (Stuart St.), in the Courtyard Boston Downtown Hotel.* ☎ *617/338-7699. www. royaleboston.com. Cover $15–$30. T: Green Line to Boylston. Map p 116.*

Gay & Lesbian Bars & Clubs

★★ **Club Café** SOUTH END   A club, video bar, cabaret and restaurant under one roof, this upscale spot is the city's top gay nightlife destination. Thursday is see-and-be-seen night. *209 Columbus Ave. (Berkeley St.).* ☎ *617/536-0966. www.clubcafe.com. No cover. T: Orange Line to Back Bay. Map p 116.*

★ **Jacques** BAY VILLAGE   Boston's only drag club, on a side street between the Theater District and the Back Bay, also books performance artists and live music. No credit cards. *79 Broadway (off Charles St. S.).* ☎ *617/426-8902. www.jacques-cabaret.com. Cover $6–$10. T: Green Line to Arlington. Map p 116.*

★ **The Ramrod** FENWAY Upstairs is a bar with a pool table,

Local and international artists, including Buckwheat Zydeco and Madeleine Peyroux, play at Regattabar.

downstairs is a crowded dance club, leather is required in the back room (jackets don't count), and a cruisey atmosphere prevails throughout. *1254 Boylston St. (Ipswich St.).* ☎ *617/266-2986. www.ramrod-boston.com. T: Green Line D to Fenway. Map p 116.*

Jazz Clubs

★★★ **Regattabar** CAMBRIDGE A large, elegant room in a swanky hotel, the Regattabar is engaged in a long-running battle with Scullers (see next listing) to book the biggest names in jazz. Everybody wins. *1 Bennett St. (Eliot St.), Cambridge, in the Charles Hotel.* ☎ *617/395-7757. www.regattabarjazz.com. Tickets $10–$35. T: Red Line to Harvard. Map p 115.*

★★★ **Scullers Jazz Club** ALLSTON   Without easy access to the T, Scullers is harder to reach than the Regattabar (see previous listing)—which means these patrons *really* want to be here. *400 Soldiers*

Field Rd. (Mass. Turnpike Cambridge exit), in the DoubleTree Suites by Hilton Hotel. ☎ 617/562-4111. www.scullersjazz.com. Tickets $20–$50. Map p 115.

★ **Wally's Cafe** SOUTH END Hard-core jazz fans have sought out Wally's since it opened in 1947. This small, family-run place books mostly local talent and attracts a serious—and seriously diverse—crowd. 427 Massachusetts Ave. (Columbus Ave.). ☎ 617/424-1408. www.wallyscafe.com. No cover. 1-drink minimum. T: Orange Line to Massachusetts Ave. Map p 116.

Live-Music Clubs

★★★ **Club Passim** CAMBRIDGE The place for folk music is a subterranean coffeehouse—it also serves beer and wine—founded in 1958. Passim has booked every folk artist you've ever loved, and plenty you haven't heard of. Yet. 47 Palmer St. (Church St.). ☎ 617/492-7679. www.clubpassim.org. Cover usually $10–$25. T: Red Line to Harvard. Map p 115.

★★ **Great Scott** ALLSTON This ordinary-looking bar is a terrific live-music venue that also books excellent DJs. The clientele matches the neighborhood: mostly students and recent grads. No credit cards. 1222 Commonwealth Ave. (Harvard Ave.). ☎ 617/566-9014. www.greatscottboston.com. Cover $5–$15. T: Green Line B to Harvard Ave.

★ **House of Blues** FENWAY Across the street from Fenway Park, this huge club hops year-round. It books top-notch blues, rock, and pop artists; the restaurant serves the chain's familiar Southern menu, with some New England flourishes. 15 Lansdowne St. (Brookline Ave. and Ipswich St.). ☎ 888/693-2583. www.houseofblues.com/boston. Tickets $23–$55. T: Green Line B, C, or D to Kenmore.

★★★ **Johnny D's Uptown Restaurant & Music Club** SOMERVILLE The impressively varied schedule (rock, blues, bluegrass, and much more) makes this friendly, family-run club well worth the trip—just two T stops past Harvard Square. 17 Holland St. (Davis Sq.). ☎ 617/776-2004. www.johnnyds.com. Cover $5–$20 (usually

The talent at Scullers Jazz Club is worth the search.

The Middle East showcases local bands as well as national acts.

$8–$12). T: Red Line to Davis. Map p 115.

★★ **Lizard Lounge** CAMBRIDGE The "stage" at this subterranean club is on the floor, allowing the rock and folk musicians to stray into the 20- and 30-something crowd. *1667 Massachusetts Ave. (Wendell St.).* ☎ *617/547-0759. www.lizard loungeclub.com. Cover $5–$15. T: Red Line to Harvard. Map p 115.*

★★★ **The Middle East** CAM-BRIDGE Four performance spaces and bookers with an uncanny ear for promising alternative and pro-gressive artists make this the best (and possibly loudest) rock club in the Boston area. *472–480 Massachu-setts Ave. (Brookline St.).* ☎ *617/ 864-3278. www.mideastclub.com. Cover $5–$30. T: Red Line to Central. Map p 115.*

★★ **Toad** CAMBRIDGE Here you'll find top-notch local rock, rockabilly, and blues artists per-forming for a savvy crowd that appreciates the booze menu, inti-mate surroundings, and price

(free!). 1912 Massachusetts Ave. (Porter Rd.). ☎ *617/497-4950. www. toadcambridge.com. No cover. T: Red Line to Porter. Map p 115.*

Lounges

★★★ **The Bristol Lounge** BACK BAY The posh hotel restau-rant and lounge is a magnet for a well-heeled older crowd. There's live music nightly and a Saturday dessert buffet. *200 Boylston St. (Hadassah Way), in the Four Seasons Hotel.* ☎ *617/351-2037. T: Green Line to Arlington. Map p 116.*

★★★ **Top of the Hub** BACK BAY The 52nd-floor lounge is a gorgeous setting for romance, especially if you arrive in daylight and watch the sunset. Top of the Hub schedules live jazz nightly. No jeans. *Prudential Center, 800 Boylston St. (Fairfield St.).* ☎ *617/ 536-1775. www.topofthehub.net. $24/person minimum at tables. T: Green Line E to Prudential. Map p 116.*

Pool & More

★★ Flat Top Johnny's CAMBRIDGE This casual hangout is a cavernous space with a dozen pool tables and a long menu of microbrews. So cool, yet so close to MIT—go figure. *1 Kendall Sq. (Hampshire St.).* ☎ *617/494-9565. www.flattopjohnnys.com. T: Red Line to Kendall/MIT, 10-min. walk. Map p 115.*

★ Jillian's Boston FENWAY Thirty-five pool tables are the tip of the iceberg—Jillian's is also a bowling alley, dance club, sports bar, and restaurant. Children are admitted, but only during the day. *145 Ipswich St. (Lansdowne St.).* ☎ *617/437-0300. www.jilliansboston.com. T: Green Line B, C, or D to Kenmore, 10-min. walk. Map p 116.*

Pubs

The Black Rose FANEUIL HALL MARKETPLACE The Black Rose is usually crowded with out-of-towners, but the enthusiastic musicians

The Bristol Lounge is a great choice for a post-theater drink.

performing traditional Irish music don't care that the people singing along are mostly tourists. *160 State St. (Commercial St.).* ☎ *617/742-2286. www.blackroseboston.com. Cover $3–$10. T: Blue Line to Aquarium. Map p 116.*

★ Grafton Street Pub & Grill CAMBRIDGE The stylish room, professional crowd, and tasty comfort food make this place a neighborhood fave; the standouts are the Irish bartenders and deftly poured Guinness. *1230 Massachusetts Ave. (Bow St.).* ☎ *617/497-0400. www.graftonstreetcambridge. com. T: Red Line to Harvard. Map p 115.*

★★ Mr. Dooley's Boston Tavern FINANCIAL DISTRICT This authentically decorated pub is far enough off the tourist track to be a favorite with local office workers and homesick expats. There's live Irish music on weekend nights. *77 Broad St. (Batterymarch St.).* ☎ *617/338-5656. www.somerspubs.com. Cover (Fri–Sat) $3–$5. T: Blue Line to Aquarium. Map p 116.*

Sports Bars

★ Cask 'n Flagon FENWAY A local landmark, "the Cask" is busiest when the Red Sox are in town—they play across the street—and lively year-round. *62 Lansdowne St. (Brookline Ave.).* ☎ *617/536-4840. www.casknflagon.com. T: Green Line B, C, or D to Kenmore. Map p 116.*

★★ The Four's NORTH STATION Across the street from the TD Garden, the Four's has been a Boston favorite since 1976. It boasts tons of TVs, abundant memorabilia, and good pub grub. *166 Canal St. (Causeway St.).* ☎ *617/720-4455. www.thefours.com. T: Green or Orange Line to North Station. Map p 116.*

On game days, the line to get into Game On! stretches down the street.

★ **Game On!** FENWAY If you can't get a ticket to the game, this is a solid substitute: The high-tech "sports cafe" and its dozens of TVs are actually *in* the ballpark (there's no access to the stands). *82 Lansdowne St. (Brookline Ave.).* ☎ *617/351-7001. www.gameonboston.com. T: Green Line B, C, or D to Kenmore. Map p 116.* ●

Getting a Deal on Nightlife

Check around before you leave home to see whether discounts are available for cultural happenings that interest you. An excellent resource is ArtsBoston, which runs the **BosTix** booths at Faneuil Hall Marketplace (T: Green or Blue Line to Government Center, or Orange Line to Haymarket) and in Copley Square (T: Green Line to Copley or Orange Line to Back Bay). Same-day tickets to musical and theatrical performances are half price, subject to availability. You must pay cash, and there are no refunds or exchanges. Check the board or website for the day's offerings. The booths are open Tuesday through Saturday 10am to 6pm and Sunday 11am to 4pm. Call ☎ **617/262-8632** or visit www.bostix.org.

Boston Arts & Entertainment

Agganis Arena 2
AMC Boston Common 19 23
Bank of America Pavilion 21
Berklee Performance
  Center 10
Blue Man Group 26
BosTix Copley Square 11
BosTix Faneuil Hall
  Marketplace 18
Boston Center for the Arts 13
Boston Common 16
Boston Lyric Opera 26
Boston Opera House 22
Boston Pops 9
Boston Symphony Orchestra 9
Colonial Theatre 24
Commonwealth Shakespeare
  Company 16
Coolidge Corner Theatre 3
Cutler Majestic Theatre 25
Emmanuel Church 14
Fenway Park 4
Hatch Shell 15
Huntington Theatre Company 8

Isabella Stewart Gardner
  Museum 5
King's Chapel 19
Museum of Fine Arts 6
New England
  Conservatory 7
Orpheum Theatre 20
Paradise Rock Club 1
Shear Madness 26
Shubert Theatre 27
Symphony Hall 9
TD Garden 17
Trinity Church 12
Wang Theatre 28

Lechmere
Thorndike St.
Spring St.
Hurley St.
Charles St.
3rd St.
2nd St.
1st St.
Binney St.
Linskey Wy.
Land Blvd
Cambridge Pkwy.
Main St.
Longfellow Br.

Memorial Dr.

Charles River

Charles River
Esplanade

Storrow Dr.

BACK BAY

Storrow Dr.
Bay State Rd.
BOSTON UNIVERSITY
Beacon St.
Kenmore
Charlesgate

Marlborough St.
Commonwealth Ave.
Fairfield St.
Exeter St.
Clarendon St.
Copley
Copley
Sq.
Newbury St.
St. James Ave.
Boston
Public
Library
John
Hancock
Tower
Back Bay

Lansdowne St.
Fenway Park
Boylston St.
Hynes
Convention Center
PRUDENTIAL
CENTER
Belvidere St.
Prudential
Huntington Ave.
Darmouth St.

FENWAY
Van Ness St.
Boylston St.
Mudy R.
Westland Ave.
Symphony Rd.
Symphony
Mass.
Ave.
St. Botolph St.
W Newton St.
Carleton St.
W Canton St.
W Brookline St.

Peterborough St.
Queensberry St.
Park Dr.
Jersey St.
Back Bay
Fens
Hemenway St.
Edgerly Rd.
Gainsborough St.
St. Stephen St.
Northeastern
Forsyth St.
Columbus Ave.
Northampton St.
Tremont St.
West Concord St.
Camden St.
Lenox St.
Kendall St.
Massachusetts Ave.
W Springfield St.
Worcester St.

The Fenway
Museum of
Fine Arts
Huntington Ave.
Museum
Ruggles St.
NORTHEASTERN
UNIVERSITY
Ruggles
Melnea Cass Blvd.
Hammond St.
ROXBURY

Palace Rd.
Longwood
Ward St.
McGreevey St.
Parker St.

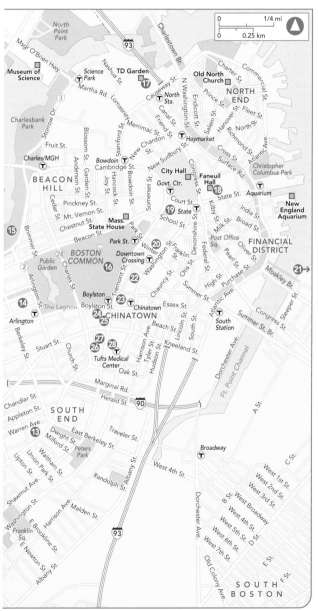

Arts & Entertainment Best Bets

Best **Concert Hall**
★★ Symphony Hall, *301 Massachusetts Ave. (p 130)*

Best **18th-Century Flashback**
★★ Handel & Haydn Society, *various locations (p 129)*

Best **Concert Venue with a View**
★★ Bank of America Pavilion, *290 Northern Ave. (p 132)*

Most **Beautiful Indoor Venue**
★★ Boston Opera House, *539 Washington St. (p 133)*

Most **Beautiful Outdoor Venues**
★ Boston Landmarks Orchestra, *various locations (p 129)*

Best **Dinner & a Show**
★★ Boston Pops, Symphony Hall, *301 Massachusetts Ave. (p 129)*

Best **Theater Deal**
★★ Commonwealth Shakespeare Company, *Boston Common (p 134)*

Best **Music Deals**
★ Longy School of Music of Bard College, *1 Follen St., Cambridge (p 131);* and ★ New England Conservatory of Music, *290 Huntington Ave. (p 129)*

Best **Pre-Broadway Showcase**
★★ American Repertory Theater, *64 Brattle St., Cambridge (p 133)*

Best **Sports Venue**
★★★ Fenway Park, *4 Yawkey Way (p 133)*

Best **Holiday Event**
★★ The Nutcracker, Boston Ballet, *Boston Opera House, 539 Washington St. (p 131)*

Best **Family Entertainment**
★ Shear Madness, *Charles Playhouse, 74 Warrenton St. (p 133)*

Best **First-Run Movie Theater**
★ AMC Loews Boston Common, *175 Tremont St. (p 131)*

Best **Art House**
★ Kendall Square Cinema, *1 Kendall Sq., Cambridge (p 131)*

Best **Revival House**
★★ Brattle Theatre, *40 Brattle St., Cambridge (p 131)*

Best **Midnight Movies**
★★ Coolidge Corner Theatre, *290 Harvard St., Brookline (p 131)*

Fenway is the oldest ballpark in the major leagues.

Arts & Entertainment **A to Z**

Keith Lockhart leads the Boston Pops.

Classical Music

★ **Boston Landmarks Orchestra** VARIOUS LOCATIONS The orchestra performs free (free!) concerts in historic settings—usually parks—around town on summer evenings. *Performances at the Hatch Shell, on Boston Common, and in other locations.* ☎ 617/520-2200. *www.landmarksorchestra.org.*

★★ **Boston Pops** BACK BAY The Boston Symphony Orchestra's playful sibling often features celebrity guest stars. Refreshments are served at tables on the floor of Symphony Hall, and there's balcony seating without food and drink. The season runs from May through the Fourth of July extravaganza, plus holiday programs in December. *301 Massachusetts Ave. (Huntington Ave.).* ☎ 888/266-1200 or ☎ 617/266-1200 (SymphonyCharge). *www.bostonpops.org.* Tickets $22–$125. T: Green Line E to Symphony. Map p 126.

★★★ **Boston Symphony Orchestra** BACK BAY The BSO is one of the five best American orchestras and one of the finest in the world. The most celebrated programs are classical music, often with a renowned guest artist or conductor. The season runs October through April. *301 Massachusetts Ave. (Huntington Ave.).* ☎ 888/266-1200 or ☎ 617/266-1200 (SymphonyCharge). *www.bso.org.* Tickets $31–$125; rehearsal $20. T: Green Line E to Symphony. Map p 126.

★★ **Emmanuel Church** BACK BAY Emmanuel's orchestra and chorus perform Bach cantatas at Sunday services (10am) from mid-September to mid-May; check the website for other dates. *15 Newbury St. (Arlington St.).* ☎ 617/536-3356. *www.emmanuelmusic.org.* Free-will offering. T: Green Line to Arlington. Map p 126.

★★ **Handel & Haydn Society** BACK BAY/FENWAY "Historically informed" concerts with period instruments and techniques might sound stodgy—until you hear the first note of a dynamic, creative performance. *Offices: 300 Massachusetts Ave.* ☎ 617/266-3605. *www.handelandhaydn.org.* Performing at *Symphony Hall (p 126)* and *New England Conservatory's Jordan Hall (p 126).*

Concert & Performance Venues

★★★ **Hatch Shell** BACK BAY The riverside amphitheater, best known as the home of the Boston Pops' Fourth of July concert, schedules other events on many summer nights. Free Friday Flicks (family movies) begin at sunset (late June–late Aug). *Charles River Esplanade (off Storrow Dr.).* ☎ 617/626-4970. *www.mass.gov/dcr.* Free admission. T: Red Line to Charles/MGH or Green Line to Arlington. Map p 126.

★ **New England Conservatory** FENWAY Students and faculty performing free classical, jazz, and chamber music dominates the

The Emmanuel Church orchestra and chorus.

schedule, which includes professional artists and companies. *290 Huntington Ave. (Gainsborough St.).* ☎ 617/585-1260. www.necmusic. edu/concerts-events. Ticket prices vary. T: Green Line E to Symphony. Map p 126.

★★ Symphony Hall BACK BAY

When the BSO and the Pops are away, acoustically perfect Symphony Hall books a wide variety of performing artists. *301 Massachusetts Ave. (Huntington Ave.).* ☎ 888/266-1200 or ☎ 617/266-1200 (SymphonyCharge). www.bso. org. Ticket prices vary. T: Green Line E to Symphony. Map p 126.

Concert Series

★ Fridays at Trinity BACK BAY

Architectural treasure Trinity Church features 30-minute organ recitals by local and visiting artists on Friday at 12:15pm. *206 Clarendon St. (Boylston St.).* ☎ 617/536-0944. www.trinitychurchboston.org. $10 donation suggested. T: Green Line to Copley. Map p 126.

★★ Isabella Stewart Gardner Museum FENWAY

The beloved museum (p 25, bullet ❸) features chamber music, jazz, "cutting-edge classical," and more from September through May. *280 The Fenway (Palace Rd.).* ☎ 617/278-5156. www. gardnermuseum.org. Tickets (including museum admission) $27 adults, $24 seniors, $12 students, $5 kids 7–17. Kids under 7 not admitted. T: Green Line E to Museum of Fine Arts. Map p 126.

How to Find Out What's On

For up-to-date entertainment listings, the web—social media in particular—has made newspapers and magazines nearly obsolete. Follow, "Like," or subscribe to e-mails from promising companies and venues, or just search Twitter for "Boston" and the term or terms that appeal to you (like "free"!). Also check daily-deal and flash-sale sites for happenings that fit your schedule. For advance tickets, visit a **BosTix booth** (see p. 126), or order from **Ticketmaster** (☎ 800/745-3000; www.ticketmaster.com), **Telecharge** (☎ 800/447-7400; www.telecharge.com), or the venue or company online or over the phone. *Tip:* If you wait until the day before or the day of a performance, you'll sometimes have access to tickets that were held back and just released for sale.

★ King's Chapel Noon Hour Recitals DOWNTOWN CROSSING
A diverse slate of organ, instrumental, and vocal performances enlivens this Freedom Trail stop. The 35-minute concerts begin at 12:15pm on Tuesday. *58 Tremont St. (School St.).* ☎ *617/227-2155. www.kings-chapel.org. $3 donation requested. T: Red or Green Line to Park St. Map p 126.*

★ Longy School of Music of Bard College CAMBRIDGE
Students and instructors from the prestigious conservatory perform at locations around the compact campus. *1 Follen St. (Garden St.).* ☎ *617/876-0956, ext. 1500. www.longy.edu. Ticket prices vary; many performances free. T: Red Line to Harvard. Map p 115.*

★★ Museum of Fine Arts FENWAY
Indoor and outdoor performances in a wide variety of genres are a great reason to visit the iconic museum (p 26, bullet ⑤). *465 Huntington Ave. (between Museum Rd. and Forsyth Way).* ☎ *800/440-6975. www.mfa.org/programs/music. Free with museum admission to $30. T: Green Line E to Museum of Fine Arts. Map p 126.*

Dance
★★ Boston Ballet THEATER DISTRICT
Best known for *The Nutcracker*, Boston Ballet is one of the top dance companies in the country. *Performances at the Boston Opera House (p 126).* ☎ *617/695-6955 (box office). www.bostonballet.org. Tickets $35–$169. T: Orange Line to Chinatown.*

Film
★ AMC Loews Boston Common 19 THEATER DISTRICT
The only first-run theater downtown boasts stadium seating and digital sound. It gets unbelievably crowded on weekend nights. *175 Tremont St. (Avery St.).* ☎ *888/AMC-4FUN or 617/423-5801. www.amctheatres.com. Tickets $7–$13. T: Green Line to Boylston. Map p 126.*

★★ Brattle Theatre CAMBRIDGE
A paragon of a revival house, the Brattle also schedules first-run independent films, talks, and readings. *40 Brattle St. (Church St.).* ☎ *617/867-6838. www.brattlefilm.org. Tickets $8–$10. T: Red Line to Harvard. Map p 115.*

★★ Coolidge Corner Theatre BROOKLINE
The Coolidge Corner books independent and international films, documentaries, revivals, and midnight shows. *290 Harvard St. (Beacon St.).* ☎ *617/734-2500. www.coolidge.org. Tickets $7–$10. T: Green Line C to Coolidge Corner. Map p 126.*

★★ Kendall Square Cinema CAMBRIDGE
The Kendall offers independent, alternative, and foreign-language films as well as excellent concessions. *1 Kendall Sq.*

Boston Ballet is one of the country's best dance companies.

The A.R.T.'s production of Pippin.

(Binney St.). ☎ 617/499-1996. www.
landmarktheatres.com. Tickets
$9–$11. T: Red Line to Kendall/MIT,
10-min. walk. Map p 115.

Opera

★ **Boston Lyric Opera** THE-
ATER DISTRICT The company
performs classical and contempo-
rary works from October through
May. *Performances at the Shubert
Theatre, 265 Tremont St. (Stuart St.).*
☎ 617/542-6772. www.blo.org.
Tickets $30–$225. T: Green Line to
Boylston. Map p 126.

Popular Music

★ **Agganis Arena** BOSTON UNI-
VERSITY Besides booking touring
rock and pop artists, the midsize
venue is BU's hockey rink. *925 Commonwealth Ave. (Harry Agganis
Way).* ☎ 617/358-7000 or ☎ 800/
745-3000 (Ticketmaster). www.
agganisarena.com. Ticket prices vary.
T: Green Line B to St. Paul St. or
Pleasant St. Map p 126.

★★ **Bank of America Pavilion**
SEAPORT DISTRICT The huge
waterfront tent is a sublime summer
setting for rock, pop, folk, country,
and more. *290 Northern Ave.*

(Congress St.). ☎ 617/728-1600 or
☎ 800/745-3000 (Ticketmaster).
www.livenation.com. Ticket prices
vary. T: Silver Line SL1/SL2 to Silver
Line Way. Map p 126.

★★ **Berklee Performance Center** BACK BAY Students and staff
members from Berklee College of
Music's noted jazz and folk programs perform here. So do touring
artists, including the school's many
famous alumni (and dropouts). *136
Massachusetts Ave. (Boylston St.).*
☎ 617/747-2261. www.berklee.edu/
BPC. Ticket prices vary; many shows
free. T: Green Line B, C, or D to
Hynes Convention Center. Map
p 126.

★ **Orpheum Theatre** DOWN-
TOWN CROSSING The 1852
building is rickety and cramped,
but the sightlines are fantastic.
1 Hamilton Place (Tremont St.).
☎ 617/482-0106 or ☎ 800/745-
3000 (Ticketmaster). www.crossroads
presents.com. Ticket prices vary. T:
Red or Green Line to Park St. Map
p 126.

★ **Paradise Rock Club** BOSTON
UNIVERSITY Rock and alternative
artists with local, regional, and
international followings play

for student-intensive crowds here. *967–969 Commonwealth Ave. (Pleasant St.).* ☎ *617/562-8800 or* ☎ *800/745-3000 (Ticketmaster). www.crossroadspresents.com. Ticket prices vary. T: Green Line B to Pleasant St. Map p 126.*

★★ Somerville Theatre

SOMERVILLE   This first- and second-run movie theater occasionally books folk, rock, and international artists in its main space. *55 Davis Sq. (Dover St.).* ☎ *617/625-5700. www.somervilletheatreonline.com. Ticket prices vary. T: Red Line to Davis. Map p 115.*

Spectator Sports

★★★ Fenway Park FENWAY

The beloved Red Sox play at the landmark ballpark from April to October. See p 24, bullet ❶. *4 Yawkey Way (Brookline Ave.).* ☎ *877/733-7699 for tickets. www.redsox.com. Tickets $12–$220. T: Green Line B, C, or D to Kenmore. Map p 126.*

★ TD Garden NORTH STATION

The city's premier arena is home to the Celtics (NBA) and Bruins (NHL) as well as ice shows and touring rock and pop artists. *100 Legends Way (Causeway St.).* ☎ *617/624-1000. www.tdgarden.com. Ticket prices vary. T: Green or Orange Line to North Station. Map p 126.*

Theater

★★ American Repertory Theater (A.R.T.) CAMBRIDGE

Founded in 1980, the nationally renowned A.R.T. (say each letter) is associated with Harvard. Performances are at the university's Loeb Drama Center and at the "theatrical club space" OBERON (0 Arrow St., off Mass. Ave.). *64 Brattle St. (Hilliard St.).* ☎ *617/547-8300. www.amrep.org. Tickets $15 and up. T: Red Line to Harvard. Map p 115.*

★★ Blue Man Group THEATER

DISTRICT   The off-Broadway phenomenon, a trio of cobalt-colored performers backed by a rock band, enlists audience members—beware if you're sitting in the first few rows. *Charles Playhouse Stage I, 74 Warrenton St.* ☎ *617/426-6912 or* ☎ *800/745-3000 (Ticketmaster). www.blueman.com. Tickets $55 and up. T: Green Line to Boylston. Map p 126.*

★★ Boston Center for the Arts SOUTH END

The city's top destination for contemporary theater, music, and dance, the BCA is a fun, funky leader in the local arts community. *539 Tremont St. (Clarendon St.).* ☎ *617/426-5000. www.bcaonline.org. Ticket prices vary. T: Orange Line to Back Bay. Map p 126.*

★★ Boston Opera House THE-

ATER DISTRICT   Built as a vaudeville theater, the cavernous, ornate Opera House mostly books touring Broadway musicals. From the day after Thanksgiving through New Year's, Boston Ballet's *Nutcracker* takes over. *539 Washington St. (Ave. de Lafayette).* ☎ *617/259-3400 or* ☎ *745-3000 (Ticketmaster). www.bostonoperahouse.com. Ticket prices vary. T: Green Line to Boylston. Map p 126.*

Commonwealth Shakespeare Company's The Last Will.

★★ **Citi Performing Arts Center** THEATER DISTRICT Three historic venues make up the non-profit Citi Center. The largest is the **Wang Theatre,** a former movie house that seats more than 3,000 and has awful sightlines from the upper balconies. Seats on the lower levels are worth the price. Across the street, the **Shubert Theatre** is a medium-size venue that's perfect for musicals and opera. The exquisite **Colonial Theatre** was built in 1900 as a legitimate stage; it has excellent sightlines and acoustics. *Wang Theatre and box office: 270 Tremont St. (Stuart St.).* ☎ *866/348-9738 or 617/482-9393. www.citi center.org. Shubert: 265 Tremont St. (Stuart St.). Colonial: 106 Boylston St. (Tremont St.). Ticket prices vary. T: Green Line to Boylston. Map p 126.*

The Citi Wang Theatre opened in 1925 and seats more than 3,000.

★★ **Commonwealth Shakespeare Company** BOSTON COMMON A highlight of summer is Commonwealth Shakespeare's annual free production, which runs Tuesday to Sunday; check for schedules and details of scaled-back performances in neighborhood locations. *Between Tremont and Beacon sts., off Charles St.* ☎ *617/426-0863. www.comm shakes.org. Free admission. T: Green Line to Boylston. Map p 126.*

★★ **Cutler Majestic Theatre** THEATER DISTRICT The exquisite 1903 Beaux Arts theater books music, dance, opera, and Emerson College student productions. *219 Tremont St. (Boylston St.).* ☎ *617/824-8000. www.cutlermajestic.org. Ticket prices vary. T: Green Line to Boylston. Map p 126.*

★★ **Huntington Theatre Company** FENWAY The high-profile professional company raised its national profile by winning a Regional Theatre Tony Award in 2013. It presents contemporary works and revivals at the Boston University Theatre, with some productions at the Boston Center for the Arts (p 133). *264 Huntington Ave. (Massachusetts Ave. and Gainsborough St.).* ☎ *617/266-0800. www.huntingtontheatre.org. Ticket prices vary. T: Green Line E to Symphony or Orange Line to Massachusetts Ave. Map p 126.*

★★ **Sanders Theatre** CAMBRIDGE Harvard's Memorial Hall holds this three-tiered space, a performance venue (and college lecture hall) that books professional folk, classical, and world-music performers and local arts companies. *45 Quincy St. (Cambridge St.).* ☎ *617/496-4595 or 617/496-2222 (Harvard Box Office). www.fas.harvard.edu/~memhall. Ticket prices vary. T: Red Line to Harvard. Map p 115.*

★ **Shear Madness** THEATER DISTRICT The audience helps solve a murder in the course of this long-running, madcap show set in a hair salon; it's great fun and never the same twice. *Charles Playhouse Stage II (downstairs), 74 Warrenton St.* ☎ *617/426-5225. www.shear madness.com. Tickets $50. T: Green Line to Boylston. Map p 126.* ●

Lodging Best Bets

Best in **Boston**
★★★ Boston Harbor Hotel $$$$
Rowes Wharf (p 140)

Best in **Cambridge**
★★★ The Charles Hotel $$$$
1 Bennett St. (p 141)

Best **Views**
★★★ The Westin Copley Place
Boston $$$ *10 Huntington Ave.
(p 148)*

Most **Romantic**
★★ Eliot Hotel $$$$ *370 Common-
wealth Ave. (p 142)*

Best for **Business**
★★★ The Langham, Boston $$$
250 Franklin St. (p 145)

Best for **Families**
★★ DoubleTree Suites by Hilton
$$–$$$ *400 Soldiers Field Rd. (p 142)*

Best Place to **See Celebrities**
★★★ Four Seasons Hotel $$$$
200 Boylston St. (p 143)

Best **Historic Hotel**
★★ The Fairmont Copley Plaza
Hotel $$$$ *138 St. James Ave.
(p 142)*

Best **Boutique Hotel**
★★ Fifteen Beacon $$$$ *15 Beacon St. (p 143)*

Most **Hospitable to Motorists**
★ MidTown Hotel $$–$$$ *220
Huntington Ave. (p 145)*

Best **Pool**
★★ Sheraton Boston Hotel $$$$
39 Dalton St. (p 148)

Best Deal **on Newbury Street**
★ Newbury Guest House $$ *261
Newbury St. (p 146)*

Best **Access to the River**
★★★ Royal Sonesta Hotel $$$ *5
Cambridge Pkwy., Cambridge (p 147)*

Best **Hidden Jewel**
★ Boston Common Hotel & Con-
ference Center $$ *40 Trinity Pl.
(p 140)*

Best for **Marathon Spectators**
★ Charlesmark Hotel $$ *655
Boylston St. (p 141)*

Best for **Red Sox Fans**
★ Residence Inn Boston Back Bay/
Fenway $$$ *500 Commonwealth
Ave. (p 146)*

Best for **Celtics and Bruins
Ticketholders**
★★★ Onyx Hotel $$$ *155 Port-
land St. (p 146)*

*If I were traveling with someone else's credit cards, I'd head straight to the Four
Seasons. Previous page: Fairmont Copley Plaza Hotel.*

Cambridge Lodging

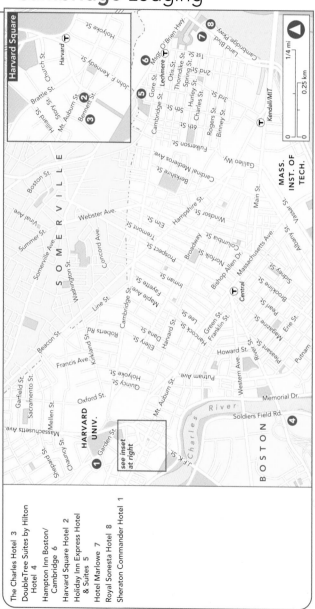

The Charles Hotel 3

DoubleTree Suites by Hilton Hotel 4

Hampton Inn Boston/Cambridge 6

Harvard Square Hotel 2

Holiday Inn Express Hotel & Suites 5

Hotel Marlowe 7

Royal Sonesta Hotel 8

Sheraton Commander Hotel 1

Boston Lodging

Anthony's Town House 4
Best Western Boston/The Inn
   at Longwood Medical 5
Boston Common Hotel &
   Conference Center 21
Boston Harbor Hotel 42
Boston Marriott Copley Place 19
Boston Marriott Long Wharf 39
Chandler Inn Hotel 24
Charlesmark Hotel & Lounge 16
Colonnade Hotel Boston 13
Copley Square Hotel 17
Courtyard Boston Brookline 2
DoubleTree Suites by Hilton Hotel 1
DoubleTree by Hilton Boston
   Downtown 28
Eliot Hotel 8
The Fairmont Copley Plaza Hotel 20
Fifteen Beacon 34
Four Seasons Hotel 26
Harborside Inn 40
Hilton Boston Back Bay 10
Hilton Boston Logan Airport 43
Hostelling International Boston 29
Hotel Commonwealth 6
Hotel 140 22
Hyatt Regency Boston 31
The Langham, Boston 41
The Lenox Hotel 15

Loews Boston Back Bay Hotel 23
Longwood Inn 3
Mandarin Oriental, Boston 14
The MidTown Hotel 12
Millennium Bostonian Hotel 38
Newbury Guest House 9
Nine Zero 32
Omni Parker House 33
Onyx Hotel 37
Residence Inn Boston Back Bay/Fenway 7
Residence Inn Boston Harbor 36
Residence Inn by Marriott Boston
   Downtown Seaport 44
Revere Hotel Boston Common 27
The Ritz-Carlton, Boston Common 30
Seaport Hotel 43
Sheraton Boston Hotel 11
Taj Boston 25
The Westin Boston Waterfront 45
The Westin Copley Place Boston 18
Wyndham Boston Beacon Hill 35

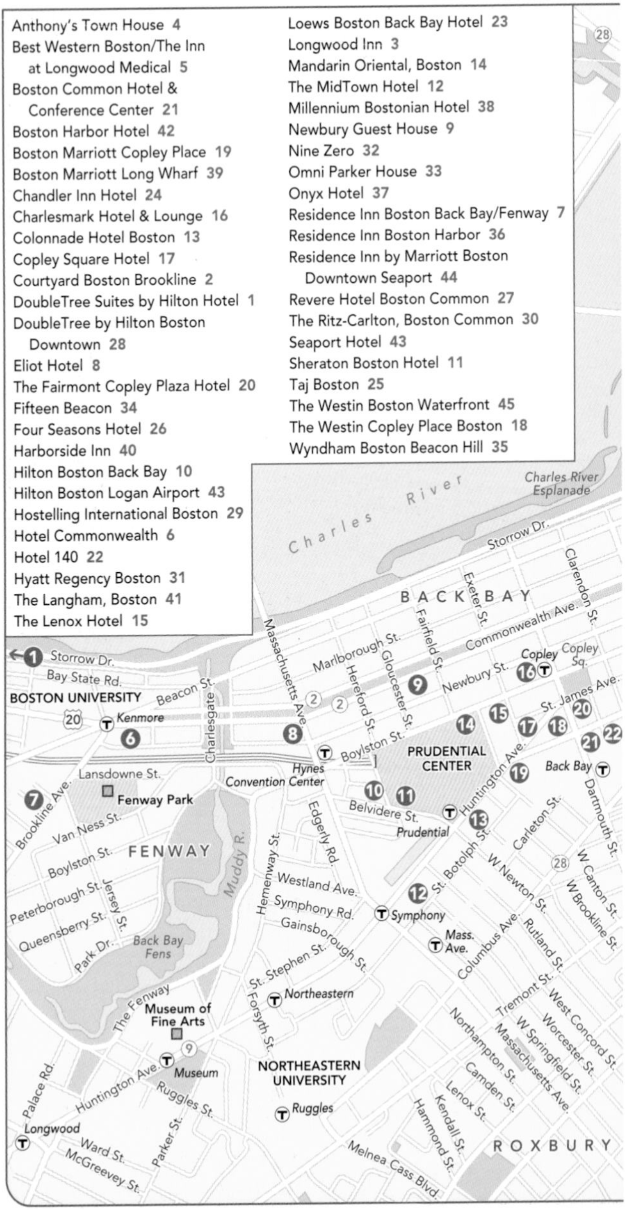

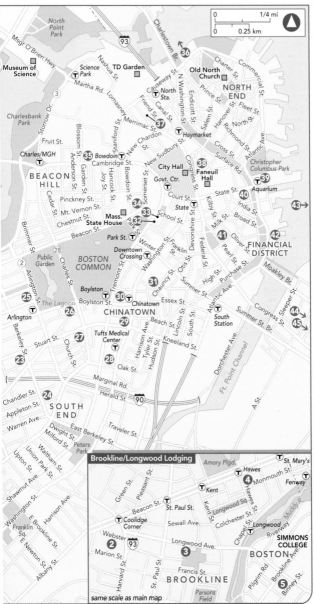

North Point Park

Museum of Science

93

Science Park Ⓣ

TD Garden

Msgr O'Brien Hwy.

Nashua St.

Martha Rd.

Lomasney Way

Charlestown Br.

36

Charter St.

Old North Church

Commercial St.

Prince St.

NORTH END

Fleet St.

Salem St.

Hanover St.

North St.

Fulton St.

Charlesbank Park

Storrow Dr.

3

Fruit St.

Charles/MGH Ⓣ

BEACON HILL

Blossom St.

St. Joseph St.

Anderson St.

Garden St.

Cedar St.

Causeway St.

North Sta. Ⓣ

Friend St.

Canal St.

Merrimac St.

37

New Chardon St.

Endicott St.

Haymarket Ⓣ

Cross St.

Richmond St.

Atlantic Ave.

Surface Rd.

Christopher Columbus Park

35

Bowdoin Ⓣ

Cambridge St.

Hancock St.

Joy St.

Bowdoin St.

New Sudbury St.

City Hall

Govt. Ctr. Ⓣ

38

Congress St.

Faneuil Hall

Ⓣ Aquarium

39

Pinckney St.

Mt. Vernon St.

Chestnut St.

Beacon St.

34

Somerset St.

Court St.

State Ⓣ

State St.

Kilby St.

Milk St.

India St.

Broad St.

40

43→

33

School St.

32

Mass. State House

Park St. Ⓣ

Devonshire St.

41

Pearl St.

Oliver St.

42

FINANCIAL DISTRICT

Brimmer St.

Public Garden

28

Charles St.

2

Arlington St.

Boston Common

Downtown Crossing Ⓣ

Winter St.

Washington St.

Tremont St.

Franklin St.

Otis St.

High St.

Federal St.

Purchase St.

Atlantic Ave.

Moakley Br.

25

Ⓣ

The Lagoon

Boylston Ⓣ

30

Boylston St.

26

31

Chauncy St.

Summer St.

Congress St.

Sleeper St.

44→

45→

Arlington Ⓣ

Berkeley St.

23

Stuart St.

Church St.

27

Tufts Medical Center Ⓣ

28

Oak St.

29

CHINATOWN

Harrison Ave.

Tyler St.

Hudson St.

Beach St.

Kneeland St.

Essex St.

Lincoln St.

South St.

South Station Ⓣ

Summer St. Br.

Dorchester Ave.

Ft. Point Channel

A St.

Chandler St.

24

Appleton St.

Warren Ave.

SOUTH END

Dwight St.

Milford St.

East Berkeley St.

Peters Park

Marginal Rd.

Herald St.

90

Traveler St.

Waltham St.

Union Park St.

Upton St.

Shawmut Ave.

Washington St.

E Brookline St.

Harrison Ave.

Franklin Sq.

E Newton St.

Albany St.

0 —— 1/4 mi
0 —— 0.25 km

Brookline/Longwood Lodging

Amory Plgd.

Ⓣ St. Mary's

Hawes

4

Monmouth St.

Ⓣ Fenway

Green St.

Pleasant St.

Ⓣ Kent

Longwood Sq.

Hawes St.

Kent St.

Beacon St.

Ⓣ St. Paul St.

Colchester St.

Chapel St.

Ⓣ Longwood

Muddy R.

Riverway

SIMMONS COLLEGE

Ⓣ Coolidge Corner

Sewall Ave.

Webster St.

2

93

Marion St.

Harvard St.

St. Paul St.

Longwood Ave.

Francis St.

3

BROOKLINE

BOSTON

Pilgrim Rd.

Brookline Ave.

5

Binney St.

Parsons Field

same scale as main map

Lodging A to Z

Anthony's Town House OUT-SKIRTS/BROOKLINE The good-size rooms at this guesthouse share bathrooms. The four-story 19th-century brownstone, which has free Wi-Fi but no elevator, boasts high ceilings and ornate yet homey interiors. *1085 Beacon St. (Hawes St.), Brookline.* ☎ *617/566-3972. www.anthonystownhouse.com. 10 units. Doubles $83–$113. No credit cards. T: Green Line C to Hawes St. Map p 138.*

★★ **kids Best Western Boston/The Inn at Longwood Medical** FENWAY This modern hotel in the heart of the Longwood Medical area is convenient to the Fenway. Rooms are large, and suites have kitchen facilities. *342 Longwood Ave. (Brookline Ave.).* ☎ *800/468-2378. www.innatlongwood.com. 161 units. Doubles $179–$269. AE, DISC, MC, V. T: Green Line D or E to Longwood. Map p 138.*

★ **Boston Common Hotel & Conference Center** BACK BAY The rooms are compact yet comfy, the rates terrific, the location (around the corner from Back Bay Station) even better. *40 Trinity Place (Stuart St.).* ☎ *617/933-7700. www.bostoncommonhotel.com. 64 units. Doubles $125–$239. AE, DISC, MC, V. T: Orange Line to Back Bay. Map p 138.*

★★★ **Boston Harbor Hotel** WATERFRONT The most beautiful hotel in town boasts gorgeous rooms with marble bathrooms, great views, courtly service, and plentiful amenities. *Rowes Wharf (Atlantic Ave. and High St.).* ☎ *800/752-7077. www.bhh.com. 230 units. Doubles $345–$795. AE, DISC, MC, V. T: Blue Line to Aquarium or Red Line to South Station. Map p 138.*

★ **kids Boston Marriott Copley Place** BACK BAY A fine hotel for business or leisure travelers, with perks for both. The generously sized rooms boast cushy bedding and contemporary furnishings. *110 Huntington Ave. (Harcourt St.).*

The Boston Harbor Hotel's landmark arch has become a symbol of Boston.

Just off Harvard Square, the Charles is the finest hotel in Cambridge.

☎ 800/228-9290. www.copley marriott.com. 1,147 units. Doubles $169–$549. AE, DISC, MC, V. T: Orange Line to Back Bay or Green Line to Copley. Map p 138.

★★ kids **Boston Marriott Long Wharf** WATERFRONT The great location and views complement the large, sunny rooms and good business features. *296 State St. (Atlantic Ave.).* ☎ 800/228-9290. www.marriott longwharf.com. 400 units. Doubles $249–$629. AE, DISC, MC, V. T: Blue Line to Aquarium. Map p 138.

★★ **Chandler Inn Hotel** SOUTH END Small but posh rooms in a convenient location help the largest gay-owned property in town sell out regularly. *26 Chandler St. (Berkeley St.).* ☎ 800/842-3450. www. chandlerinn.com. 56 units. Doubles $149–$279. AE, DISC, MC, V. T: Orange Line to Back Bay. Map p 138.

★★★ kids **The Charles Hotel** CAMBRIDGE The top-notch accommodations, service, restaurants, health club, and spa make the Charles Cambridge's finest hotel. The good-size rooms are deceptively simple: unfussy Shaker style contrasts with pampering details. *1 Bennett St. (Eliot St.), Cambridge.* ☎ 800/882-1818.

www.charleshotel.com. 294 units. Doubles $299–$599. AE, MC, V. T: Red Line to Harvard. Map p 137.

★ **Charlesmark Hotel & Lounge** BACK BAY Sleek contemporary design makes the compact rooms (many overlooking the Marathon finish line) feel huge. Custom furnishings help the boutique feel. *655 Boylston St. (Dartmouth and Exeter sts.).* ☎ 617/ 247-1212. www.thecharlesmark.com. 40 units. Doubles $129–$279 w/ breakfast. AE, DISC, MC, V. T: Green Line to Copley. Map p 138.

★★ kids **Colonnade Hotel Boston** BACK BAY Contemporary boutique style, old-fashioned service, and large guest rooms appeal to business travelers; families enjoy the rooftop pool and V.I.Kids program. *120 Huntington Ave. (W. Newton and Garrison sts.).* ☎ 800/962-3030. www.colonnade hotel.com. 285 units. Doubles $219– $459. AE, DISC, MC, V. T: Green Line E to Prudential. Map p 138.

★ **Copley Square Hotel** BACK BAY Service sets this independent hotel apart from its giant corporate neighbors. The 1891 building holds comfy, decent-size rooms done in contemporary style. *47 Huntington*

The rooftop pool is one of the distinctive features of the Colonnade Hotel Boston.

Ave. (Exeter St.). ☎ 800/225-7062. www.copleysquarehotel.com. 143 units. Doubles $179–$549. AE, DISC, MC, V. T: Green Line to Copley. Map p 138.

★ Courtyard Boston Brookline
OUTSKIRTS/BROOKLINE This business hotel lies in a fun neighborhood just 15 minutes from Boston. Rooms are large but generic. 40 Webster St. (Beacon St.), Brookline. ☎ 866/296-2296. www.brooklinecourtyard.com. 188 units. Doubles $199–$399. AE, DISC, MC, V. T: Green Line C to Coolidge Corner. Map p 138.

★★ kids DoubleTree Suites by Hilton Hotel
OUTSKIRTS/BROOKLINE Each sizable two-room suite has a fridge; the T isn't nearby, but this is a deal if you're driving. 400 Soldiers Field Rd. (at Mass. Pike Brighton/Cambridge exit). ☎ 800/222-8733. www.hilton familyboston.com. 308 units. Doubles $129–$339. AE, DISC, MC, V. Map p 137.

★★ kids DoubleTree by Hilton Boston Downtown
CHINATOWN The modern, centrally located DoubleTree has compact rooms and gives guests access to the huge YMCA next door. 821 Washington St. (Oak and Stuart sts.). ☎ 800/222-8733. www.hiltonfamilyboston.com. 267 units. Doubles $159–$349. AE, DISC, MC, V. T: Orange Line to New England Medical Center. Map p 138.

★★★ Eliot Hotel
BACK BAY Most units are large, romantic suites with antique furnishings, giving the Eliot a residential feel; the gracious staff completes the illusion. 370 Commonwealth Ave. (Mass Ave.). ☎ 800/443-5468. www.eliot hotel.com. 95 units. Doubles $235–$545. AE, MC, V. T: Green Line B, C, or D to Hynes Convention Center. Map p 138.

★★ The Fairmont Copley Plaza Hotel
BACK BAY Ornate decor and courtly service make this hotel, built in 1912, a Boston classic. Posh fabrics and custom furnishings will make you feel at home—especially if "home" is a mansion. 138 St. James Ave. (Dartmouth St. and Trinity Pl.). ☎ 800/257-7544. www.fairmont.com/copley plaza. 383 units. Doubles from $289. AE, MC, V. T: Green Line to Copley or Orange Line to Back Bay. Map p 138.

★★ Fifteen Beacon BEACON
HILL Over-the-top luxury and contemporary style make this the city's premier boutique property. Management bends over backward to keep demanding guests happy. *15 Beacon St. (Somerset St.).* ☎ *877/ XV-BEACON. www.xvbeacon.com. 60 units. Doubles from $395. AE, DISC, MC, V. T: Red or Green Line to Park St. Map p 138.*

★★★ Four Seasons Hotel
BACK BAY The best hotel in New England offers its pampered guests everything they could ever want— for a price. *200 Boylston St. (Hadassah Way).* ☎ *800/819-5053. www. fourseasons.com/boston. 272 units. Doubles from $445. AE, DISC, MC, V. T: Green Line to Arlington. Map p 138.*

★ kids Hampton Inn Boston/ Cambridge CAMBRIDGE This
business-traveler favorite is in a convenient if unattractive area. Rooms are generic but quite comfortable. *191 Msgr. O'Brien Hwy. (Water St.), Cambridge.* ☎ *800/ 426-7866. www.bostoncambridge. hamptoninn.com. 114 units. Doubles $169–$359 w/breakfast. AE, DISC, MC, V. T: Green Line to Lechmere. Map p 137.*

★ Harborside Inn WATERFRONT
A renovated 19th-century warehouse near Faneuil Hall Marketplace, this hotel is a good value. Rooms facing the sky-lit atrium are quietest. *185 State St. (Atlantic Ave.).* ☎ *617/723-7500. www. harborsideinnboston.com. 54 units. Doubles $139–$299. AE, DISC, MC, V. T: Blue Line to Aquarium. Map p 138.*

★ Harvard Square Hotel
CAMBRIDGE You're paying for the fantastic location, not the well-maintained but utilitarian accommodations. *110 Mount Auburn St. (Eliot St.).* ☎ *800/458-5886. www. harvardsquarehotel.com. 73 units. Doubles $159–$279. AE, DISC, MC, V. T: Red Line to Harvard. Map p 137.*

★★ Hilton Boston Back Bay
BACK BAY The 26-story business hotel, with large rooms featuring oversized work desks, also suits families. Higher-floor views are spectacular. *40 Dalton St. (Belvidere St.).* ☎ *800/HILTONS. www.boston backbay.hilton.com. 390 units. Doubles $199–$699. AE, DISC, MC, V. T: Green Line B, C, or D to Hynes Convention Center. Map p 138.*

The Eliot Hotel offers large, romantic suites.

The Fairmont Copley Plaza—the "grande dame" of Boston.

★ **Hilton Boston Logan Airport** AIRPORT An excellent business choice, this is a good fallback for vacationers priced out of downtown. *1 Hotel Dr. (Terminal Rd.).* ☎ *800/445-8667. www.hiltonfamilyboston.com. 599 units. Doubles $159–$399. AE, DISC, MC, V. T: Blue Line to Airport, shuttle bus. Map p 138.*

★ **Holiday Inn Express Hotel & Suites** CAMBRIDGE Weigh the location and price (which includes parking) against the limited services and amenities; this is a solid option. *250 Msgr. O'Brien Hwy. (Sciarappa St.).* ☎ *800/439-4745. www.hiexpress.com/bos cambridgema. 112 units. Doubles $150–$289 w/breakfast. AE, DISC, MC, V. T: Green Line to Lechmere. Map p 137.*

★ **Hostelling International Boston** THEATER DISTRICT Surprisingly comfortable (and air-conditioned), the centrally located six-story hostel is popular year-round. Private units have en suite bathrooms. *19 Stuart St. (Washington St.).* ☎ *888/464-4872. www.bostonhostel.org. 481 beds. Dorm beds $43–$63, private units*

$170–$200 w/breakfast. MC, V. T: Green Line to Boylston or Orange Line to Tufts Medical Center. Map p 138.

★★ **Hotel Commonwealth** BACK BAY The lavishly appointed guest rooms overlook Kenmore Square or (across the Mass. Pike) Fenway Park. The traditional-looking hotel is convenient to Boston University and the Fenway. *500 Commonwealth Ave. (Kenmore St.).* ☎ *866/784-4000. www.hotel commonwealth.com. 150 units. Doubles $209–$489. AE, DISC, MC, V. T: Green Line B, C, or D to Kenmore. Map p 138.*

★★ **kids Hotel Marlowe** CAMBRIDGE This posh business hotel near MIT also appeals to families. The good-sized rooms are elegantly decorated with funky accents. *25 Land Blvd. (Cambridge Pkwy.).* ☎ *800/825-7140. www.hotelmarlowe.com. 236 units. Doubles $199–$449. AE, DISC, MC, V. T: Green Line to Lechmere or Red Line to Kendall. Map p 137.*

★ **Hotel 140** BACK BAY The contemporary-style rooms run small (some hold just a full-size bed), but the price is right. *140 Clarendon St. (Stuart St.).* ☎ *800/714-0140. www. hotel140.com. 59 units. Doubles $129–$339 w/breakfast. AE, MC, V. T: Orange Line to Back Bay. Map p 138.*

★ Hyatt Regency Boston
DOWNTOWN CROSSING The business-oriented Hyatt slashes weekend prices. Rooms are large, with luxurious European-style appointments. *1 Ave. de Lafayette (Washington St.).* ☎ *800/233-1234. www.regencyboston.hyatt.com. 500 units. Doubles $199–$469. AE, DISC, MC, V. T: Red or Orange Line to Downtown Crossing. Map p 138.*

★★ The Langham, Boston
FINANCIAL DISTRICT The city's top business hotel, in an unbeatable location, does a lot of weekend leisure business. *250 Franklin St. (Post Office Sq.).* ☎ *800/791-7761. www.boston.langhamhotels. com. 318 units. Doubles $175–$495. AE, DISC, MC, V. T: Blue or Orange Line to State. Map p 138.*

★★ The Lenox Hotel
BACK BAY Victorian style and 21st-century features make the eco-conscious Lenox

Hotel 140 offers cozy rooms at bargain (for Boston) prices.

a good alternative to the neighborhood's behemoths. Spacious, high-ceilinged rooms feature custom furniture. *61 Exeter St. (Boylston St.).* ☎ *800/225-7676. www.lenoxhotel. com. 212 units. Doubles $215–$425. AE, DISC, MC, V. T: Green Line to Copley. Map p 138.*

★★ Loews Boston Back Bay Hotel
BACK BAY Plush lodgings make the Loews Boston (formerly a Doyle Collection hotel) a top choice for business travelers. The conveniently located building used to be police headquarters. *350 Stuart St. (Berkeley St.).* ☎ *855/495-6397. www. loewshotels.com. 225 units. Doubles $215–$589. AE, DISC, MC, V. T: Orange Line to Back Bay. Map p 138.*

★ kids Longwood Inn
OUTSKIRTS/BROOKLINE This sprawling Victorian guesthouse in a residential neighborhood has comfy-cozy rooms and backs up to a playground. *123 Longwood Ave. (Marshall St.).* ☎ *617/ 566-8615. www.longwood-inn.com. 22 units. Doubles $99–$169. AE, DISC, MC, V. T: Green Line D to Longwood. Map p 138.*

★★ Mandarin Oriental, Boston
BACK BAY Feng shui prevails at this luxurious property connected to the Prudential Center. Service befitting the price tag drives international repeat business. *776 Boylston St. (Fairfield St.).* ☎ *866/ 796-5475. www.mandarinoriental. com/boston. 148 units. Doubles from $495. AE, DISC, MC, V. T: Green Line to Copley. Map p 138.*

★ kids The MidTown Hotel
BACK BAY This motel-like hotel has large rooms, small bathrooms, a seasonal outdoor pool, and relatively cheap parking. *220 Huntington Ave. (Cumberland St.).* ☎ *800/ 343-1177. www.midtownhotel.com. 159 units. Doubles $129–$329. AE, DISC, MC, V. T: Green Line E to Symphony. Map p 138.*

The sleek atmosphere of the Nine Zero hotel is a welcome departure for Boston.

★ Millennium Bostonian Hotel

FANEUIL HALL MARKETPLACE
Three renovated 19th-century
buildings make up this unexpectedly elegant business hotel. Rooms
vary in size; all have top-of-the-line
furnishings and amenities. *26 North
St. (Clinton St.).* ☎ *866/866-8086.
www.millenniumhotels.com. 201
units. Doubles $189–$449. AE, DISC,
MC, V. T: Orange or Green Line to
Haymarket. Map p 138.*

★ Newbury Guest House BACK

BAY This sophisticated inn, housed
in a trio of converted 1880s town
houses, offers comfortable accommodations at relatively modest rates.
Reserve early. *261 Newbury St. (Fairfield and Gloucester sts.).* ☎ *800/437-
7668. www.newburyguesthouse.com.
32 units. Doubles $179–$269 w/break-
fast. AE, DISC, MC, V. T: Green Line B,
C, or D to Hynes Convention Center.
Map p 138.*

★★ Nine Zero DOWNTOWN

CROSSING Superb service and a
great location make the Nine Zero
a Boston favorite; the contemporary style evokes SoHo or South
Beach. *90 Tremont St. (Bromfield
St.).* ☎ *866/906-9090. www.nine
zero.com. 190 units. Doubles $219–
$600. AE, DISC, MC, V. T: Red or
Green Line to Park St. Map p 138.*

★ kids Omni Parker House

DOWNTOWN CROSSING In
business since 1855, the Parker
House offers a wide range of
rooms, from compact to dazzling.
Most aren't huge, but all are nicely
appointed and well maintained. *60
School St. (Tremont St.).* ☎ *800/444-
OMNI. www.omniparkerhouse.com.
551 units. Doubles $189–$349. AE,
DISC, MC, V. T: Green or Blue Line
to Government Center. Map p 138.*

★★ Onyx Hotel NORTH STA-

TION The hotel's contemporary
boutique decor contrasts with the
business amenities and gentrifying
neighborhood. *155 Portland St.
(Causeway St.).* ☎ *866/660-6699.
www.onyxhotel.com. 112 units. Doubles $179–$399. AE, DISC, MC, V. T:
Green or Orange Line to North Station. Map p 138.*

★ kids Residence Inn Boston Back Bay/Fenway FENWAY

Across the street from Fenway
Park, the Residence Inn targets
extended-stay travelers as well as
families with a kitchen in every unit.
125 Brookline Ave. (Overland St.).
☎ *888/236-2427. www.marriott.
com/bosfn. 175 units. Doubles $139–
$449 w/breakfast. AE, DISC, MC, V.
T: Green Line B, C, or D to Kenmore.
Map p 138.*

★★ **kids** **Residence Inn Boston Harbor** CHARLESTOWN This all-suite hotel on the water is a good alternative to downtown. Many of the generously sized rooms have harbor views. *34–44 Charles River Ave. (Chelsea St.).* ☎ *866/296-2297. www.marriott.com/bostw. 168 units. Doubles $189–$449 w/breakfast. AE, DISC, MC, V. T: Orange Line to Community College. Map p 138.*

★ **Residence Inn by Marriott Boston Downtown Seaport** SOUTH BOSTON In a renovated 1901 warehouse less than a mile from the convention center, the well-appointed hotel has a kitchen in every unit. *370 Congress St. (Thomson Place).* ☎ *888/236-2427. www.marriott.com/bosfp. 120 units. Doubles $199–$419 w/breakfast. AE, DISC, MC, V. T: Silver Line SL1/SL2 to Court House. Map p 138.*

★ **Revere Hotel Boston Common** THEATER DISTRICT Large guest rooms with balconies and great views help make up for the less-than-scenic neighborhood around this oversize boutique hotel (a former Radisson). *200 Stuart St. (Charles St. S.).* ☎ *855/673-8372. www.reverehotel.com. 356 units. Doubles $219–$605. AE, DISC, MC, V. T: Green Line to Boylston. Map p 138.*

Parker House rolls and Boston cream pie were invented at the Omni Parker House.

★★ **The Ritz-Carlton, Boston Common** THEATER DISTRICT The luxurious, contemporary accommodations take up floors 9 through 12 of a high-rise tower; public areas, including the spectacular health club, are near the street. *10 Avery St. (Tremont and Washington sts.).* ☎ *800/241-3333. www.ritzcarlton.com. 193 units. Doubles from $395. AE, DISC, MC, V. T: Green Line to Boylston. Map p 138.*

★★ **kids** **Royal Sonesta Hotel** CAMBRIDGE This luxurious hotel offers easy access to Boston, MIT, the Museum of Science, and the Charles. The spacious, modern

The Onyx Hotel has a custom-designed (by her mom) Britney Spears room.

The Best Lodging

rooms offer lovely river and city views. *40 Edwin H. Land Blvd. (CambridgeSide Pl.).* ☎ *800/766-3782. www.sonesta.com/boston. 400 units. Doubles $225–$369. AE, DISC, MC, V. T: Green Line to Lechmere. Map p 137.*

★★ kids **Seaport Hotel** SOUTH BOSTON A business-traveler favorite in a newly hot neighborhood. The kid-savvy staff, pool, and proximity to the Children's Museum draw families. *1 Seaport Lane (Seaport Blvd./Northern Ave.).* ☎ *800/440-3318. www.seaportboston.com. 426 units. Doubles $189–$449. AE, DISC, MC, V. T: Silver Line SL1/SL2 to World Trade Center. Map p 138.*

★★ kids **Sheraton Boston Hotel** BACK BAY This huge, well-appointed hotel has something for everyone. Large, contemporary rooms offer gorgeous views from the higher floors. *39 Dalton St. (Belvidere St.).* ☎ *800/325-3535. www.sheraton.com/boston. 1,220 units. Doubles $149–$409. AE, DISC, MC, V. T: Green Line E to Prudential. Map p 138.*

Rooms at the luxe Royal Sonesta are artful and tech-savvy.

★ **Sheraton Commander Hotel** CAMBRIDGE Traditional in every detail, from the colonial-style decor to the helpful service, this hotel is a Cambridge classic. *16 Garden St. (Berkeley St.).* ☎ *800/325-3535. www.sheraton.com/commander. 174 units. Doubles $139–$479. AE, DISC, MC, V. T: Red Line to Harvard. Map p 137.*

★★ **Taj Boston** BACK BAY Known for its luxe accommodations, great location, and courteous staff, this property was a Ritz-Carlton before the Indian luxury chain made it even fancier. *15 Arlington St. (Newbury St.).* ☎ *877/482-5267. www.tajhotels.com/boston. 273 units. Doubles from $195. AE, DISC, MC, V. T: Green Line to Arlington. Map p 138.*

★★ **The Westin Boston Waterfront** SOUTH BOSTON With direct access to the convention center, the Westin has all the features you'd expect, including a solicitous staff. *425 Summer St. (D St.).* ☎ *800/WESTIN-1. www.westin.com/bostonwaterfront. 793 units. Doubles $149–$555. AE, DISC, MC, V. T: Silver Line SL1/SL2 to World Trade Center. Map p 138.*

★★ kids **The Westin Copley Place Boston** BACK BAY The views are so good (the best in town) that the spacious rooms and business amenities are almost an afterthought. *10 Huntington Ave. (Dartmouth St.).* ☎ *800/WESTIN-1. www.westin.com/copleyplace. 803 units. Doubles $200–$569. AE, DISC, MC, V. T: Green Line to Copley. Map p 138.*

★ **Wyndham Boston Beacon Hill** BEACON HILL Adjacent to Mass. General Hospital, this well-equipped business hotel (formerly a Holiday Inn) has a seasonal outdoor pool. *5 Blossom St. (Cambridge St.).* ☎ *877/999-3223. www.wyndham.com. 303 units. Doubles $160–$400. AE, DISC, MC, V. T: Red Line to Charles/MGH. Map p 138.* ●

Concord

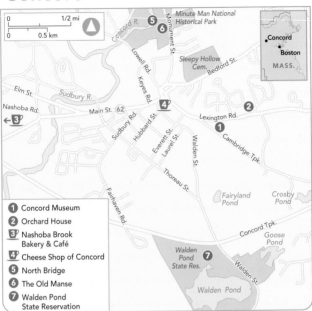

0 — **1/2 mi**
0 — **0.5 km**

- Concord R.
- Minute Man National Historical Park
- **5** Monument St.
- **6**
- Lowell Rd.
- Sleepy Hollow Cem.
- Bedford St.
- Keyes Rd.
- Elm St.
- Sudbury R.
- Nashoba Rd.
- Main St. 62
- **4**
- **2**
- Lexington Rd.
- Sudbury Rd.
- Hubbard St.
- Everett St.
- Laurel St.
- **1**
- Cambridge Tpk.
- Walden St.
- Thoreau St.
- **3**
- Fairyland Pond
- Crosby Pond
- Concord Tpk.
- Goose Pond
- Farhaven Rd.
- Walden Pond State Res.
- **7**
- Walden St.
- Walden Pond

- Concord
- Boston
- MASS.

1 Concord Museum
2 Orchard House
3 Nashoba Brook Bakery & Café
4 Cheese Shop of Concord
5 North Bridge
6 The Old Manse
7 Walden Pond State Reservation

Over the course of three-plus centuries, Concord (say "conquered") has grown from a country village to a prosperous suburb of about 18,000. The first official battle of the Revolutionary War took place at the North Bridge on April 19, 1775. By the mid-19th century, an impressive constellation of literary stars—Ralph Waldo Emerson, Henry Wadsworth Longfellow, Henry David Thoreau, and Louisa May Alcott—called the town home. Present-day Concord preserves and honors that rich history. START: **Jump in the car and follow Route 2 from Cambridge until you see signs for Lincoln; where the road takes a sharp left, go straight, following signs for historic Concord. If it's not rush hour, the trip from Boston takes 30 to 40 minutes.**

1 ★★ kids **Concord Museum**

The museum tells the story of the town in informative exhibits that incorporate intriguing artifacts, murals, films, maps, and documents. A onetime Native American settlement, Concord is best known

as a Revolutionary War battleground. In the 19th century, it was a literary and intellectual center with a thriving clock-making industry. The town was also an important player in the 20th-century historic preservation movement. Many

Previous page: Bridge over a stream.

museum displays focus on the big names: You'll see one of the lanterns Longfellow immortalized in "Paul Revere's Ride" ("one if by land, and two if by sea"), the contents of Emerson's study, and a large collection of Thoreau's belongings. The period furniture, silver, clocks, and (my favorites) embroidery samplers offer an engaging look at the lives of regular people. If you're traveling with kids, check ahead for info on family activities. ○ 1–1½ hrs. 53 Cambridge Turnpike (Lexington Rd.). ☎ 978/369-9609 (recorded info) or ☎ 978/369-9763. www.concordmuseum.org. Admission $10 adults, $8 seniors and students, $5 kids 6–18, free for kids under 6. June–Aug daily 9am–5pm; Apr–May & Sept–Dec Mon–Sat 9am–5pm, Sun noon–5pm; Jan–Mar Mon–Sat 11am–4pm, Sun 1–4pm.

❷ ★★★ kids Orchard House

Louisa May Alcott lives! Well, the beloved author did live here, where she wrote and set her novel *Little Women* (1868). Louisa and her sisters—the models for *Little Women*'s March family—called Orchard House home from 1858 to 1877.

They come to life on the guided tour, the only way to see the house. Numerous heirlooms survive; I especially like Louisa's little desk and the miniature pieces of furniture that appear to be from a dollhouse (they're actually a salesman's samples). Check ahead for information on the extensive schedule of special events and holiday programs. ○ 1 hr. On autumn Saturdays, try to arrive before noon. 399 Lexington Rd. ☎ 978/369-4118. www.louisamayalcott.org. Guided tours $9 adults, $8 seniors and students, $5 kids 6–17, free for kids under 6, $25 families. Apr–Oct Mon–Sat 10am–4:30pm, Sun 1–4:30pm; Nov–Mar Mon–Fri 11am–3pm, Sat 10am–4:30pm, Sun 1–4:30pm.

❸ Now it's picnic time. My top choice is in West Concord: Nashoba **Brook Bakery & Café** (152 Commonwealth Ave.; ☎ 978/318-1999; www.slowrise.com; $), which makes its own bread, pastries, soups, salads, and sandwiches. In downtown Concord, the ❹ **Cheese Shop of Concord** (29 Walden St.; ☎ 978/369-5778; www.concordcheeseshop.com;

Orchard House, the setting of Little Women.

$) sells sandwiches, soups, and all the trimmings, including chocolates. While you stock up, grab a snack for later (I'll be sending you to Walden Pond, which doesn't have a food concession). Tote your treats to Monument Square or proceed to the North Bridge, our next stop.

⑤ ★ kids North Bridge Off Monument Street outside Concord Center, a path leads to the North Bridge, a reproduction of the wooden structure that spanned the Concord River in April 1775, when the Revolutionary War began. Tune out the chatter of visitors and the hum of engines, and you can almost imagine the battle commemorated in Ralph Waldo Emerson's poem "Concord Hymn," the first stanza of which is engraved on the base of the *Minute Man* statue near the bridge. Daniel Chester French (sculptor of the John Harvard statue in Cambridge and the seated Abraham Lincoln at the president's memorial in Washington, D.C.) created the iconic image of the militia member with a musket in one hand and a plow handle in the other. A plaque on the other side of the bridge honors the British soldiers who died in the battle. Up the hill at the National Park Service visitor center, a diorama and video program illustrate the battle, and rangers are on duty if you have questions. To get there, you can walk across the grounds or return to the car for the 2-minute ride. ⏱ *45 min. Minute Man National Historical Park, North Bridge Visitor Center, 174 Liberty St. (off Monument St.).* ☎ *978/369-6993. www.nps.gov/mima. Free admission. Apr–Oct daily 9am–5pm; check ahead for winter hours. Grounds: Year-round daily sunrise–sunset.*

The Rev. William Emerson watched the Battle of Concord from the yard of the Old Manse.

⑥ ★ The Old Manse A longtime family home, the Old Manse figures in Concord's literary history. The Rev. William Emerson built the Old Manse (1770) and watched the Battle of Concord from here, and his grandson Ralph Waldo Emerson later worked on the essay "Nature" in the study. Newlywed Nathaniel Hawthorne moved here in 1842; he looks forbidding and serious in most of his portraits, but on the guided tour of the Old Manse (the only way to see the interior), you'll meet a lighthearted Hawthorne who collaborated with his new bride, Sophia Peabody, to scratch messages with her diamond ring on two windows. Henry David Thoreau planted a vegetable garden as a wedding present for the Hawthornes, and a re-creation of that project is on the grounds today. **Note:** The Old Manse wasn't the permanent home of any of the town's big names. You've already seen Louisa May Alcott's; if you're interested in visiting Emerson's or Hawthorne's, ask at the Chamber of Commerce office or visit the chamber website for information. ⏱ *1 hr. 269 Monument St. (at North Bridge).* ☎ *978/369-3909. www.old manse.org. Guided tour $8 adults, $7*

Concord: Practical Matters

Driving is the most efficient way to get to and around Concord. You can also take the **MBTA** commuter rail (☎ 800/392-6100 or ☎ 617/222-3200; www.mbta.com) from Boston's North Station or Porter Square in Cambridge. Note that service is limited, especially on weekends. The **Chamber of Commerce,** 15 Walden St., Suite 7 (☎ 978/369-3120; www.concordchamberofcommerce.org), maintains a visitor center at 58 Main St., 1 block south of Monument Square. It's open daily 10am–4pm April through October; public restrooms in the same building are open daily 7am to 8pm year-round. The chamber office is open year-round Monday through Friday; hours vary, so call ahead.

seniors and students, $5 kids 6–12, free for kids 5 and under, $25 families. House: Late May to Oct Tue–Sun noon–5pm; mid-Mar to mid-May & Nov–Dec Sat–Sun noon–5pm; other times by appointment. Grounds: Year-round daily dawn–dusk.

❼ ★★ kids Walden Pond State Reservation On the way back to Boston, stop at one of the most famous places in New England. Walden Pond was home to eccentric author Henry David Thoreau for 2 years, 2 months, and 2 days in the mid-1840s, and if not for that association, the area around the pond would likely have become valuable residential real estate many years ago. Instead, the legacy of the founder of the conservation movement is a gorgeous, surprisingly unspoiled state park property that allows hiking, picnicking, swimming, fishing, and other low-impact activities but not pets or bikes. ⏱ 1 hr. Arrive early or late in the day or call ahead in the summer and fall, when the park closes to newcomers after reaching capacity (1,000). 915 Walden St. (Rte. 126), off Route 2. ☎ 978/369-3254. www.mass.gov/dcr. Free admission. Parking $5 (cash only). Daily 5am–sunset.

Reconstructed cabin of Thoreau at Walden Pond.

Salem

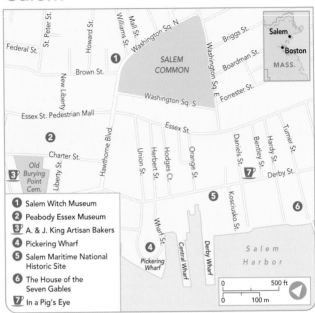

1 Salem Witch Museum
2 Peabody Essex Museum
3 A. & J. King Artisan Bakers
4 Pickering Wharf
5 Salem Maritime National Historic Site
6 The House of the Seven Gables
7 In a Pig's Eye

I f you know Salem only because of its association with witches, you're in for a delightful surprise. Salem has been haunted (sorry) by the witch trials since 1692, but it has far more to offer. It was a center of merchant shipping at the height of the post–Revolutionary War China trade, and today Salem celebrates its maritime history at the same time that it preserves and honors the memory of the victims of the witch trials. START: **From downtown Boston, take I-93 north to I-95 north, or take the Callahan Tunnel to Route 1A and follow it to Route 1 north. (The hotel staff can tell you which approach is easier.) From I-95 or Route 1, follow signs to Route 128 north. Exit at Route 114 east, and continue to downtown Salem. From Boston, the trip takes about 45 minutes if it isn't rush hour.**

1 ★★ kids **Salem Witch Museum** Start here for an excellent overview of the 1692 witch-trial hysteria. The museum centers on a well-researched audiovisual presentation—a series of dioramas, populated with life-size human figures that light up in sequence as

recorded narration describes the pertinent events. The story gets scary (one of the convicted "witches" was pressed to death by stones piled on a board on his chest), but the anti-prejudice message is both clear and timeless. ⏱ 1 hr. 19½ Washington Sq. (Rte.

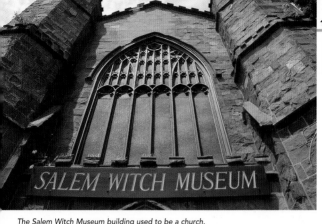

The Salem Witch Museum building used to be a church.

1A and Brown St.). ☎ 978/744-1692. www.salemwitchmuseum.com. Admission $9 adults, $7.50 seniors, $6 kids 6–14, free for kids 5 and under. Daily July–Aug 10am–7pm; Sept–June 10am–5pm; check ahead for extended Oct hours.

② ★★★ **Peabody Essex Museum** The Peabody Essex is one of the best art museums in New England, with a national reputation for its extensive collections of Asian art and photography, American art and architecture, maritime art, and Asian, African, and Native American art. It also books an exceptional slate of traveling museum shows. The Peabody Essex embraces a curatorial philosophy that emphasizes placing objects in context, demonstrating the interplay of influences across time and cultures. Perhaps the best-known object in the museum's collections is an 18th-century Qing Dynasty house. **Yin Yu Tang,** as the house is known, was shipped to Salem from rural China and is the only example of Chinese domestic architecture outside that country. Take the audio tour to enjoy an intriguing look at 2 centuries of life in China while you explore the house. Also allow time to check out some lower-profile exhibits: The Peabody Essex originated as a maritime museum (the Peabody) and the county historical society (the Essex Institute), and some of my favorite objects date to those days. I especially like the collections of ship figureheads, furniture, and dollhouses. ⏱ 3 hr. Build your visit around your timed ticket to Yin Yu Tang. East India Sq. (off Hawthorne Blvd. at Essex St.). ☎ 866/745-1876 or

A bedroom in the Yin Yu Tang house at the Peabody Essex Museum.

The "sky well" of the Yin Yu Tang house.

☎ 978/745-9500. www.pem.org. Admission $15 adults, $13 seniors, $11 students, free for kids 16 and under. Yin Yu Tang admission $5 with museum admission. Tues–Sun and Mon holidays 10am–5pm (until 9:30pm 3rd Thu of every month).

3 **A. & J. King Artisan Bakers** Not far from the museum, this cozy cafe serves out-of-this-world sweets and substantial sandwiches on delectable house-made bread. Consider grabbing a loaf to go. *48 Central St. (Charter St.).* ☎ *978/744-4881. www.ajkingbakery.com. $.*

4 ★ kids Pickering Wharf The waterfront complex offers just enough retail and dining options to be interesting but not overwhelming, against the backdrop of a beautiful marina. 🕐 *1 hr. Derby and Congress sts.* ☎ *978/740-6990. www.pickering wharf.com. Daily year-round; shop and restaurant hours vary.*

5 ★ kids Salem Maritime National Historic Site Alongside the National Park Service's water-front center, in a renovated ware-house, is a uniquely memorable exhibit: a ship. A full-size replica of

a 1797 East Indiaman merchant ves-sel, the 171-foot (52m) *Friendship* is open to visitors on the guided ranger tour; you can also study it from the shore if you don't want to climb on. Tours—you can also use the audio download available on the website—visit other buildings in the complex and touch on Salem's literary history (Nathaniel Haw-thorne worked in the Custom House). If this location is closed, visit the NPS regional center at 2 New Liberty St., a 5-minute walk away. 🕐 *1 hr. 193 Derby St. (Orange and Kosciusko sts.).* ☎ *978/740-1660. www.nps.gov/sama. Free admission and tours. Summer daily 9am–5pm; winter weekdays 1–5pm, weekends 9am–5pm.*

6 ★ kids The House of the Seven Gables Nathaniel Haw-thorne wrote the 1851 novel that inspired the name of this attraction, and if you haven't read it since high school (or haven't read it at all), I'm here to tell you: It's scary. Don't worry if you don't know the story; begin your visit with the audiovisual program that recaps the book (and—spoiler alert—gives away the ending). The rambling 1668 house holds six rooms of period furniture,

Salem: Practical Matters

Driving in Salem offers the most flexibility, but it is also accessible by public transit and easy to negotiate on foot. The **MBTA** (☎ 800/392-6100 or ☎ 617/222-3200; www.mbta.com) operates commuter trains from North Station and buses from Haymarket. From late May through October, the **Salem Ferry** (☎ 877/733-9425 or ☎ 617/227-4321; www.salemferry.com) is an excellent alternative. Always be sure you know the schedule for your return trip. Tourist information is widely available. Visit the **National Park Service Regional Visitor Center,** 2 New Liberty St. (☎ 978/740-1650; www.nps.gov/sama), open daily from 9am to 5pm; download or request a visitor's guide from **Destination Salem** (☎ 877/SALEM-MA or ☎ 978/744-3663; www.salem.org); or check with the **Salem Chamber of Commerce,** 265 Essex St., Suite 101 (☎ 978/744-0004; www.salem-chamber.org), open weekdays from 9am to 5pm.

including pieces referred to in the novel. Guides point them out on the informative tour, which includes interesting descriptions of what life in the 1700s was like and more Q-and-A than many other house tours allow. The high point of the tour is the secret staircase, but one of my favorite things about visiting this property is the opportunity to poke around the grounds after the tour. The modest home where Hawthorne was born has been moved here, and the lovely period gardens overlook the harbor. ⏲ *1½ hrs. 54 Turner St. (off Derby St.). ☎ 978/744-0991. www.7gables.org. Guided tour of house and grounds $12.50 adults, $11.50 seniors, $7.50 kids 5–12, free for kids 4 and under. July–Oct daily 10am–7pm; Nov–June daily 10am–5pm. Closed first 2 weeks of Jan.*

The House of the Seven Gables belonged to Nathaniel Hawthorne's cousin.

7 ★★ **In a Pig's Eye** After a busy day of sightseeing, unwind at this friendly neighborhood tavern with a wide-ranging menu (including Mexican specialties Mon–Tues). *148 Derby St. (Daniels St.). ☎ 978/741-4436. www.inapigseye.com. $–$$.*

Plymouth

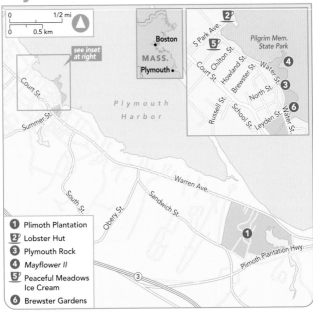

0   1/2 mi
0   0.5 km

see inset at right

Boston
MASS.
Plymouth •

Pilgrim Mem. State Park

S Park Ave.
Court St.
Chilton St.
Howland St.
Brewster St.
Water St.
North St.
Russell St.
School St.
Leyden St.
Water St.

Plymouth Harbor

Court St.

Summer St.

Warren Ave.

South St.

Oberry St.

Sandwich St.

Plimoth Plantation Hwy.

❶ Plimoth Plantation
❷ Lobster Hut
❸ Plymouth Rock
❹ *Mayflower II*
❺ Peaceful Meadows Ice Cream
❻ Brewster Gardens

Did you wear a construction-paper hat or a feathered head-dress in the Thanksgiving pageant? If you attended grade school in the United States before the heyday of political correctness, you probably did—and you probably know a little something about Plymouth. The Pilgrims. The *Mayflower*. The Rock. Refreshingly, this town honors its history but isn't trapped in the past; it's a lively contemporary community that happens to have a lot of historic attractions. START: **Take I-93 south and merge onto Route 3 south. To go directly to Plimoth Plantation, take Exit 4. Use Exit 6A (Route 44 east) to go straight to downtown Plymouth. If it isn't rush hour, the trip from Boston takes about an hour.**

❶ ★★ kids **Plimoth Plantation**
Until we perfect time travel, a visit here is the best way to experience the Pilgrims' daily life. A re-creation of a 1627 village, Plimoth Plantation approximates the conditions in the early days of the little community, which was settled in 1620. Visitors wander the farm area, visiting homes and gardens constructed with careful attention to historic detail. The "Pilgrims" are actors who assume the personalities of original community members, and they take their roles seriously—kids get a kick out of their mystified reactions to questions about innovations such as TV or airplanes. You

Plymouth Rock.

can watch them framing a house, splitting wood, shearing sheep, preserving foodstuffs, or cooking over an open hearth, as all as it was done in the 1600s, using only the equipment available then. You'll be walking a lot, so wear comfortable shoes. **Note:** If you plan to visit the *Mayflower II* (later in this tour), buy a combination ticket. ⏱ *3 hr. Be here when the gates open, especially in summer. 137 Warren Ave. (Rte. 3).* ☎ *508/746-1622. www.plimoth.org. Admission (good for 2 consecutive days) $26 adults, $24 seniors, $15 kids 6–12, kids 5 and under free. Plimoth Plantation and Mayflower II or Plimoth Grist Mill admission $30 adults, $27 seniors, $19 kids 6–12, free for kids 5 and under. Late Mar–Nov daily 9am–5pm. Closed Dec to mid-Mar.*

2' ★ kids **Lobster Hut** The deck overlooking the harbor is the place to be at this self-service seafood restaurant, which is popular with out-of-towners and locals alike. *25 Town Wharf (off Water St.).* ☎ *508/746-2270. $–$$.*

3 ★★★ kids **Plymouth Rock** Tradition tells us that the original Plymouth Rock was the landing place of the *Mayflower* passengers in 1620. From a hunk 15 feet (5m) long and 3 feet (.9m) wide, the boulder shrank over the years through several relocations. In 1867, the rock wound up here, perched at tide level on the peaceful shore. It's a model attraction: easy to understand, quick to visit, and unexpectedly affecting. In honor of the tercentennial (300th anniversary) of the Pilgrims' arrival, the Colonial Dames of America commissioned the enclosure, a templelike structure designed by McKim, Mead & White. ⏱ *10 min. Pilgrim Memorial State Park, Water St. (Leyden and North sts.).* ☎ *508/747-5360. www.mass.gov/dcr. Daily 24 hr.*

4 ★ kids **Mayflower II** Every time I come here, I marvel: This

Costumed actors portraying colonists stroll the grounds of Plimoth Plantation.

Exhibits aboard Mayflower II *describe and illustrate the Pilgrims' journey and experience.*

ship is *tiny*. A full-scale reproduction of the type of vessel that brought the Pilgrims to America in 1620, *Mayflower II* is just 106½ feet (32m) long. Costumed guides assume passengers' identities to discuss the vessel and its perilous voyage, while other interpreters provide a contemporary perspective. This is a great place to introduce children to the idea that history is a true story—about real people. To start, ask them to imagine sharing such a small space with 101 people. ⏱ *1 hr. State Pier.*

☎ *508/746-1622. www.plimoth.org. Admission $10 adults, $9 seniors, $7 kids 6–12. Plimoth Plantation (good for 2 consecutive days) and Mayflower II admission $30 adults, $27 seniors, $19 kids 6–12, free for kids 5 and under. Late Mar–Nov daily 9am–5pm. Closed Dec to mid-Mar.*

5 ★ **kids** **Peaceful Meadows Ice Cream** A family business that dates to 1962, Peaceful Meadows is a tasty place to refuel. Take your ice cream (fresh peach—yum) to our final stop. *170 Water St. (opposite Town Wharf).* ☎ *508/746-2362. www.peacefulmeadows.com. $.*

6 ★ **kids** **Brewster Gardens** Backtrack along Water Street to wind down at this lovely park, on the site of the garden of an original settler, William Brewster. Settle in to enjoy the greenery, or follow Town Brook up the hill to Jenney Pond, where the waterwheel powers the Plimoth Grist Mill. ⏱ *1 hr. Water and Leyden sts.* ☎ *508/830-4095.* ●

Plymouth: Practical Matters

Driving to Plymouth is vastly preferable to taking public transit. Plymouth and Brockton **buses** (☎ 508/746-0378; www.p-b.com) serve the park-and-ride lot at Exit 5 off Route 3. The **MBTA** commuter rail (☎ 800/392-6100 or ☎ 617/222-3200; www.mbta.com) from Boston's South Station serves Cordage Park, north of downtown Plymouth, on weekdays only. From either stop, the local bus (☎ 800/483-2500; www.gatra.org) takes you the rest of the way—but it doesn't run on Sunday. The year-round visitor information center at Exit 5 covers the whole region; for Plymouth-specific information, visit the seasonal **visitor center** at 130 Water St. (☎ 508/747-7525), across from the town pier. Information is available year-round from **Destination Plymouth** (☎ 800/USA-1620 or ☎ 508/747-7533; www.seeplymouth.com).

The
Savvy Traveler

Before You Go

Tourist Offices

Contact the **Greater Boston Convention & Visitors Bureau,** 2 Copley Place, Suite 105, Boston, MA 02116 (☎ 888/SEE-BOSTON or ☎ 617/536-4100; www.bostonusa.com), for tons of information online, over the phone, and by mail. Other good resources are the **Cambridge Office for Tourism,** 4 Brattle Street, Suite 208, Cambridge, MA 02138(☎ 800/862-5678or ☎ 617/441-2884; www.cambridgeusa.org), and the **Massachusetts Office of Travel and Tourism,** 10 Park Plaza, Suite 4510, Boston, MA 02116 (☎ 800/227-MASS or ☎ 617/973-8500; www.massvacation.com).

Apps

Before leaving home, you can download countless iOS and Android apps for (among many other things) events, attractions, businesses, municipalities, universities, and the MBTA—but don't get carried away. You're here to see Boston, not your mobile device. The time you spend picking just a few apps that meet your needs can save you hours when you're on the road. Good starting points include the National Park Service and the Greater Boston Convention & Visitors Bureau (search "BostonUSA").

The Best Times to Go

Conventions, special events, and school vacations make Boston busy virtually year-round. The best weather and largest crowds coincide during foliage season, from mid-September to early November. Spring is unpredictable (snow sometimes falls in April) but overall has smaller crowds than the fall, and decent weather. July and August are family vacation time, with large

crowds at most attractions. The "slow" season is January through March, when many hotels offer great deals, especially on weekends.

Festivals & Special Events

SPRING. The third Monday of April is **Patriots Day,** a state holiday that commemorates the events of April 18 and 19, 1775, when the Revolutionary War began. Ceremonies and reenactments take place in Boston's North End at the **Old North Church** (☎ 617/523-6676; www.oldnorth.com) and the **Paul Revere House** (☎ 617/523-2338; www.paulreverehouse.org). In suburban Lexington, a skirmish breaks out on the field now known as the Battle Green, and hostilities rage at the North Bridge in Concord. Consult the **Battle Road Committee** (www.battleroad.org) or contact the **Lexington Chamber of Commerce** (☎ 781/862-1450; www.lexington chamber.org) or the **Concord Chamber of Commerce** (☎ 978/369-3120; www.concordchamberofcommerce.org) for information. Beyond New England, Patriots Day is best known for the **Boston Marathon** (www.bostonmarathon.org), one of the oldest and most famous in the world. The race begins in Hopkinton, Massachusetts, and ends on Boylston Street just outside Boston's Copley Square. The lead runners break the tape around noon. On the Saturday before Patriots Day, the **Swan Boats** (☎ 617/522-1966; www.swanboats.com) in the Public Garden open their season. **Mayfair in Harvard Square** (www.harvardsquare.com), on the first Sunday of the month, is a massive street festival with live music and multiple beer gardens. The second or third weekend of May brings

Previous page: Washington Statue.

Useful Websites

- **Boston.com** (the *Boston Globe* and other resources): www. boston.com
- **Boston-to-English Dictionary:** www.universalhub.com/ glossary
- **Greater Boston Convention & Visitors Bureau:** www.boston usa.com and www.twitter.com/bostoninsider
- **MBTA** (subway, trolley, bus, ferry, and commuter-rail schedules and route maps): www.mbta.com
- **National Park Service:** www.nps.gov
- **Open Table** (restaurant reservations): www.opentable.com
- **Yelp:** www.yelp.com/boston

Lilac Sunday to the Arnold Arboretum (☎ 617/524-1717; www. arboretum.harvard.edu). It's the only day of the year that the arboretum allows picnicking.

SUMMER. The second week of June culminates in the **Boston Pride Parade** (☎ 617/262-9405; www. bostonpride.org), the largest gaypride parade in New England. Also in mid-June, the **Dragon Boat Festival** (www.bostondragonboat.org) brings the colorful vessels to the Charles River near Harvard Square; spectators celebrate Chinese culture and food on the riverbank. The following weekend, the arts-oriented **Cambridge River Festival** (☎ 617/349-4380; www.cambridge artscouncil.org) takes over the banks of the Charles. The high point of the summer calendar is **Boston Harborfest** (☎ 617/227-1528; www.bostonharborfest.com), the city's weeklong Fourth of July party. Events include concerts, children's activities, cruises, fireworks, the Boston Chowderfest, guided tours, talks, and USS *Constitution*'s turnaround cruise. The big day ends with a beloved tradition, the **Boston Pops Concert and Fireworks Display** (www.july4th.org). The musicians play at the Hatch Shell

amphitheater, on the Esplanade; the spectators spread out along both banks of the river and the bridges across the Charles River basin. The program includes the *1812 Overture*, with real cannon fire and church bells. The North End is home to another tradition, the **Italian-American feasts** that dominate weekends from late July through August. The street fairs feature live music, dancing, carnival food, tacky souvenirs, and lively crowds of locals and out-of-towners happily mingling. The two biggest events are the **Fisherman's Feast** (www. fishermansfeast.com) and the **Feast of St. Anthony** (www.saintanthonys feast.com), in mid- and late August.

AUTUMN. On the third weekend of October, the **Head of the Charles Regatta** (☎ 617/868-6200; www. hocr.org) dominates Cambridge and, to a lesser extent, Boston. Rowing teams and individuals vie to beat the clock (they start one at a time, not all together) as they race from the Charles River basin to West Cambridge. Hundreds of thousands of fans line the shore and the bridges. October is party time in Salem, where **Haunted Happenings** (☎ 877/SALEM-MA; www.hauntedhappenings.org) lasts

BOSTON'S AVERAGE TEMPERATURES & RAINFALL						
	JAN	FEB	MAR	APR	MAY	JUNE
Temp. (°F)	30	31	38	49	59	68
Temp. (°C)	-1	-1	3	9	15	20
Rainfall (in.)	3.8	3.5	40	3.7	3.4	3.0
	JULY	AUG	SEPT	OCT	NOV	DEC
Temp. (°F)	74	72	65	55	45	34
Temp. (°C)	23	22	18	13	7	1
Rainfall (in.)	2.8	3.6	3.3	3.3	4.4	4.2

all month. Halloween celebrations include parades, parties, a special commuter-rail ride from Boston, fortunetelling, cruises, and tours.

WINTER. Boston's holiday season begins the day after Thanksgiving, when Boston Ballet kicks off its annual performances of **The Nutcracker** (☎ 617/695-6955; www.bostonballet.org). In mid-December, the **Boston Tea Party Reenactment** at the Old South Meeting House (☎ 617/482-6439; www.oldsouthmeetinghouse.org) and the Boston Tea Party Ships & Museum (☎ 855/TEA-1773; www.bostonteapartyship.org) brings history alive by enlisting audience members in the debate over taxation without representation. The **Christmas Revels** show (☎ 617/972-8300; www.revels.org), a multicultural celebration of the winter solstice, takes place at Harvard's Sanders Theatre (☎ 617/496-2222). It illuminates the customs of a different culture each year. The year ends with **First Night,** the original arts-oriented, no-alcohol, citywide New Year's Eve celebration, which traditionally includes ice sculptures, arts performances, a parade, and midnight fireworks. The nonprofit that had run the event for 37 years shut down in 2013; check the city website (www.cityofboston.gov) for up-to-date information and schedules.

The Weather

New England weather is famously changeable—variations from day to day and even hour to hour can be enormous. Always dress in layers. Spring and fall are the best bets for moderate temperatures, but spring (also known as mud season) doesn't usually settle in until early May. Summers are hot, especially in July and August, and can be uncomfortably humid. Fall is when you're most likely to catch a comfortable run of dry, sunny days and cool nights. Winters are cold and usually snowy—bring a warm coat and sturdy boots.

Cellphones

Cellphones (mobiles) with tri-band GSM capabilities work in the United States; call your service provider before departing your home country to ensure that the international call bar has been switched off and to check call charges, which can be extremely high. Also remember that you will be charged for calls you receive on a U.K. mobile used abroad. The least expensive way to keep in touch, if you don't need to know your number in advance, is with a pay-as-you-go phone. American electronics stores, such as the ubiquitous **Radio Shack** (☎ 800/843-7422; www.radioshack.com), sell a variety of these so-called throwaway or "burner" phones at reasonable prices. Before you leave the store, make sure the one you select can call your home country. U.K. visitors can also rent a U.S. phone before leaving home. Contact **Cellhire** (☎ 0800/610-610; www.cellhire.co.uk). One good wireless-rental company is **InTouch Global** (☎ 800/872-7626 or ☎ 703/222-7161; www.intouchglobal.com).

Car Rentals

For booking rental cars online, the best deals are usually on rental-car company websites. U.K. visitors should check **Holidayautos** (☎ 0800/224-8001; www.holidayautos.co.uk). Companies with offices at Boston's Logan Airport—which is scheduled to open a centralized car-rental facility in late 2014—include **Alamo** (☎ 888/233-8749; www.alamo.com), **Avis** (☎ 800/633-3469; www.avis.com), **Budget** (☎ 800/218-7992; www.budget.com), **Dollar** (☎ 800/800-4000; www.dollar.com), **Hertz** (☎ 800/654-3131; www.hertz.com), and **National** (☎ 877/222-9058; www.nationalcar.com). **Enterprise** (☎ 800/261-7331; www.enterprise.com) and **Thrifty** (☎ 800/847-4389; www.thrifty.com) are nearby but not on the grounds. If you belong to **Zipcar** or another car-sharing service at home, check ahead to see whether your membership is good in the Boston area.

Getting **There**

By Plane

Boston's **Logan International Airport** (airport code BOS) is in East Boston at the end of the Sumner, Callahan, and Ted Williams tunnels, 3 miles (4.8km) across the harbor from downtown. For information, including real-time flight arrivals and departures, go to www.flylogan.com. Wi-Fi is free all over the airport.

Getting to & from the Airport

General Info: The Massachusetts Port Authority, or **MassPort** (☎ 800/23-LOGAN; www.flylogan.com), coordinates airport transportation. The 24-hour toll-free line and the website's GetUthere feature provide information about getting to the city and to many nearby suburbs. In addition, airport representatives staff the information booth near the baggage claim area in each terminal daily from about 7am to 11:45pm.

Taxis: Just getting into a cab at the airport costs $10.10 ($7.50 in fees plus the initial $2.60 fare). The total fare to downtown or the Back Bay runs $20 to $45. Depending on traffic, the driver might use the Ted Williams Tunnel for destinations outside downtown, like the Back Bay.

Public Transit: The Silver Line SL1 bus stops at each airport terminal and runs directly to South Station, where you can connect to the Red Line subway and the commuter rail to the southern suburbs. It takes about 20 minutes, not including waiting time. At press time, service leaving the airport is free. The subway takes just 10 minutes to reach downtown; free shuttle buses run from each terminal to the Airport subway station on the Blue Line of the T from 5:30am to 1am every day, year-round. The Blue Line stops at Aquarium, State Street, and Government Center, downtown points where you can exit or transfer to the other lines. The bus or subway fare is $2.50 with a CharlieTicket (or cash, on buses only), $2 with a CharlieCard.

Ferries & Boats: The trip to the downtown waterfront in a weather-protected **boat** takes about 7 minutes and costs $10 one-way. The free no. 66 shuttle bus connects the airport terminals to the Logan ferry dock. Two on-call water-taxi companies serve the airport, the downtown waterfront, and other points around the harbor: **City Water Taxi** (☎ 617/422-0392; www.citywatertaxi.com) and **Rowes Wharf Water Transport** (☎ 617/406-8584; www.roweswharfwatertransport.com). Leaving the airport, ask the shuttle-bus driver to radio ahead for water-taxi pickup; on the way back, call ahead for service.

Shuttle Vans: The Logan Airport website (www.flylogan.com) lists numerous companies that serve local hotels. One-way prices start at $15 per person and are subject to fuel surcharges.

By Car

Three major highways converge in Boston. **I-90,** also known as the Massachusetts Turnpike or "Mass. Pike," is an east-west toll road that originates at Logan Airport and links up with the New York State Thruway. **I-93/U.S. 1** extends north to Canada. **I-93/Route 3,** the Southeast Expressway, connects Boston with the south, including Cape Cod. To avoid driving downtown, exit the Mass. Pike at Cambridge/Allston or at the Prudential Center in the Back Bay. I-95 (Massachusetts Rte. 128) is

a beltway about 11 miles (18km) from downtown that connects Boston to highways in Rhode Island, Connecticut, and New York to the south, and New Hampshire and Maine to the north.

Approaches to Cambridge include **Storrow Drive** and **Memorial Drive,** which run along either side of the Charles River. Storrow Drive has a Harvard Square exit that leads across the Anderson Bridge to John F. Kennedy Street and into the square. Memorial Drive intersects with JFK Street; turn away from the bridge to reach the square.

By Train & Bus

Boston has three rail centers: **South Station,** on Atlantic Avenue at Summer Street; **Back Bay Station,** on Dartmouth Street between Huntington and Columbus avenues; and **North Station,** on Causeway Street. **Amtrak** (☎ 800/USA-RAIL; www.amtrak.com) serves all three stations, each of which is also an MBTA subway stop.

The bus terminal (www.southstation.net), formally the **South Station Transportation Center**, is on Atlantic Avenue next to the train station. The major bus lines that serve Boston are **Greyhound** (☎ 800/231-2222 or ☎ 617/526-1801; www.greyhound.com) and **Peter Pan** (☎ 800/343-9999; www.petertpanbus.com).

Getting **Around** on Foot

This is the way to go if you can manage it. Even the tallest hills aren't too steep, and vehicular traffic is brutal. Wear comfortable shoes.

By Bike

Purchase a short- or long-term pass and you can hit the streets on two wheels with Boston's bike-sharing program, **Hubway** (www.thehubway.com).

By Public Transportation

The **Massachusetts Bay Transportation Authority,** or MBTA (☎ 800/392-6100 or ☎ 617/222-3200; www.mbta.com), runs subways, trolleys, buses, and ferries in Boston and many suburbs, as well as the commuter rail, which extends as far as Providence, Rhode Island. The stored-value fare system uses paper CharlieTickets and plastic CharlieCards. CharlieTickets are easier to get (they're available from kiosks at every station and every airport terminal), but users pay more. With a CharlieTicket, the subway fare is $2.50, the bus fare $2. With a CharlieCard—available from employees who staff most downtown subway stations and from retail locations listed on the website—subway riders pay $2, bus passengers $1.50. At press time, the MBTA is converting the ferry fare system to accept cards and passes. Commuter-rail tickets are available at stations and (subject to a surcharge) on the train, but downloading and using the smartphone app is quicker.

The subway system (called "the T" by locals) consists of the Red, Green, Blue, and Orange lines. The commuter rail to the suburbs is purple on system maps and sometimes called the Purple Line. The Silver Line is a fancy name for a bus line. Service begins at around 5:15am and ends around 12:30am.

Buses and "trackless trolleys" (buses with electric antennae) provide service around town and many suburbs. The Silver Line looks like a branch of the subway on some maps and on the MBTA website but is a bus line. Riders on the Washington Street branches (SL4 and SL5) pay bus fares; on the Waterfront branches (SL1 and SL2), subway fares prevail.

The Boston Harbor water shuttle (☎ 617/227-4321) is a commuter ferry that connects Long Wharf, near the New England Aquarium, with the Charlestown Navy Yard. The one-way fare is $3.

The water taxis that serve the airport also connect stops around the harbor; one-way fares run $10 to $20. Contact **City Water Taxi** (☎ 617/422-0392; www.citywatertaxi.com) or **Rowes Wharf Water Transport** (☎ 617/406-8584; www.roweswharfwatertransport.com). Call ahead from the dock for pickup.

By Taxi

Taxis can be tough to hail on the street. Your best bet is to call a dispatcher, seek out a hotel or cabstand, or use an app. To call ahead, try the **Independent Taxi Operators Association,** or **ITOA** (☎ 617/426-8700; www.itoataxi.com); **Boston Cab** (☎ 617/536-5010; www.bostoncab.us); **Top Cab/City Cab** (☎ 617/266-4800 or ☎ 617/536-5100); or **Metro Cab** (☎ 617/782-5500; www.boston-cab.com). In Cambridge, call **Ambassador Brattle/Yellow Cab** (☎ 617/492-1100 or 617/547-3000; www.ambassadorbrattle.com) or **Checker Cab** (☎ 617/497-9000; www.checkercabcambridge.com).

By Car

If you plan to visit only Boston and Cambridge, there's no reason to have a car. With its pricey parking, confusing streets, and widespread construction, Boston in particular is a motorist's nightmare. Drive to Cambridge only if you're feeling flush—you'll pay to park there, too. If you drive to the Boston area, park at the hotel and use the car for day trips. If you want to rent a car for day trips, see "Car Rentals," above for more information.

Fast **Facts**

AREA CODES Boston proper, **617** and **857**; immediate suburbs, **781** and **339**; northern and western suburbs, **978** and **351**; southern suburbs, **508** and **774.** To make a local call, you must dial all 10 digits.

ATMS/CASHPOINTS Before you leave home, find out your daily withdrawal limit. Unless you can find an ATM operated by your own bank, expect to pay a $1.50 to $3 access fee. **Cirrus** (☎ 800/4CIRRUS; www.mastercard.com), **PLUS** (☎ 800/THE-PLUS; www.visa.com), and **NYCE** (www.nyce.net) cover most Boston-area banks.

BABYSITTERS Many hotels maintain lists of babysitters; check at the front desk or with the concierge. Local agencies aren't a cost-effective option; most impose a steep annual fee and daily referral charge on top of the sitter's hourly wage and expenses. If you're in town on business, ask whether the company you're visiting has a corporate membership in an agency.

B&BS Try **B&B Agency of Boston** (☎ 800/248-9262, ☎ 617/720-3540, or ☎ 0800/89-5128 from the U.K.; www.boston-bnbagency.com).

BANKING HOURS Most are open weekdays 9am–5pm, and sometimes Saturday morning.

CLIMATE See "The Weather," earlier in this chapter.

CONSULATES & EMBASSIES Embassies are in Washington, D.C. Some consulates are in major U.S. cities, and most nations have a mission to the United Nations in New York City. For addresses and phone numbers of embassies in Washington, D.C., call ☎ 202/555-1212 or visit **www.embassy.org/embassies**. The following are Boston-area addresses: The **Canadian consulate**

is at 3 Copley Place, Suite 400, Boston, MA 02116 (☎ 617/247-5100; www.boston.gc.ca). The **Irish consulate** is at 535 Boylston St., 5th floor, Boston, MA 02116 (☎ 617/267-9330, www.consulategeneral ofirelandboston.org). The **U.K. consulate** is at 1 Memorial Dr., Cambridge, MA 02142 (☎ 617/245-4500; www.ukinusa.fco.gov.uk).

CUSTOMS National customs agencies strictly regulate what visitors to the United States may bring with them and take home. For details regarding U.S. Customs and Border Protection, consult your nearest U.S. embassy or consulate or visit www.cbp.gov.

DENTISTS The desk staff or concierge at your hotel should be able to suggest a dentist. The **Massachusetts Dental Society** (☎ 800/342-8747; www.massdental.org) can point you toward a member.

DOCTORS The desk staff or concierge at your hotel can direct you to a doctor. You can also try the physician referral service at one of the area's many hospitals. Among them are **Brigham and Women's** (☎ 800/294-9999) and **Massachusetts General** (☎ 800/711-4644).

DRINKING LAWS See "Liquor Laws," below.

ELECTRICITY Like Canada, the United States uses 110–120 volts AC (60 cycles), compared with 220–240 volts AC (50 cycles) in most of Europe, Australia, and New Zealand. Downward converters that change 220–240 volts to 110–120 volts are difficult to find in the United States, so bring one with you.

EMBASSIES See "Consulates & Embassies," above.

EMERGENCIES Call ☎ 911 for fire, ambulance, or police. This is a free call from pay phones. For the state police, call ☎ 617/523-1212, or ☎ 911 from a cellphone. The toll-free number for the **Poison Control Center** is ☎ 800/222-1222.

HOLIDAYS Banks, government offices, post offices, and some stores, restaurants, and museums close on the following legal national holidays: January 1 (New Year's Day), the third Monday in January (Martin Luther King, Jr., Day), the third Monday in February (Presidents' Day, Washington's Birthday), the last Monday in May (Memorial Day), July 4th (Independence Day), the first Monday in September (Labor Day), the second Monday in October (Columbus Day), November 11 (Veterans' Day/Armistice Day), the fourth Thursday in November (Thanksgiving Day), and December 25 (Christmas Day). Also, the Tuesday following the first Monday in November is Election Day and is a federal government holiday in presidential-election years (held every 4 years, next in 2016). In Massachusetts, state offices close for Patriots Day on the third Monday in April.

INSURANCE Whether or not you choose to invest in travel insurance depends on numerous factors, including how far you're traveling, how much you're spending, how set your schedule is, and your physical condition. In particular, international travelers should note that unlike many other countries, the United States does not usually offer free or low-cost medical care to visitors (or citizens). For information about traveler's insurance, trip-cancellation insurance, and medical insurance while traveling, please visit www.frommers.com/tips/health_and_travel_insurance.

HOSPITALS **Massachusetts General Hospital,** 55 Fruit St. (☎ 617/726-2000; www.massgeneral.org), and **Tufts Medical Center,** 800 Washington St. (☎ 617/636-5000; www.tuftsmedicalcenter.org), are closest to downtown. At the Harvard Medical Area on the Boston–Brookline border are **Beth Israel Deaconess Medical Center,** 330 Brookline Ave. (☎ 617/667-7000; www.bidmc.org); **Brigham and Women's Hospital,** 75 Francis St. (☎ 617/732-5500; www.brighamandwomens.org); and **Boston Children's Hospital,** 300 Longwood Ave. (☎ 617/355-6000; www.childrenshospital.org). In Cambridge are **Mount Auburn Hospital,** 330 Mount Auburn St. (☎ 617/492-3500; www.mountauburnhospital.org), and **Cambridge Hospital,** 1493 Cambridge St. (☎ 617/665-1000; www.cambridgehospital.org).

INTERNET Wireless access is widely available throughout Boston, often for no charge. There's free service at Logan Airport and in numerous outdoor spaces, including the Rose Kennedy Greenway. Your hotel may have a public terminal, and many hotels offer on-premises access (often for a daily fee). **FedEx Office** (www.fedexoffice.com) offers free Wi-Fi and rental computer workstations at most branches. Locations include 2 Center Plaza, Government Center (☎ 617/973-9000); 10 Post Office Sq., Financial District (☎ 617/482-4400); 187 Dartmouth St., Back Bay (☎ 617/262-6188); and 1 Mifflin Place, off Mount Auburn Street near Eliot Street, Harvard Square (☎ 617/497-0125).

LIQUOR LAWS The legal drinking age in Massachusetts (and the rest of the U.S.) is 21. Many bars, particularly those near college campuses, check the ID of everyone who enters. Liquor stores and the liquor sections of other stores are open

Monday through Saturday and open at noon on Sunday in communities where that's legal. Last call typically is 30 minutes before closing time (1am in bars, 2am in clubs).

MAIL & POSTAGE At press time, domestic postage rates are 33¢ for a postcard and 46¢ for a letter. For international mail, a first-class letter of up to 1 ounce or a postcard costs $1.10. The main post office, at 25 Dorchester Ave. (☎ 617/654-5302), next to South Station, is open daily 24 hours.

MONEY / TRAVELER'S CHECKS Credit cards and debit cards are more popular, but traveler's checks are widely accepted in the U.S. In tourist-friendly Boston, you won't have much trouble using them at any business. International visitors should carry traveler's checks denominated in U.S. dollars; foreign-currency checks are often difficult to exchange. You can buy traveler's checks at most banks. If you carry them, keep a record of the serial numbers separate from your checks in the event that they are stolen or lost. You'll get a refund faster if you know the numbers.

PARKING The traffic is awful, but parking is the real reason not to drive around Boston. Most spaces on the street are metered (and patrolled until at least 6pm Mon–Sat) and are open to nonresidents for 2 hours or less between 8am and 6pm. The penalty is a $45 ticket—even the most expensive garage is cheaper. The rate is usually $1.25 per hour. Most meters take quarters only; some locations, including streets with pay-and-display kiosks, also accept credit and debit cards. Time limits range from 15 minutes to 2 hours.

A full day at most garages costs no more than $35, but some downtown facilities charge as much as $45, and hourly rates can be exorbitant. Try the city-run garage under **Boston Common** (☎ 617/954-2098); the entrance is at Zero Charles St., between Boylston and Beacon streets. You get a slight break on the price if you buy something at the shopping centers associated with the **Prudential Center** garage (☎ 617/236-3060), with entrances on Boylston Street, Huntington Avenue, and Exeter Street, and at the Sheraton Boston Hotel; the **Copley Place** garage (☎ 617/369-5025), off Huntington Avenue; and the **75 State Street Garage** (☎ 617/443-2817), near Faneuil Hall Marketplace. Good-size garages downtown are at **Government Center,** 50 New Sudbury St. off Congress Street (☎ 617/227-0385); 136 Blackstone St., entrance off **Sudbury Street** at Congress Street (☎ 617/973-0421); and **Zero Post Office Square** in the Financial District (☎ 617/423-1430). In the Back Bay, there's a large facility near the Hynes Convention Center at **50 Dalton St.** (☎ 617/723-1488).

PASSPORTS Always keep a photocopy of your passport with you when you're traveling. If your passport is lost or stolen, having a copy facilitates the reissuing process at a local consulate or embassy. Keep your passport and other valuables in the hotel or room safe. See "Consulates & Embassies," above, for more information.

RESTROOMS Most tourist attractions, hotels, department stores, malls, and public buildings have public restrooms. The CambridgeSide Galleria, Copley Place, Prudential Center, and Quincy Market shopping areas; the central branch of the Boston Public Library in Copley Square; and most fast-food restaurants and coffee bars have clean restrooms. Some restaurants and bars, including those in tourist areas, display a sign saying that toilets are for the use of patrons only. Paying for a cup of coffee or a soft drink qualifies you as a patron. You'll find free-standing, self-cleaning **pay toilets** (25¢) at various locations around downtown. Check these facilities carefully before using them; despite regular patrols, drug users have been known to take advantage of the generous time limits.

SAFETY Boston and Cambridge are generally safe, but you should always take the same precautions you would in any other large North American city. As in any city, stay out of parks (including Boston Common, the Public Garden, the Esplanade, and the Rose Kennedy Greenway) at night unless you're in a crowd. Specific areas to avoid at night include Boylston Street between Tremont and Washington streets, and Tremont Street from Stuart to Boylston streets. Try not to walk alone late at night in the Theater District or on the side streets around North Station. Public transportation in the areas you're likely to visit is busy and safe, but service stops between 12:30am and 1am.

SMOKING Massachusetts is an anti-tobacco stronghold. State law bans smoking in all workplaces, including restaurants, bars, and clubs. Some buildings forbid smoking within a 10- to 25-foot radius of the entrance.

TAXES The 6.25% state sales tax in Massachusetts applies to everything except groceries, prescription drugs, newspapers, and clothing that costs less than $175. The tax on meals and take-out food varies by community; in Boston and Cambridge, it's 7%. The lodging tax is 14.45% in Boston and Cambridge.

TELEPHONES For directory assistance or information, dial ☎ 411. Pay phones, which are becoming increasingly scarce, usually charge 50¢ for a 3-minute call.

TIPPING In hotels, tip **bellhops** at least $1 per bag and tip the **housekeeping staff** at least $2 per person per day. Tip the **doorman** or **concierge** only for a specific service (for example, calling a cab for you or obtaining difficult-to-get theater tickets). Tip the **valet-parking attendant** $1 or $2 every time you get your car. In restaurants, bars, and nightclubs, tip **service staff** 15% to 20% of the check, tip **bartenders** 10% to 15%, and tip **checkroom attendants at least** $1 per garment. Tip **cab drivers** at least 15% of the fare, tip **skycaps** at airports at least $1 per bag, and tip **hairdressers** and **barbers** 15% to 20%.

TOILETS See "Restrooms," above.

TOURIST INFORMATION OFFICES The Boston National Historical Park operates the **Faneuil Hall Visitor Center** (☎ 617/242-5642; www.nps. gov/bost; daily 9am–5pm), at Faneuil Hall Marketplace off Congress Street near North Street. The **Greater Boston Convention & Visitors Bureau** (☎ 888/SEE-BOSTON or ☎ 617/536-4100; www.bostonusa. com) operates the **Boston Common Information Center,** 148 Tremont St., on the Common (Mon–Fri 8:30am–5pm, Sat 9am–5pm) and the **Visitor Information Desk** on the main level of the Shops at Prudential Center, 800 Boylston St. (Mon–Sat 9am–6pm, Sun 10am–6pm).

TRANSIT INFO The MBTA runs the subways, local buses, and commuter rail (☎ 800/392-6100 or ☎ 617/222-3200; www.mbta.com), and the Massachusetts Port Authority coordinates airport transportation (☎ 800/23-LOGAN; www. flylogan.com).

TRAVELERS WITH DISABILITIES Boston Cab (☎ 617/536-5010; www. boston.us) has wheelchair-accessible vehicles; advance notice is recommended. An **Airport Accessible Van** (☎ 617/561-1769) operates within Logan Airport. Newer subway stations are wheelchair accessible; contact the **MBTA** (☎ 800/392-6100 or ☎ 617/222-3200; www.mbta.com) to see if the stations you need are accessible. All MBTA buses have lifts or kneelers; call

☎ 800/LIFT-BUS for more information. To learn more, contact the **Office for Transportation Access** (☎ 800/533-6282, ☎ 617/222-5123, or ☎ TTY 617/222-5415). An excellent resource is "the state organization on arts and disability," **VSA Massachusetts** (☎ 617/350-7713 or ☎ TTY 617/350-6535; www.vsamass.org).

Boston: **A Brief History**

1630 John Winthrop leads settlers to present-day Charlestown. Seeking better water, they push on to Shawmut, which they call Trimountain. On September 7, they name it Boston in honor of the English hometown of many Puritans. On October 19, the first town meeting attracts 108 voters.

1635 Boston Latin School, America's first public school, opens.

1636 Harvard College is founded.

1638 America's first printing press is established in Cambridge.

1639 The country's first post office opens in Richard Fairbank's home.

1704 America's first regularly published newspaper, the *Boston News Letter*, is founded.

1770 On March 5, five colonists are killed outside what is now the Old State House, an incident soon known as the Boston Massacre.

1773 On December 16, during the Boston Tea Party, colonists dump 342 chests of tea into the harbor from three British ships.

1775 On April 18, Paul Revere and William Dawes spread the word that the British are marching toward Lexington and Concord. The next day, "the shot heard round the world" is fired. On June 17, the British win the Battle of Bunker Hill but suffer heavy casualties.

1776 On March 17, royal troops evacuate by ship. On July 18, the Declaration of Independence is read from the balcony of the Old State House.

1831 William Lloyd Garrison publishes the first issue of the *Liberator*, a newspaper dedicated to emancipation.

1870 The Museum of Fine Arts is founded.

1872 The Great Fire burns 65 acres (65 hectares), consumes 800 buildings, and kills 33 people.

1876 Boston University professor Alexander Graham Bell invents the telephone.

1881 The Boston Symphony Orchestra is founded.

1895 The Boston Public Library opens on Copley Square.

1897 The first Boston Marathon is run. The first subway in America opens—a 1¾-mile (2.8km) stretch beneath Boylston Street.

1918 The Red Sox celebrate their World Series victory; a championship drought begins.

1930S The Great Depression devastates what remains of New England's industrial base.

1946 Boston's First Congressional District sends John F. Kennedy to Congress.

1957 The Boston Celtics win the first of their 16 NBA championships.

1958 The Freedom Trail is mapped out and painted.

1959 Construction of the Prudential Center begins, and with it, the transformation of the skyline.

1966 Massachusetts attorney general Edward Brooke, a Republican, becomes the first black elected to the U.S. Senate in the 20th century.

1969 Students protesting the Vietnam War occupy University Hall at Harvard.

1974 Twenty years after the U.S. Supreme Court made school segregation illegal, school busing begins citywide, sparking unrest in Roxbury and Charlestown.

1976 The restored Faneuil Hall Marketplace opens.

1988 The Central Artery/Third Harbor Tunnel Project, better known as the Big Dig, is approved.

1990S The murder rate plummets, the economy booms, and Boston again becomes a "hot" city.

1995 The first complete piece of the Big Dig, the Ted Williams Tunnel, opens.

1999 School busing ends with a court order.

2001 The 2000 Census shows Boston with a population of 589,141, 49.5% of which is white. On September 11, both planes used in the terrorist attacks on New York's World Trade Center originate in Boston.

2002 The New England Patriots win the Super Bowl.

2003 The state supreme court rules that forbidding same-sex civil marriage violates the state constitution. The Leonard P. Zakim–Bunker Hill Bridge, the signature structure of the Big Dig and a symbol of 21st-century Boston, opens to traffic. Demolition of the elevated Central Artery begins.

2004 The Red Sox win the World Series for the first time in 86 years. The Patriots win another Super Bowl. Massachusetts bans workplace smoking. Same-sex marriage becomes law.

2005 The Patriots win yet another Super Bowl. The Red Sox quell rumors by formally announcing that the team will stay at Fenway Park. Boston-based Gillette is acquired by Cincinnati-based Procter & Gamble.

2006 Deval Patrick becomes the second African-American elected governor in the United States (after Douglas Wilder of Virginia). The Institute of Contemporary Art opens the first new art museum in Boston in nearly a century, a dramatic structure on the South Boston waterfront. The final piece of the elevated Expressway comes down, effectively completing the Big Dig.

2007 Red Sox fans pinch themselves as the team wins another World Series.

2008 The Celtics win the NBA title, breaking a 22-year dry spell. The Rose Fitzgerald Kennedy Greenway officially opens. Massachusetts voters decriminalize marijuana possession.

2009 Edward M. "Ted" Kennedy, whom Massachusetts voters sent to the U.S. Senate nine times, dies after a 46-year career.

2011 After 39 years without an NHL title, the Boston Bruins win their sixth Stanley Cup.

2013 Two bombs explode near the Boston Marathon finish line, killing three spectators and injuring dozens. The world rallies around the city, which embraces the slogan "Boston Strong."

Boston **Art & Architecture**

N ew York has the Statue of Liberty. Paris has the Eiffel Tower. Seattle has the Space Needle. Boston has . . . red brick.

You'll see many other building materials, of course, but in forming a mental picture of the city, most people return inexorably to red brick. It's everywhere, from the **Old North Church** (1723) to the **John Joseph Moakley United States Courthouse** (1999). Those buildings bookend the central waterfront, irresistibly drawing the eye to their dramatic architecture. The church is small compared with the office towers and condo complexes nearby, but as ever, it dwarfs its closest neighbors. The courthouse, across the Fort Point Channel from downtown, is the gateway to the rapidly developing South Boston waterfront/Seaport District.

Boston's wide variety of architecture makes it a visual treat even as its lack of coherence torments architects. Fashions change, buildings disappear, urban renewal leads to questionable decisions, but everywhere you go, there's always something interesting to look at.

Built around 1680, the **Paul Revere House** in the North End is a reminder that for Boston's first 2 centuries, buildings were mostly made of wood, and huge portions of the town regularly burned to the ground. The house is colonial in age but Tudor, rather than typically "colonial," in style. The casement windows and overhanging second floor are medieval features. In 1770, and when the Reveres moved in, the house was no longer fashionable. The one next door would have been, though: the **Pierce/ Hichborn House,** constructed of brick around 1711, is a good example of the Georgian architecture popular in 18th-century Boston.

After the Revolution, from 1780 to 1820, the Federal style dominated. In Boston the new style was closely associated with architect Charles Bulfinch. His work is all over Boston, most conspicuously in the **State House** (1797) and in many Beacon Hill residences. The new Americans rejected British influence after the war and turned to classical antiquity (filtered through the Scottish architect Robert Adam) for the austere features that characterize the style: Ionic and Corinthian detailing, frequently in white against red brick or clapboard; fanlights over doors; and an almost maniacal insistence on symmetry. In the first **Harrison Gray Otis house** (1796), now a museum, at 141 Cambridge St., Bulfinch even devised a room with one false door to balance the real one. Bulfinch also designed **St. Stephen's Church** (1804) in the North End, Harvard's **University Hall** (1814), and the central part of Massachusetts General Hospital, now known as **Bulfinch Pavilion** (1818). He also planned the 1805 enlargement of **Faneuil Hall,** which made it three times the size it was when it opened in 1742.

No other architect is as closely associated with Boston as Bulfinch, but in a brief visit you're likely to see just as much of the work of several others. Alexander Parris designed **Quincy Market** (1826), the Greek Revival centerpiece of Faneuil Hall Marketplace. It was renovated and reopened in 1976 for the nation's Bicentennial celebration. Across town**, Trinity Church** (1877), the Romanesque showpiece in Copley Square, is H. H. Richardson's masterwork.

Fascinating architectural areas lie north and south of Copley Square. To the north is the **Back Bay,** built on landfill, which permitted a logical street pattern. The grid—an anomaly in Boston—was planned in the 1860s and 1870s mostly by Arthur Gilman, and the Parisian flavor of the boulevards reflects his interest in French Second Empire style. It's also evident in Gilman's design (with Gridley J. F. Bryant) of **Old City Hall** (1862) on School Street. Its mansard roof is an early example of a style duplicated on hundreds of town houses in the Back Bay. Heading south from Copley Square, you come to

the **South End,** another trove of Victoriana whose park-studded layout owes more to London than to Paris. It's the country's oldest and largest Victorian neighborhood

The architecture of the building boom that started in the 1960s owes a great deal to the fertile mind of a former Harvard instructor, **I. M. Pei.** His firm was responsible for much of the new construction, usually to good effect. The **Christian Science Center** (1973), the **John F. Kennedy Presidential Library and Museum** (1979), and the **Lynde Family Wing** for Contemporary Art at the Museum of Fine Arts (1981) are rousing successes. The **John Hancock Tower** (1974) is the most dramatic point in the Boston skyline, but it began its life by shedding panes of glass onto the street below (the problem has been corrected). The **Moakley courthouse** appears relatively modest from the street, but the side of the building that faces Boston Harbor is a spectacular curving wall of glass.

Government Center dates to the early 1960s and offends many Bostonians' sensibilities less for its inelegant plainness than because it replaced Scollay Square. That gritty, congested area was filled with theaters, shops, and burlesque houses. Old-timers recall its decrepitude and appeal with equal affection. Government Center's greatest offense is that it surrounds **City Hall,** a utilitarian monstrosity whose numerous sins are just starting to be corrected. The vast brick wasteland of City Hall Plaza has been broken up by a small park, but it's still no prize. It does allow you to do a little trick, though: Facing the building from the plaza or from Faneuil Hall, hold up the "tails" side of a nickel. The resemblance to Monticello (Thomas Jefferson's Virginia estate) is eerie.

The **Big Dig** highway-construction project that dominated the downtown area in the late 20th century and well into the 21st is finally finished. It left behind the picturesque **Rose Fitzgerald Kennedy Greenway** and the **Leonard P. Zakim–Bunker Hill Memorial Bridge,** the gorgeous white structure that spans the Charles River. The bridge is gaining recognition as a symbol of Boston, but it hasn't quite managed to eclipse our old friend red brick. Maybe it never will.

Toll-Free Numbers & Websites

Airlines

AER LINGUS
☎ 800/474-7424
☎ 0818/365-000 *in Ireland*
www.aerlingus.ie

AIR CANADA
☎ 888/247-2262
www.aircanada.ca

AIRTRAN AIRWAYS
☎ 800/247-8726
www.airtran.com

ALITALIA
☎ 800/223-5730
www.alitalia.com

AMERICAN AIRLINES
☎ 800/433-7300
www.aa.com

BRITISH AIRWAYS
☎ 800/247-9297
☎ 0844/493-0787 *in the U.K.*
www.britishairways.com

DELTA AIR LINES
☎ 800/221-1212
www.delta.com

JETBLUE AIRWAYS
☎ 800/538-2583
www.jetblue.com

LUFTHANSA
☎ 800/645-3880
www.lufthansa.com

UNITED
☎ 800/241-6522
www.united.com

US AIRWAYS
☎ 800/428-4322
www.usairways.com

VIRGIN AMERICA
☎ 877/359-8474
www.virginamerica.com

VIRGIN ATLANTIC AIRWAYS
☎ 800/862-8621
☎ 0844/209-7777 *in the U.K.*
www.virginatlantic.com

Car-Rental Agencies

ALAMO
☎ 877/222-9075
www.alamo.com

AVIS
☎ 800/633-3469
www.avis.com

BUDGET
☎ 800/218-7992
www.budget.com

DOLLAR
☎ 800/800-4000
www.dollar.com

ENTERPRISE
☎ 800/261-7331
www.enterprise.com

HERTZ
☎ 800/654-3131
www.hertz.com

NATIONAL
☎ 888/501-9010
www.nationalcar.com

THRIFTY
☎ 800/367-2277
www.thrifty.com

Major Hotel & Motel Chains

BEST WESTERN INTERNATIONAL
☎ 800/780-7234
www.bestwestern.com

CLARION HOTELS
☎ 877/424-6423
www.choicehotels.com

COMFORT INN & SUITES
☎ 877/424-6423
www.choicehotels.com

COURTYARD BY MARRIOTT
☎ 888/236-2427
www.marriott.com

DAYS INN
☎ 800/225-32976
www.daysinn.com

DOUBLETREE HOTEL
☎ 855/560-7753
www.doubletree.com

FAIRMONT HOTELS & RESORTS
☎ 800/257-7544
www.fairmont.com

FOUR SEASONS
☎ 800/819-5053
www.fourseasons.com

HAMPTON
☎ 800/560-7809
www.hampton.com

HILTON HOTELS & RESORTS
☎ 800/445-8667
www.hilton.com

HOLIDAY INN
☎ 888/HOLIDAY
www.holidayinn.com

HOWARD JOHNSON
☎ 800/221-5801
www.hojo.com

HYATT HOTELS & RESORTS
☎ 888/233-1234
www.hyatt.com

INTERCONTINENTAL HOTELS & RESORTS
☎ 800/439-4745
www.intercontinental.com

KIMPTON HOTELS & RESTAURANTS
☎ 800/546-7866
www.kimptonhotels.com

LE MERIDIEN
☎ 800/543-4300
www.starwoodhotels.com

MARRIOTT HOTELS
☎ 888/236-2427
www.marriott.com

OMNI HOTELS & RESORTS
☎ 888/843-6664
www.omnihotels.com

RADISSON
☎ 800/967-9033
www.radisson.com

RAMADA WORLDWIDE
☎ 800/854-9517
www.ramada.com

RENAISSANCE
☎ 888/236-2427
www.marriott.com

RESIDENCE INN BY MARRIOTT
☎ 888/236-2427
http://renaissance-hotels.marriott.com

RITZ-CARLTON
☎ 800/542-8680
www.ritzcarlton.com

SHERATON HOTELS & RESORTS
☎ 800/325-3535
www.starwoodhotels.com

WESTIN HOTELS & RESORTS
☎ 800/937-8461
www.starwoodhotels.com

WYNDHAM HOTELS & RESORTS
☎ 877/999-3223
www.wyndham.com

Index

Photo **Credits**

p ii, top: © Shutterstock/Jorge Salcedo; p ii, second: © Museum of Fine Arts, Boston, Massachusetts, USA/ Gift of Mr. and Mrs. Henry Lee Higginson/The Bridgeman Art Library; p ii, middle: © Wikimedia Commons/Wsvan; p ii, fourth: © Shutterstock/Marcio Jose Bastos Silva; p ii, bottom: © Shutterstock/Albert Pego; p iii, top: © Shutterstock/hawkeye978; p iii, second: © Union Oyster House; p iii, middle: © Shutterstock/Stephen Orsillo; p iii, fourth: © T. Charles Erickson/Huntington Theatre Company; p iii, bottom: © Fairmont Copley Plaza; p viii-1: © Shutterstock/Jorge Salcedo; p 3: © Shutterstock/Christopher Penler; p 4: © Shutterstock/Stephen Orsillo; p 5: © Museum of Fine Arts, Boston, Massachusetts, USA/ Gift of Mr. and Mrs. Henry Lee Higginson/The Bridgeman Art Library; p 7: © Flickr/wallyg; p 8, top: © Shutterstock/George Burba; p 8, bottom: © Shutterstock/Vlad G; p 9: © Shutterstock/Mwaits; p 10: © Flickr/julz91; p 11: © Shutterstock/lsantilli; p 13: © Museum of Fine Arts, Boston, MA, USA/ The Hayden Collection-Charles Henry Hayden Fund/ The Bridgeman Art Library; p 14: © Shutterstock/Kevin M. Kerfoot; p 15, top: © Shutterstock/aceshot1; p 15, bottom: © Shutterstock/col; p 17: © Flickr/Ochinko; p 18: © James Maskell; p 19: © Wikimedia Commons/Wsvan; p 21, top: © Flickr/skasuga; p 21, bottom: © Yoshiki Hase; p 22: © S. Cheng; p 23: © Karin Hansen/Boston Children's Museum; p 25, top: © Shutterstock/Christopher Penler; p 25, bottom: © Isabella Gardner Museum; p 26, top: © Isabella Stewart Gardner Museum, Boston, MA USA/ The Bridgeman Art Library; p 26, bottom: © Museum of Fine Arts, Boston, MA; p 27: © Museum of Fine Arts, Boston, MA, USA/ Picture Fund/ The Bridgeman Art Library; p 29, top: © Shutterstock/col; p 29, bottom: © Shutterstock/col; p 30: © Shutterstock/col; p 31: © Shutterstock/col; p 33, top: © Flickr/Thomas Hawk; p 33, bottom: © Taj Boston; p 34: © Della M. Huff; p 35: © Stephanie's on Newbury; p 37: © Flickr/marc_buehler; p 39: © Flickr/Global Jet; p 40: © Marie Morris; p 41: © Shutterstock/Jeremy Wee; p 43: © Shutterstock/Michelle Marsan; p 44: © Shutterstock/Paula Stephens; p 45: © Shutterstock/Marcio Jose Bastos Silva; p 47: © Shutterstock/Jorge Salcedo; p 49, top: © Café Vanille; p 49, bottom: © Della M. Huff; p 51: © Flickr/Eric Lumsden; p 52, top: © Shutterstock/Jorge Salcedo; p 52, bottom: © Shutterstock/spirit of america; p 53: © Shutterstock/David Davis; p 55: © Shutterstock/Kalim Saliba; p 57: © Shutterstock/Christopher Penler; p 58: © Flickr/mbaylor; p 59: © Shutterstock/Jorge Salcedo; p 61, top: © Shutterstock/col; p 61, bottom: © Shutterstock/col; p 63, top: © Robert Blackie; p 63, bottom: © Mount Auburn Cemetery; p 65: © Courtesy Boston Center for the Arts; p 66, top: © Della M. Huff; p 66, bottom: © Flickr/nsub1; p 67: © Matthew X. Kiernan/Strata-art; p 69: © Shutterstock/Zorylee Diaz-Lupitou; p 70: © Matthew X. Kiernan/Strata-art; p 71: © Della M. Huff; p 72: © Flickr/Muffet; p 73: © Shutterstock/Albert Pego; p 74: © Flickr/afagen; p 79: © International Poster Gallery; p 80: © Della M. Huff; p 81: © Flickr/wallyg; p 82: © Courtesy of The Society of Arts and Crafts; p 83: © Flickr/senomoto; p 85: © Della M. Huff; p 86: © Museum of Fine Arts, Boston, MA, USA/Anonymous gift in memory of Mr. and Mrs. Edwin S. Webster/The Bridgeman Art Library; p 87: © Flickr/ninniane; p 88: © Flickr/SoWa Sundays; p 89: © Shutterstock/hawkeye978; p 91: © Shutterstock/SeanPavonePhoto;: ; p 92: © Flickr/cdrin; p 93, top: © Shutterstock/Stephen Orsillo; p 93, bottom: © Shutterstock/col; p 95, top: © Shutterstock/Christopher Penler; p 95, bottom: © Flickr/wallyg; p 97: © Shutterstock/Jesse Kunerth; p 98: © Shutterstock/jiawangkun; p 99: © Union Oyster House; p 100: © Durgin-Park; p 105: © Union Oyster House; p 106: © Davio's; p 107, top: © Shutterstock/endeavor; p 107, bottom: © Ron Dauphin; p 108, top: Courtesy of Jacob Wirth; p 108, bottom: © Shutterstock/lsantilli; p 109: © Flickr/NinJA999; p 111: © Della M. Huff; p 112: © Union Oyster House; p 113: © Shutterstock/Stephen Orsillo; p 114: © Top of the Hub; p 118: © Cheers; p 119: © Emmanuel Huybrechts; p 120: © Rich Gastwirt; p 121: © "Cowboy" Ben Alman; p 122: © Four Seasons Hotel, Boston; p 123: © Erin Caruso/The Middle East ; p 124: © Game On Fenway; p 125: © T. Charles Erickson/Huntington Theatre Company; p 128: © Shutterstock/fmua; p 129: © Stu Rosner; p 130: © Julian and Marion Bullitt/Emmanuel Music; p 131: © Gene Schiavone/Boston Ballet; p 132: © Michael Lutch /American Repertory Theater; p 133: © Andrew Brilliant/Brilliant Pictures; p 134: © Wang Center; p 135: © Fairmont Copley Plaza; p 136: © Four Seasons Hotel, Boston; p 140: © Greg Kushmerek; p 141: © The Charles Hotel; p 142: © The Colonnade, Boston; p 143: © The Eliot Hotel; p 144: © Fairmont Copley Plaza; p 145: © Hotel 140; p 146: © Nine Zero Hotel; p 147, top: © Omni Parker House; p 147, bottom: © Onyx Hotel; p 148: © Royal Sonesta Hotel; p 149: © Christian Delbert; p 151: © John J. Althouse/Louisa May Alcott's Orchard House; p 152: © Old Manse; p 153: © Flickr/MiguelVieira; p 155, top: © Flickr/pag2525@yahoo.com; p 155, bottom: © Dennis Helmar/Yin Yu Tang, Peabody Essex Museum; p 156: © Dennis Helmar/Yin Yu Tang, Peabody Essex Museum; p 157: © Laura Stone; p 159, top: © Marcio Jose Bastos Silva; p 159, bottom: © Shutterstock/Suchan; p 160: © Andreas Juergensmeier; p 161: © Flickr/Loco Steve.